I0901773

IMAGES
of America

BARREN COUNTY

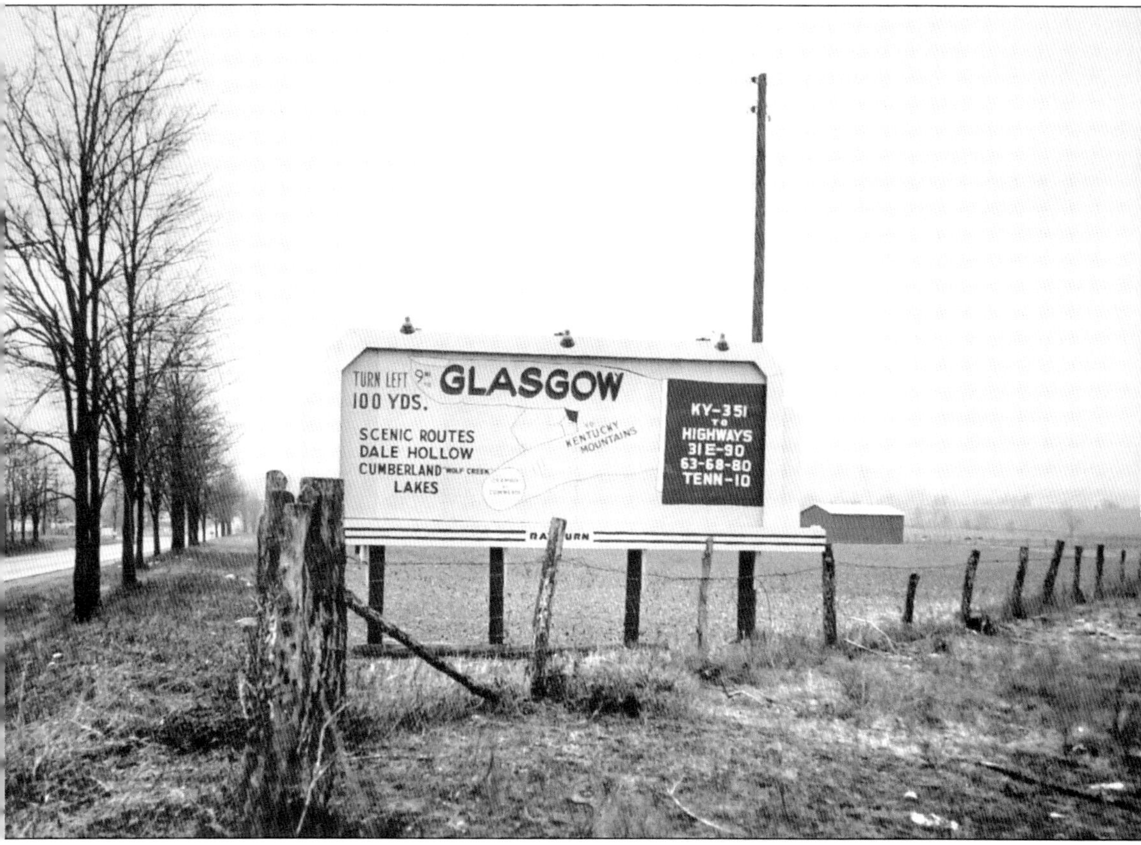

THIS WAY TO GLASGOW. Signs erected by the chamber of commerce left no doubt about how to get to Glasgow. It was noted as a beautiful stop along the way to other scenic sights, with an advertising campaign of "Breaks-Lakes-Parks." (Courtesy of the Glasgow–Barren County Chamber of Commerce.)

ON THE COVER: The Kentucky Federation of Homemakers established the first county organizations in 1925, with the Temple Hill Homemaker's Club being the first to be organized in Barren County in 1939. The groups provided a voice for women, as well as leadership and charitable opportunities. The clubs raised money for various projects by preparing and serving food at dinners, banquets, and festivals such as the annual Tobacco Festival. Their booth was always one of the most popular. The members of the Barren County Homemakers association are, from left to right, Alaska Graven, Christine Huffman, Paulene Huffman, Sally Ward, Gladys Harbison, Myrtie Whitlow, Cloteel Davis, Josephine Steen, Emma Bybee, unidentified, Mary Elizabeth Button, Geneva Goode, Anna Spillman, Dorothy Matthews, Anna Katherine Strader, and Lois Richey. Webster Smith, a Coca-Cola delivery man, is in the background. (Courtesy of the Glasgow–Barren County Chamber of Commerce.)

IMAGES
of America

BARREN COUNTY

Nancy Richey and
the Kentucky Library

ARCADIA
PUBLISHING

ISBN 978-0-7385-8592-5

Published by Arcadia Publishing
Charleston SC, Chicago IL, Portsmouth NH, San Francisco CA

Printed in the United States of America

Library of Congress Control Number: 2009942415

For all general information contact Arcadia Publishing at:
Telephone 843-853-2070
Fax 843-853-0044
E-mail sales@arcadiapublishing.com
For customer service and orders:
Toll-Free 1-888-313-2665

Visit us on the Internet at www.arcadiapublishing.com

For my father, Ish H. Richey,
whose love of learning was so contagious I became quickly infected;
and to my Uncle Millard Richey,
who sweetened my childhood days with his love;
and lastly for my son, Shane,
who travels the world but never leaves my heart.

Contents

ACKNOWLEDGMENTS

Any book such as this is not an orphan but is the product of many parents, and I gratefully acknowledge the encouragement of the director of the Kentucky Library and Museum, Timothy Mullin, and my library colleagues, Nancy Baird, Suellyn Lathrop, Jonathan Jeffrey, and Sue Lynn McDaniel. The Kentucky Library has a good collection of images from the county, but there were many individuals who graciously contributed photographs and assistance in finding others. Their names will appear throughout the book with their contributed photographs. Particular thanks to James and Olene Richey for traipsing the county for me. A very special thank-you is sent to the Glasgow–Barren County Chamber of Commerce and its staff, Ernie Myers, Gayle Meek, and Ann Stewart, for graciously allowing me to use their wonderful scrapbooks. I also wish to thank my editor at Arcadia Publishing, Amy Perryman, for all her kind and encouraging assistance. Lastly, without the constant efforts and helpful advice of my lifelong friend Gary Bewley this book would not have come to fruition. It is a great pleasure to publicly say thank you.

Unless otherwise noted, all images appear courtesy of the Kentucky Library and Museum.

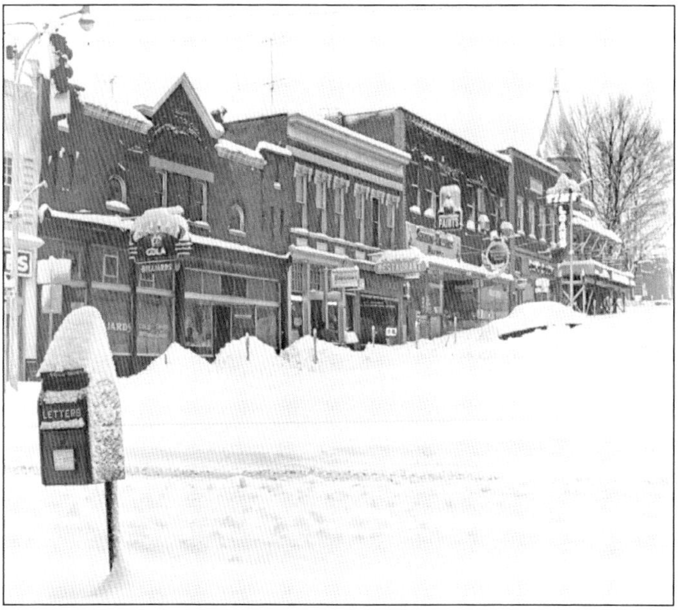

SNOW WAY. With the recent concern over global warming, many have forgotten that the area did receive several heavy snows, as shown in this image from the early 1950s. Notice the parked car at the top of the hill to gauge the depth of the snow.

INTRODUCTION

Barren County, in its formation, was taken from parts of Green and Warren Counties and became the 37th county in Kentucky. In turn, its original 1,500 square miles have been taken to create the surrounding counties of Allen, Hart, Metcalfe, and Monroe. Today, though a cohesive community, it has many parts represented by the small towns that make up the whole. Communities such as Park City, Cave City, Austin Tracy, Etoile, Eighty-Eight, Hiseville, and Temple Hill remain vibrant today because of their cultural traditions. The county and its residents also help preserve their sense of place and love of the land. The natural features of the landscape have made agriculture the primary industry for the county, though manufacturing, retail, and medicine are fast encroaching as economic diversification continues. Tobacco production is dwindling in the county, but Barren still ranks at the top of beef and dairy cattle production in the state.

The love of history and heritage is evident in the county as Barren holds strongly to its history, rural roots, and family ties. Many of its first settlers were Revolutionary War soldiers who received military service land grants. The county retains much of the verdant beauty that was noted by early travelers. One commenting in 1840, after an excursion through the entire region, noted "none but a recreant to nature, and undeserving of its pleasures, could remain indifferent to the charms in such lavish profusion around." The traveler further commented on the "healthiness of the climate, the fine range for cattle, the facilities for raising swine, the culture of tobacco, and the growth and preservation of the timber," as reason enough to totally disagree with the appellation of the "Barrens."

Census and other records show more settlers of Scottish ancestry, coming by way of Virginia, established Barren County. Thus the county retains and celebrates this cultural heritage through its popular Highland Games. The games, complete with bagpipes, kilts, and competitive athletic events, have become so popular that the Kentucky Tourism Council recently named the event as one of the Top Ten Festival Events of the summer. The county seat also bears the name of Glasgow, though there is disagreement if the designation comes from Glasgow, Scotland, or Glasgow, Virginia. An early visitor to the county seat remarked at the beauty and cleanliness of the town and its environs, as well as noting, "there are more beautiful, accomplished and intelligent women in Glasgow than in any other town of size in Kentucky." Quite a compliment! The love of community, service, and philanthropy is also evident. County-wide there are more than 40 different types of active clubs, organizations, societies, and community groups such as the Lions, Rotary, Kiwanis, South Central Kentucky Historical and Genealogical Society, and business and professional women's clubs. Glasgow, established in 1799, is located near the geographical center of the state and is approximately 100 miles south of Louisville and 85 miles north of Nashville. The town, as will be shown in the following photographs, has seen many changes through time but remains today the economic, social, and cultural center of the county.

The most notable land features in this region of Karst topography are its numerous sinkholes and caves. Barren County is also home to parts of Mammoth Cave National Park and has benefited greatly from its proximity to this natural wonder since it is Kentucky's No. 1 tourist destination, with more than 2 million visitors each year. The cave, a World Heritage Site, is the world's longest known cave system, with 367 miles of explored passageways. Other than tourism, caves have also provided county residents with income through the production of saltpeter, or potassium nitrate. The chemical was a necessary component in the production of gunpowder and reached its peak manufacture during the War of 1812 in caves in Temple Hill, Freedom, and Austin locations. The county has also sought to preserve its natural heritage by managing the Brigadoon State Nature Preserve, which represents and maintains some of the best of the county's native species and significant natural resources.

Though there is no central theme to the selection of photographs chosen for this book, the beauty of the land and its people shine through. I have tried to represent all areas of the county and have included many of the notables who have proudly called Barren County, the county of their birth. Unfortunately, it is difficult to find early photographic records of the many distinguished African Americans who have called the county home, but a preliminary listing would include the following: pioneer female pilot Willa Chappell; Negro National League Baseball player Theodore "Terrible Ted" Page; civil rights activists S. E. Smith and William S. Dotson; National Association of Teachers in Colored Schools president Francis M. Wood; pioneer settlers of Minnesota townships Greenberry and Charlotte Chambers; and one of the first African Americans to seek public office in the county, John Walden.

A myriad of activities are represented by the photographs as people go about their everyday tasks of making a living by harvesting tobacco, making molasses, sawing timber, or enjoying the simple pleasures of country life. Education has been, and continues to be, of vital significance, as the photographs showcase many students as they proudly stand with their teachers and other visitors in front of their schools. The significance of the one-room school in the community cannot be understated. It was once said that one could claim the hallmarks of greatness if you were born in a log cabin or attended a one-room school, as had Abraham Lincoln. Many Barren residents have this benchmark. The importance of the social gatherings are noted in the photographs of people as they meet for religious ceremonies, family reunions, shopping, ball games, fairs, and parades.

It is a distinctly southern Kentucky tradition to quickly reply the county of origin, not the city, if asked, "Where are you from?" My own ancestors came to Kentucky in 1796 and settled in Barren County area soon after, and so my love and admiration of the county and its citizenry runs deep. In the captions and this pictorial history, I have tried to include significant and interesting facts about the county and its people. I also hope the reader will develop a perspective that showcases the personality of this south central Kentucky county that is defined in the words of family, home, church, school, and kinship, and also see the land as it still is today, beautiful and productive.

One

Glasgow "The Heart of the Barrens"

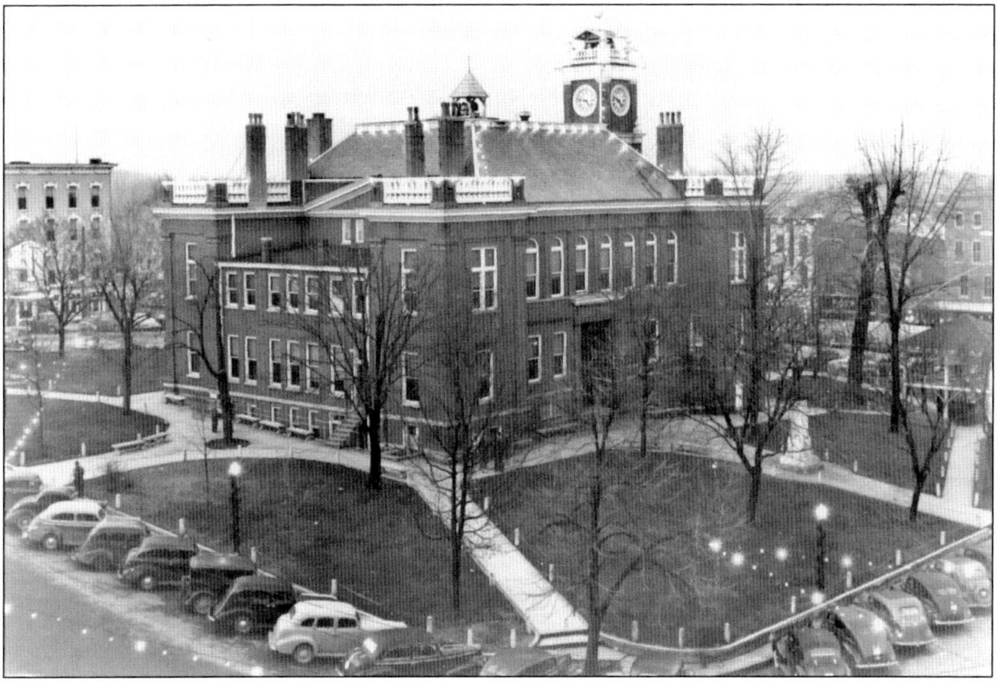

Bright Lights. Barren County's fifth courthouse is shown here decorated for the Christmas season. It was built in 1896 under the administration of Judge G. M. Bohannon. In 1962, the citizens voted to build a new sixth courthouse, as the fifth structure was considered unsafe. It was later dismantled in 1964. The current Georgian-style courthouse replaced it in 1965. (Courtesy of the Glasgow–Barren County Chamber of Commerce.)

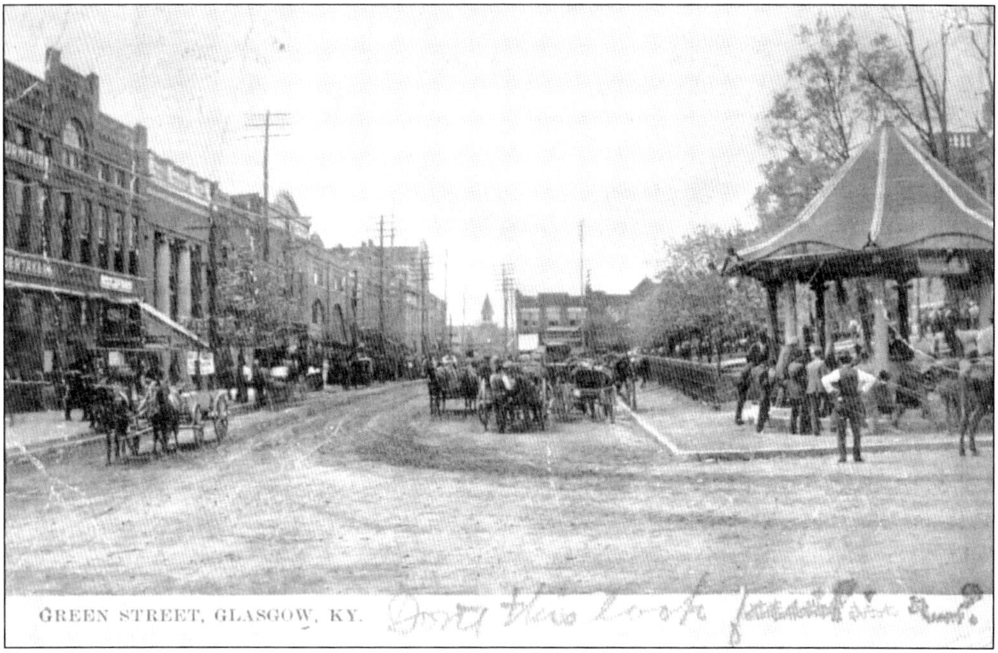

LOOKING SOUTH. Glasgow's Green Street is shown in a postcard image from the early 1900s. This shows "Fountain Corner," which was a favorite gathering spot, with its water tank and ornate bandstand.

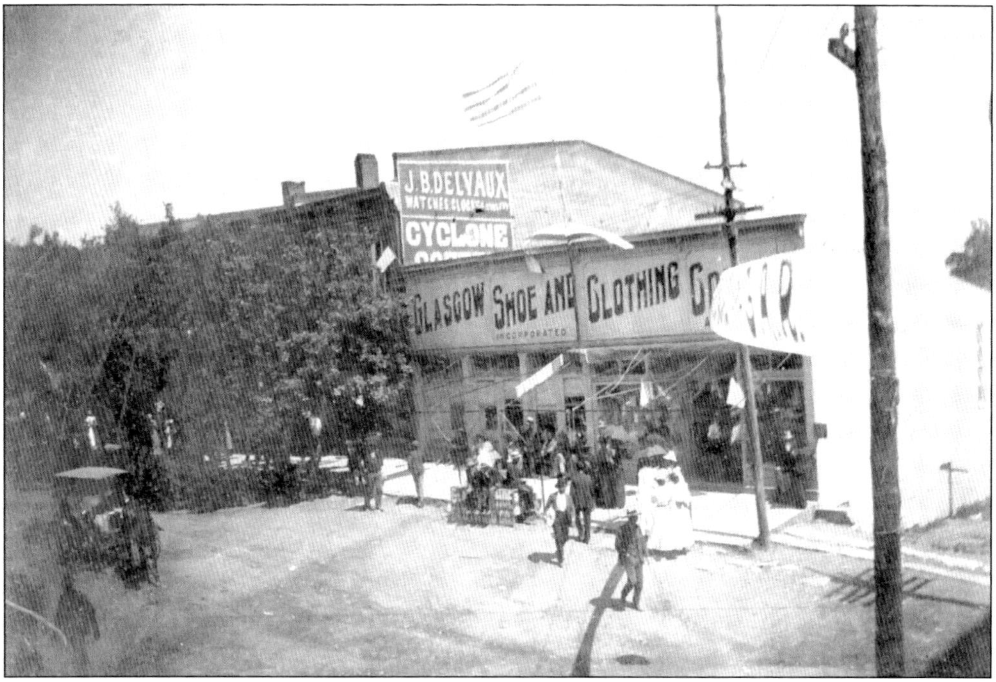

SIDEWALK SALE. Shown before the beginning of the 20th century, Glasgow's square was home to many businesses such as the Glasgow Shoe and Clothing Store. The shop has its wares set out on the street, ready for the crowds that will be coming for the Grand Army of the Republic (GAR) parade, which is seen being advertised on the banner.

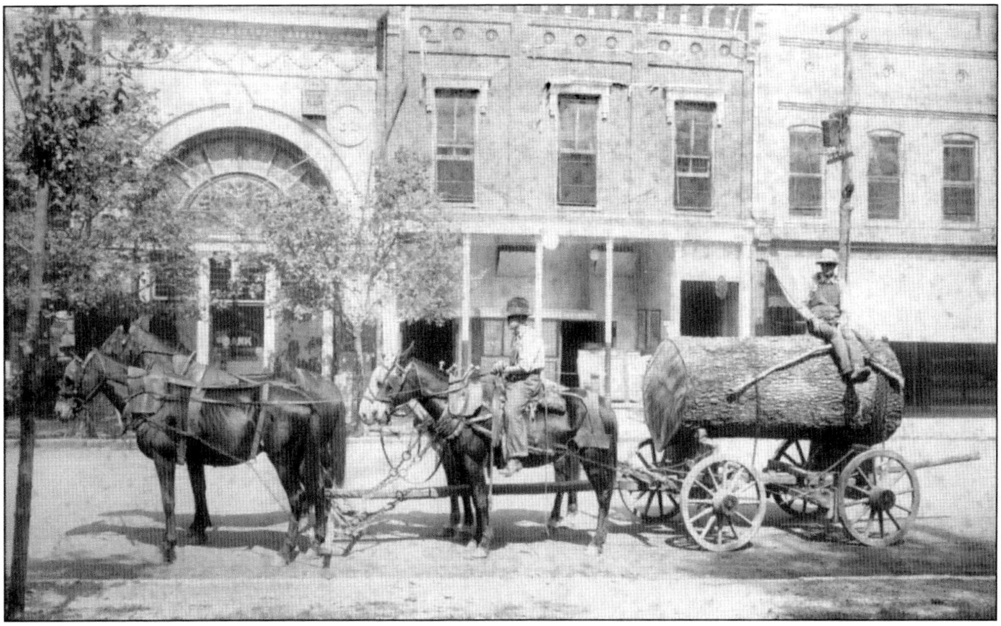

Country Meets City. Barren County, it was said by early explorers, was "two thirds covered with large and stately trees, and the Barrens were dotted with magnificent groves of the finest timber." Harvesting these trees produced many enormous logs to sell and enabled a farmer to supplement his income. Willard Carver is shown astride a mule in front of Glasgow's first theater, the Lion, while Willis Berry enjoys a topside ride. (Courtesy of Runell Houchen.)

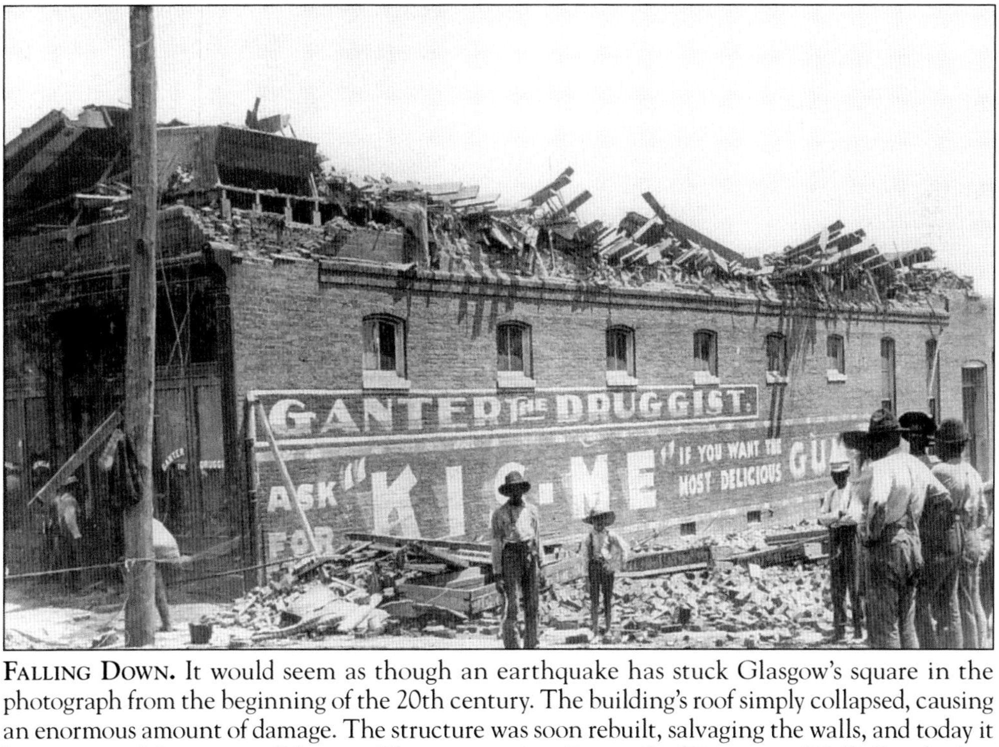

Falling Down. It would seem as though an earthquake has stuck Glasgow's square in the photograph from the beginning of the 20th century. The building's roof simply collapsed, causing an enormous amount of damage. The structure was soon rebuilt, salvaging the walls, and today it houses one of the most well-known Glasgow eateries, George J's. (Courtesy of D. T. Froedge.)

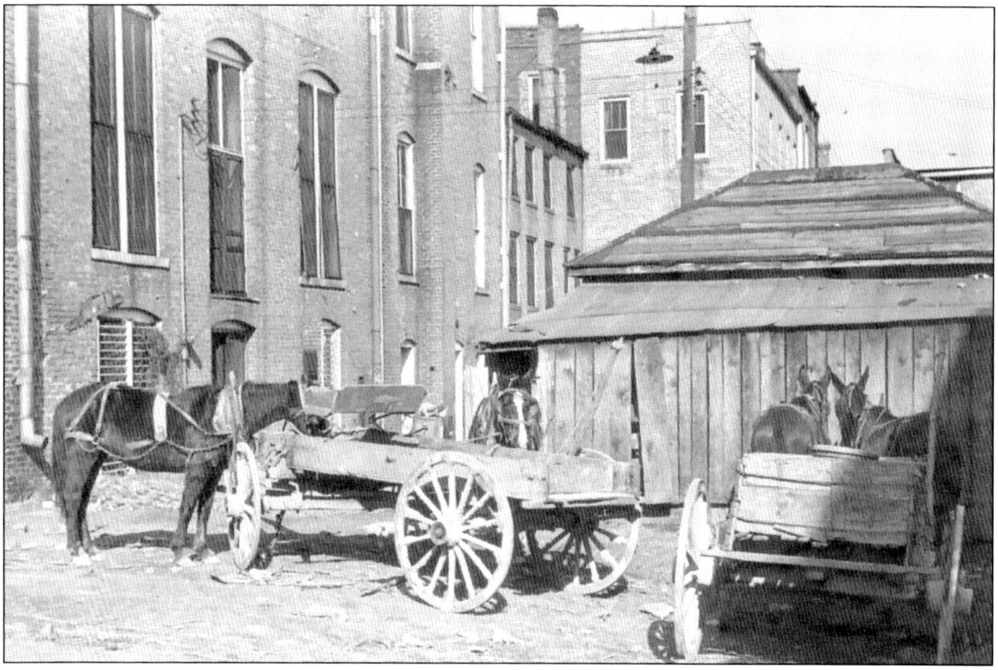

BEHIND THE SCENES. Photographs such as these, which were taken at the beginning of the 20th century, give a glimpse of what it looked like behind the buildings on Glasgow's square. The owners of the rigs had come to town, bringing their families and neighbors, to see an exciting event or to pick up a week's supplies.

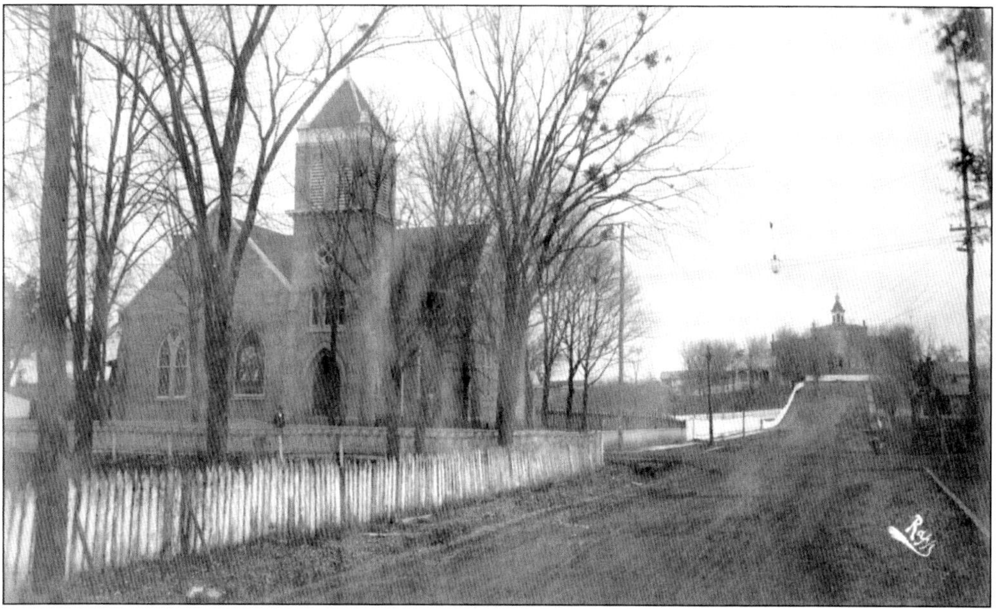

A LONG VIEW. Glasgow's second-oldest church, the Glasgow Baptist Church was organized in 1818. After the first building was torn down, this impressive two-story building, with its pointed turret and arched windows, was soon erected. The iconic church is the largest church in Glasgow. Also seen in the photograph is Liberty Female College, which was founded in 1875. (Courtesy of Special Collections: Ekstrom Library, University of Louisville.)

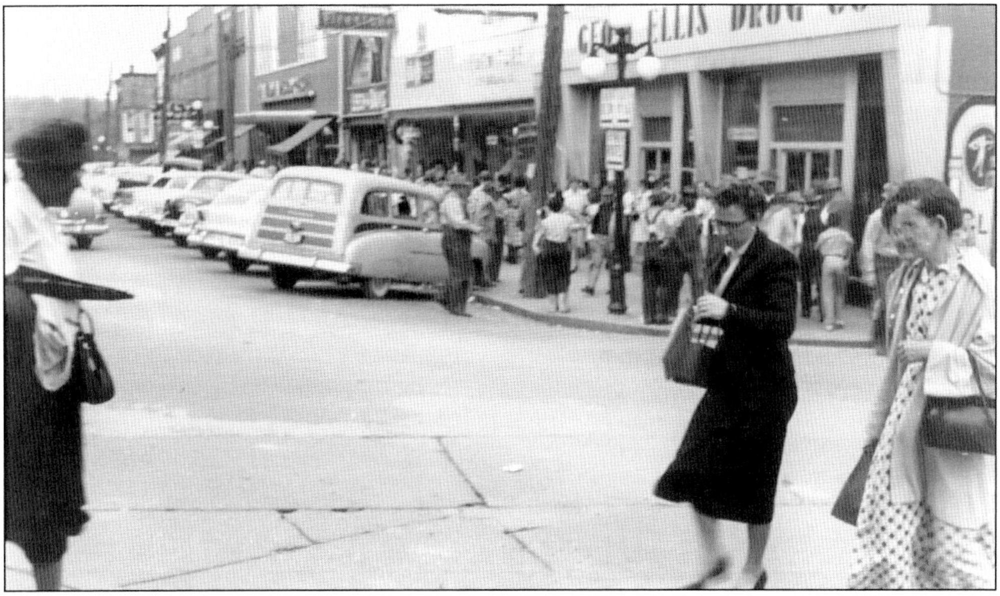

BUSY DOWNTOWN. The Glasgow Square in the 1940s and 1950s bustled, as it was the shopping hub of many counties. These photographs show busy Saturdays with people from Tompkinsville, Munfordville, Cave City, Horse Cave, and Edmonton enjoying the food, fun, and excitement that always seemed to be there. Since the malls and larger stores have drawn people away from the town square and markets, it is a sight now unfamiliar to many. Both photographs show the square with the familiar George J. Ellis Drug Company. Of particular interest in the photograph below is the poster, "America Calling, Take Your Place in Civil Defense," which was created for the war effort in 1941. (Above, courtesy of Winston Nunn; below, courtesy of D. T. Froedge.)

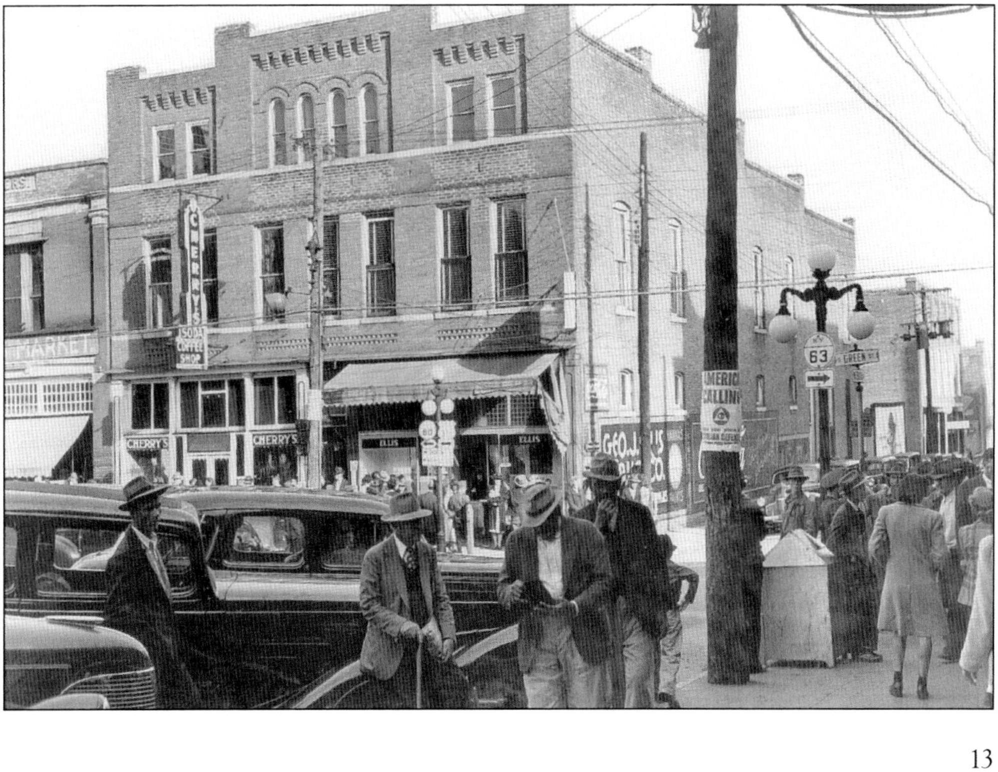

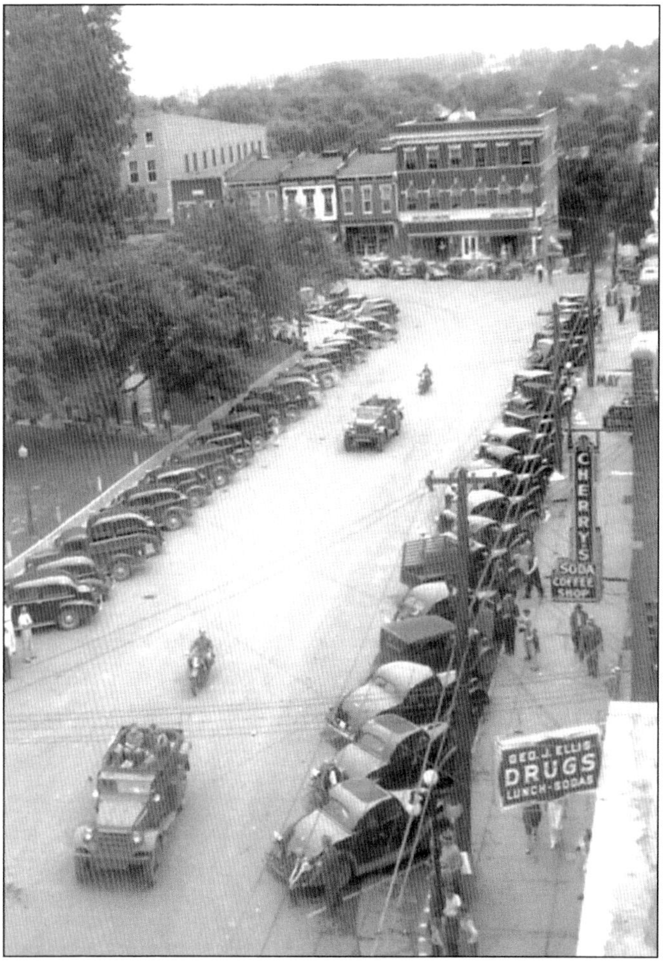

Converted Criminal. Ex-convict and evangelist Emmett "Texas Slim" Vestal visited the county as part of the HAAG Circus, which offered family entertainment, no dancing girls, and no gambling. Vestal was the last surviving member of the bank robbing Tom Slaughter gang. Slaughter had lived for a time in Park City and was successful in robbing the Peoples Bank of $8,500. In Vestal's 1934 memoir, *Ten Years in Hell*, he recounted his exploits that lead him to being sentenced to death two times, with a pardon coming only four minutes before his last scheduled execution. He regaled his audiences with his trademark statement about his bullet-riddled body, "I am glad I am a sieve for the Lord; they used to pump lead at me but now I pump the Bible at them." Reverend Vestal announces his coming via loudspeaker in the image below.

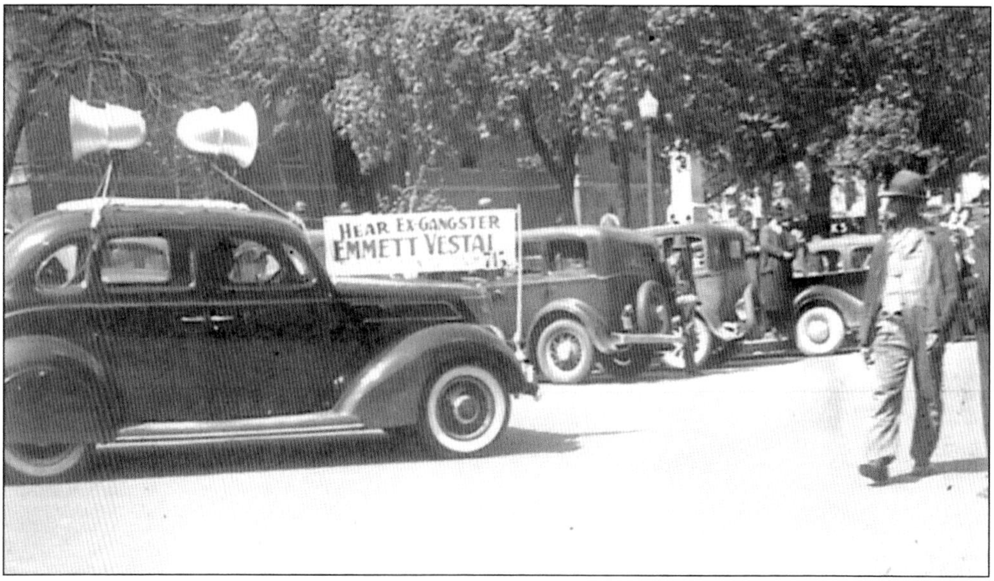

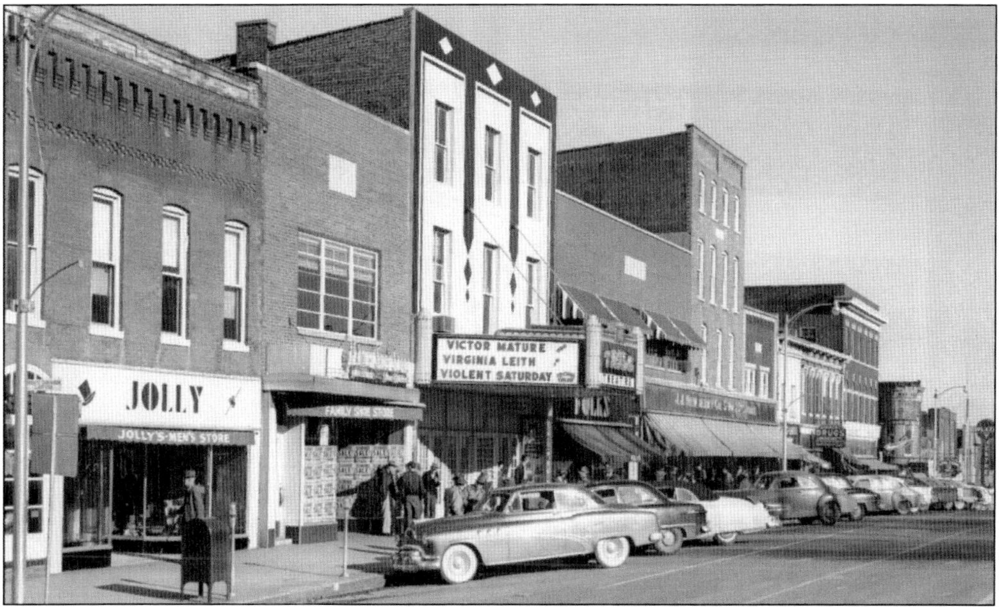

The Way It Used to Be. This exciting Glasgow Square still lives on in the memory of many Barren residents. The photograph above shows some of the favorite stores on the North Public Square, which include the following: Jolly's Men's Store, Folks, Simmons Drugs, and Newberry's. It was a time of growth and expansion for both the city and county, which were aided by an active chamber of commerce. At the time of this photograph, the chamber had just won a prize for distinction in the Kentucky Chamber of Commerce Community Development Contest. The photograph below shows the east side of the square, with its beloved Ben Franklin, National Store, Ely Drugs, and other stores. Look carefully; parking was at a premium, as there were no open spots on a busy day. (Both, courtesy of the Glasgow–Barren County Chamber of Commerce.)

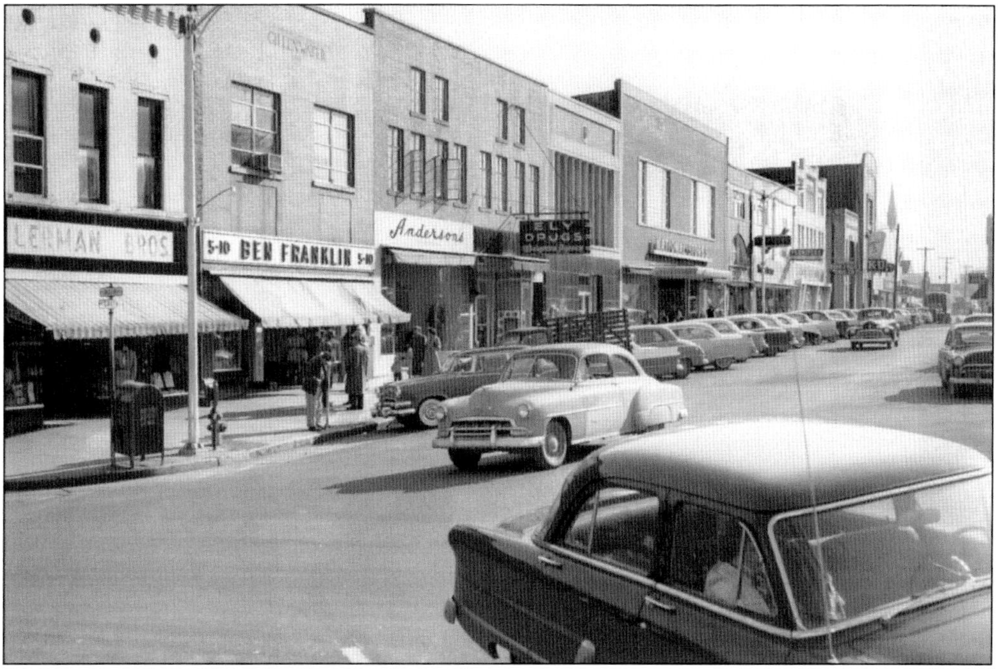

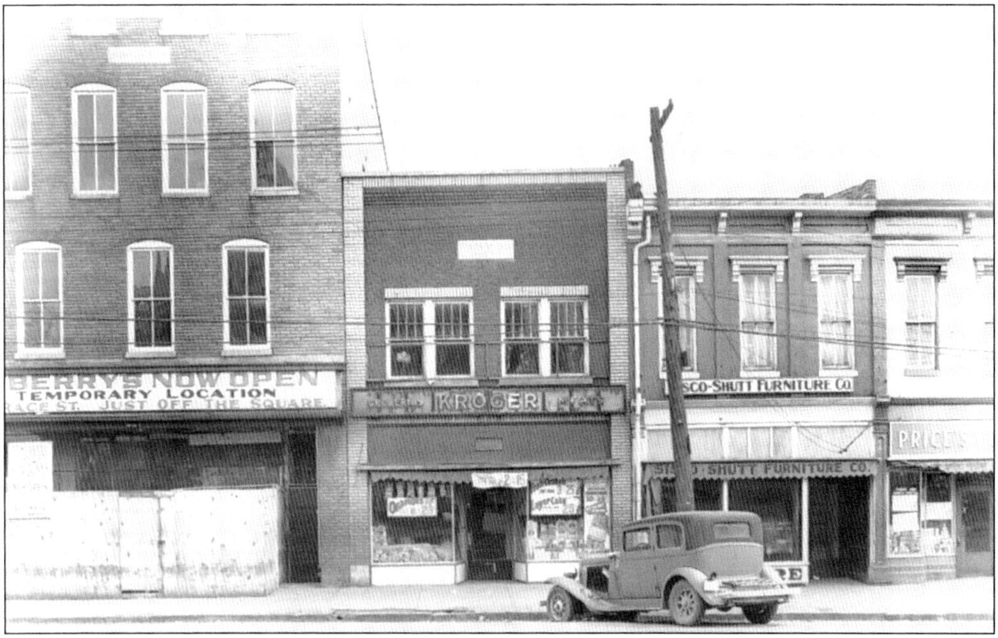

DISAPPEARING ACT. This Kroger store is a sight not seen in Barren County. At the time of this photograph, Kroger was operating 5,575 stores, the most in its history, and chose Glasgow as one of its locations. Local competition from homegrown stores caused people to fear the rapid growth of chains and their consequent power over this industry, and to this day, Kroger does not have a store in Barren County.

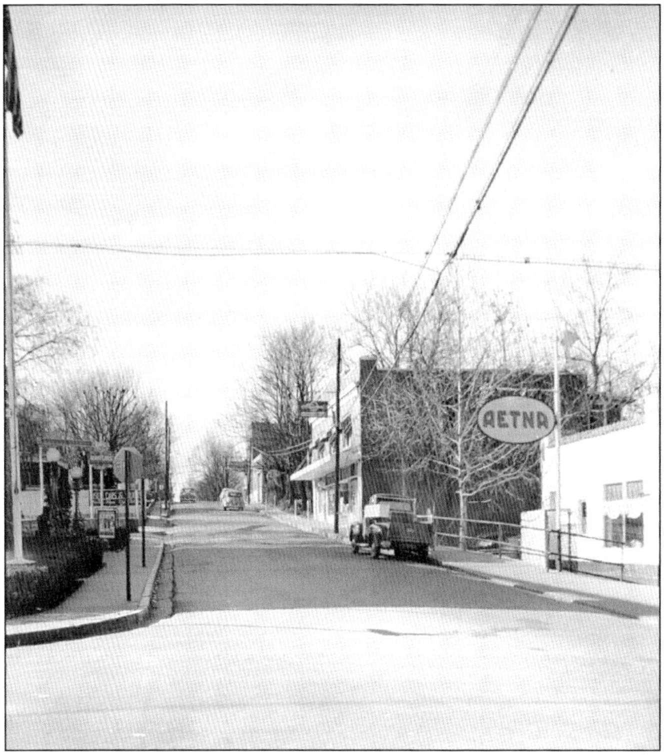

LOOKING AHEAD. This view of Washington Street in Glasgow will look familiar to residents. The business names have changed, but many of the buildings remain. The former post office building at 202 West Washington Street now houses the Barren County Board of Education offices. The Colonial Revival–style building is listed on the National Register of Historic Places. (Courtesy of the Glasgow–Barren County Chamber of Commerce.)

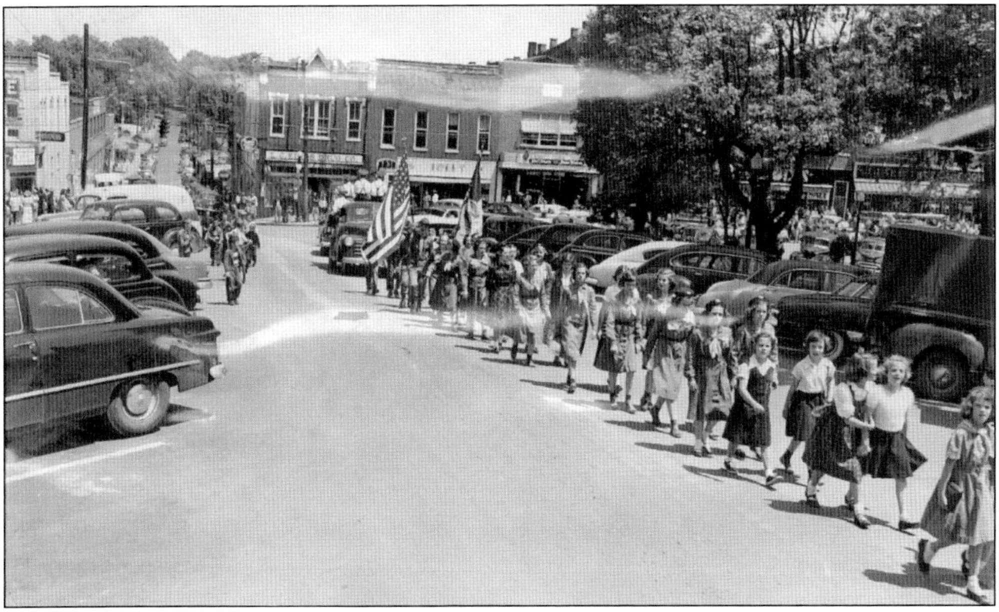

CLEANING UP. As they come up North Race Street, scouts of all ages lead the "Clean Up Campaign" parade. Their mothers and other ladies were also a part of the effort. City leaders brought together local businesses, organizations, and schools, asking that everyone aide in the efforts to make sure their little corner of the world was as clean and bright as possible. The campaigns usually lasted a week and, in some cases, included prizes or badges for those collecting the most cans or bottles. These types of activities continue today, as scout organizations conduct similar educational programs, tree planting, and other environmental projects throughout the county. (Both, courtesy of the Glasgow–Barren County Chamber of Commerce.)

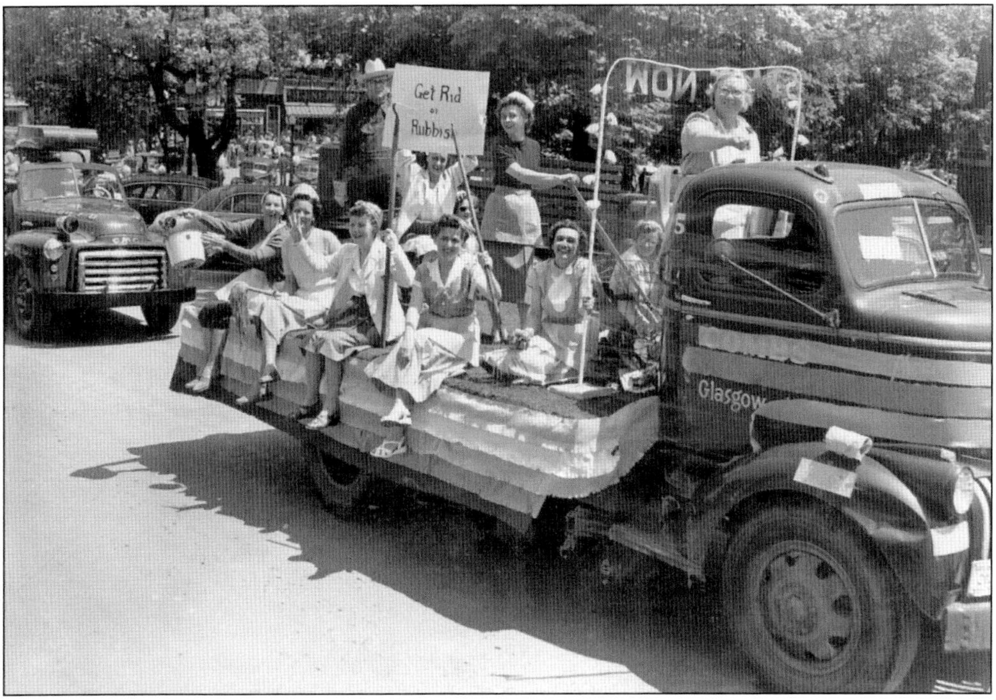

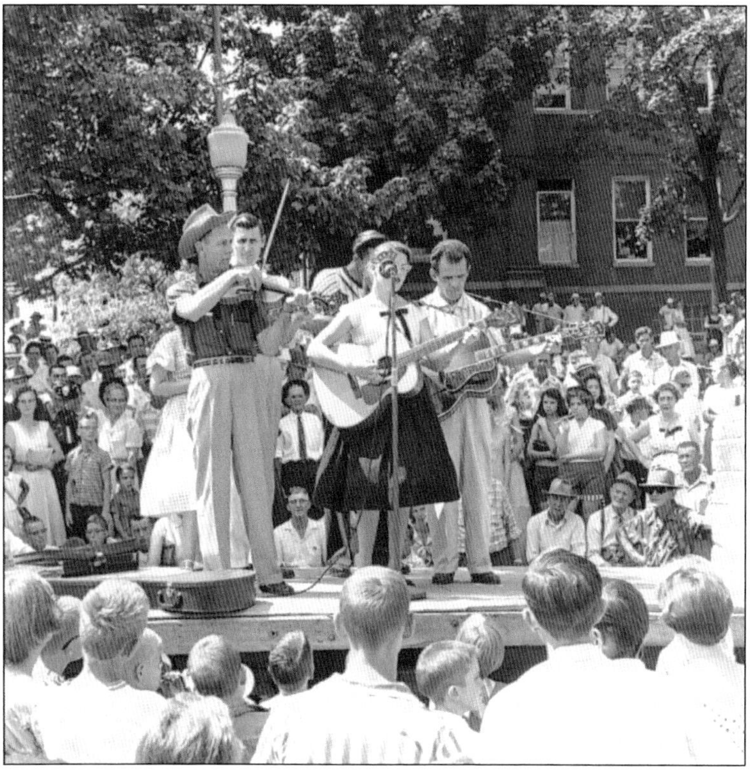

Let Me Entertain You. The county attracted many professional and amateur acts, which drew large crowds to the downtown area and merchants. This group performs on the bed of a farm wagon as their performance is broadcast over WKAY Radio. The station was Glasgow's first radio station, and its opening ceremonies were on September 25, 1946. Performers are, from left to right, Pat Kingrey, Bill Wagoner, Iola Weaver, and Troy Basil.

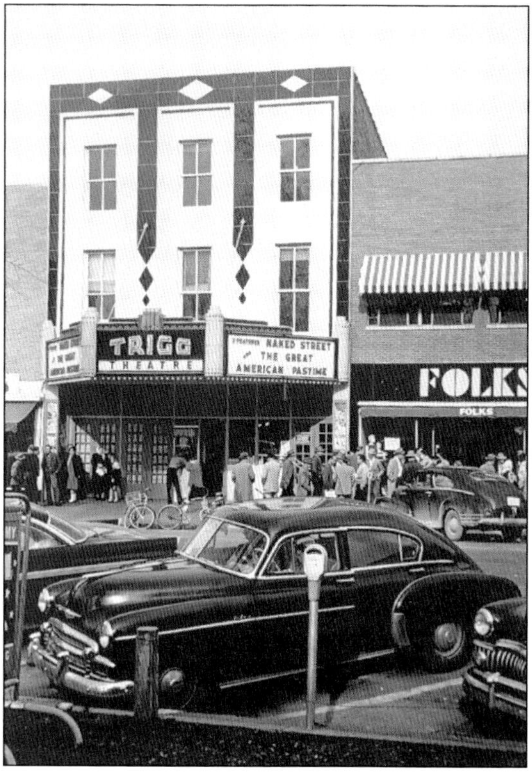

Best in Show. The Trigg Theater provided many hours of entertainment for county residents. In 1916, Bruce Aspley opened it in the spot previously occupied by the county's first theater, the Lion. One of the first air-conditioning systems made it an even more wonderful place to visit during the summer. The theater closed in 1956, though the art deco–style facade can still be seen today. (Courtesy of the Glasgow–Barren County Chamber of Commerce.)

Charity Begins at the Theater. The Plaza Theater, one of Glasgow's treasured landmarks, opened in August 1934. Seating 1,200 in wonderful air-conditioned comfort, the theater charged a nickel for the shows during the 1930s and 1940s. The theater was sold to the City of Glasgow in 2001 and extensively restored. Today it is used for many different types of events and programs. In the 1937 photograph below, members of the Lions Club, ministers, merchants, school teachers, and other members of fraternal organizations spearheaded food drives around the holidays to collect food for the needy in the community or for school lunch programs. The Plaza Theater offered a free show to all bringing in a nonperishable food item. Bags of sugar, flour, meal, and large sacks of potatoes are prominent in the image, as well as many home-canned items. (Right, courtesy Glasgow–Barren County Chamber of Commerce.)

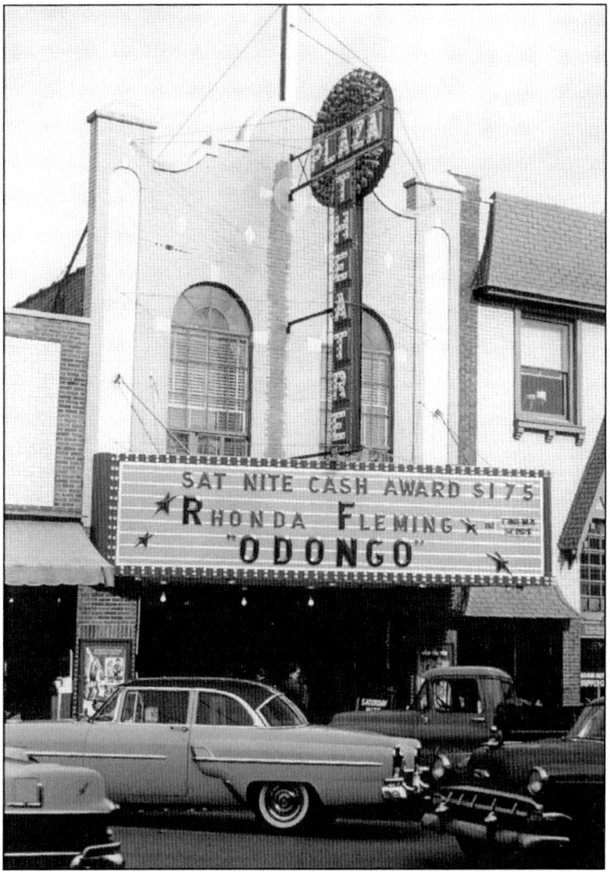

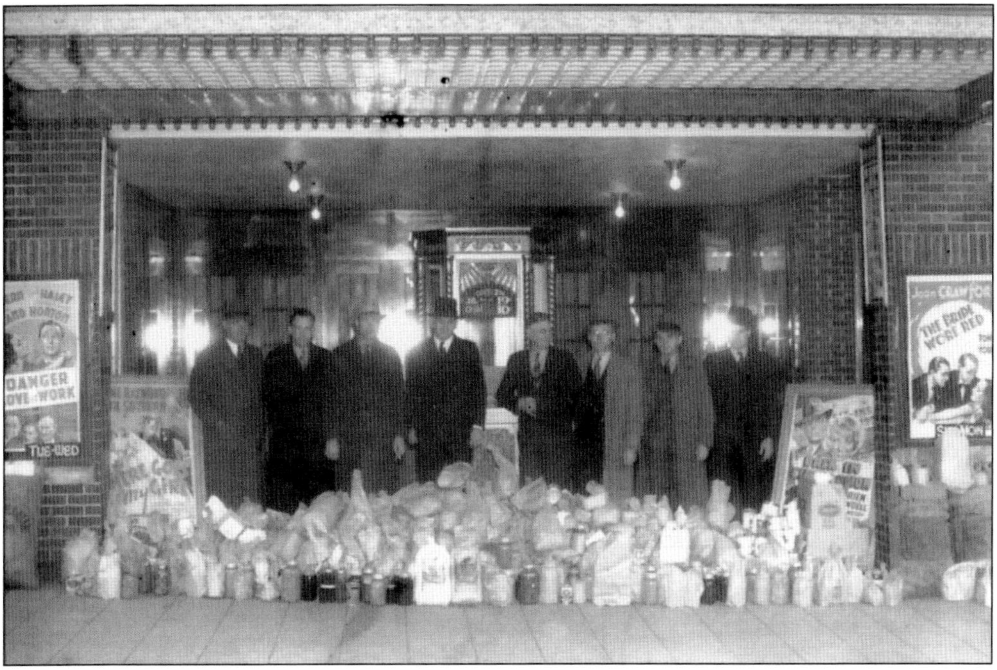

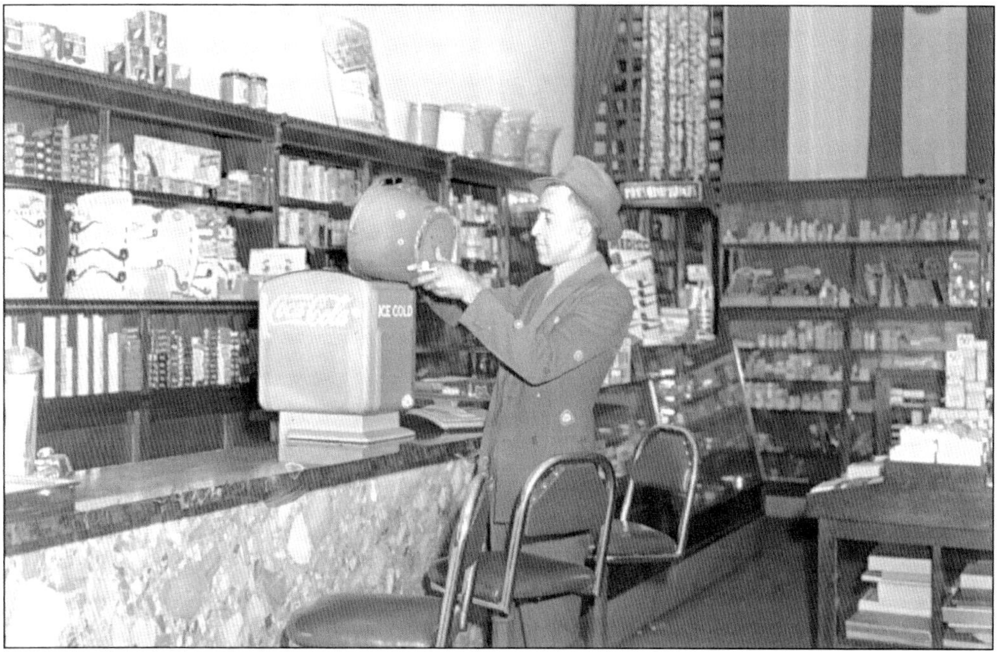

Filler-Up. George Bransford fills up the ice machine so that the wording on the Coca-Cola dispenser will ring true. Bransford was a staple at the George J. Ellis drugstore and took care of the many tasks involved in keeping the popular business running smoothly.

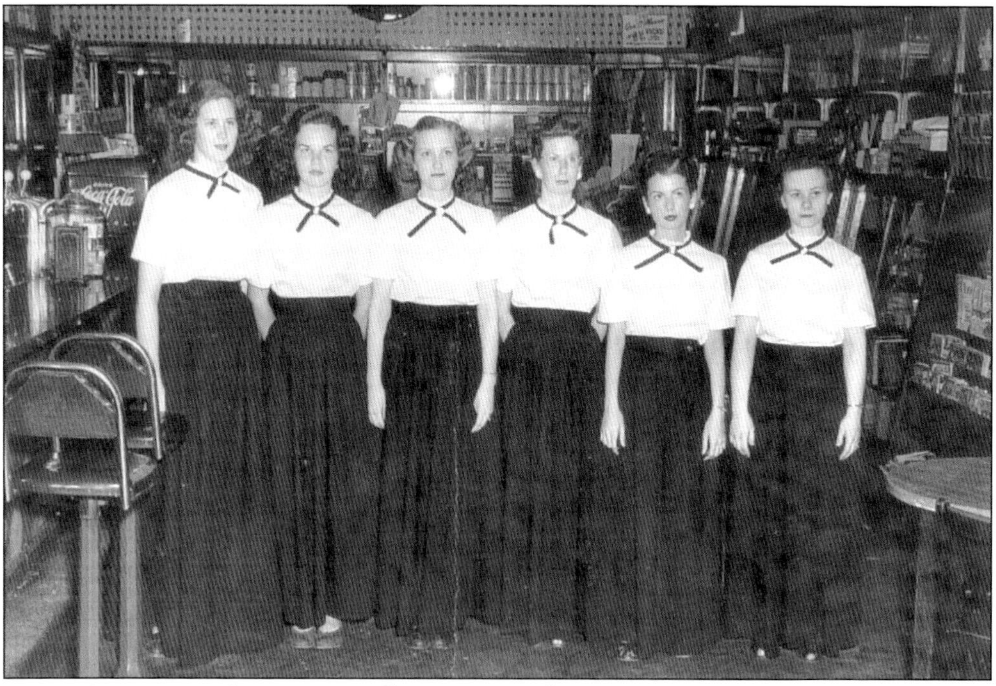

Let Us Serve You. The waitress staff at George J. Ellis was instantly recognizable in their crisp white shirts and collared ties. The staff members in 1948 were, from left to right, Violet Spillman Stevens, Shirley Morrison Bacon, Bernette Payne Bowles, Margaret Bragg Huskinson, unidentified, and Rena May Shelton Galloway. (Courtesy of D. T. Froedge.)

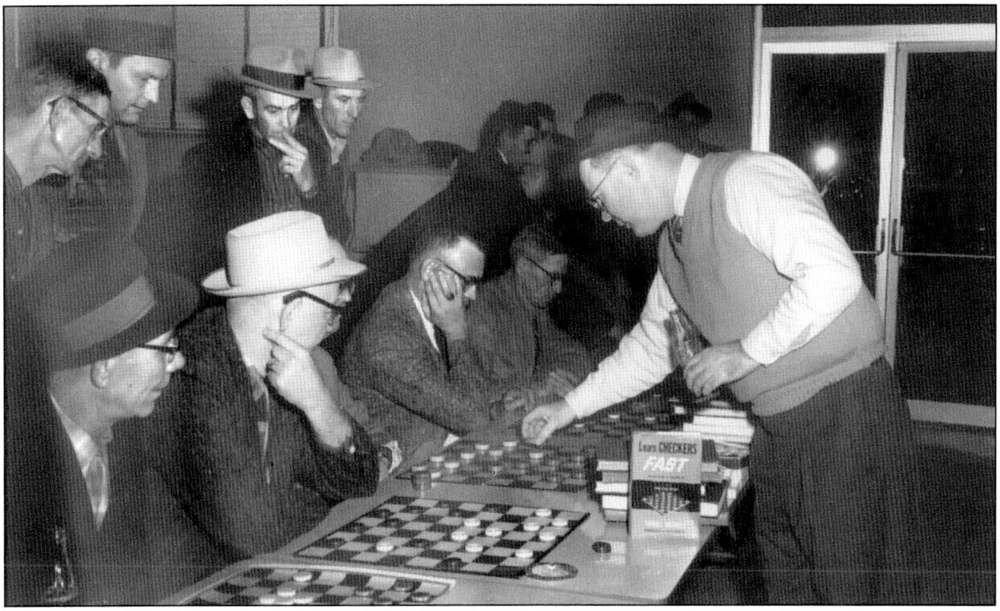

CHECKERS ANYONE? The competition could be furious in tournaments. The well-known player Col. Tom Wiswell, who was the world checker champion at one time, made appearances in town. He would play all comers, and a challenger only had to bring a board. Some of the players apparently learned on the spot, as can be seen by the book entitled *Learn Checkers Fast*. Grandmaster checker champion Don Morgan Lafferty was born in Barren County.

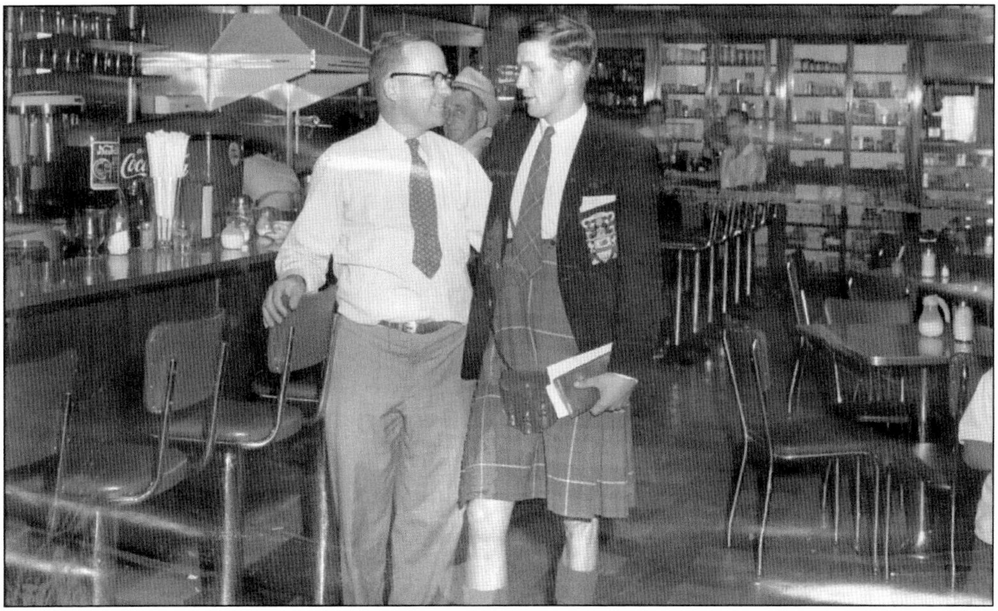

CULTURAL EXCHANGE. Though there is some disagreement about the naming of Glasgow after the Scottish town, the ties of friendship were evident, as shown in this photograph of exchange student Andrew Hamilton of Lanarkshire. Hamilton was representing the Young Farmers Club of Scotland and was the guest of the Hermon Barlow family of Cave City at their Bar-Lu farm. It was said Hamilton charmed everyone with his wit and humor. (Courtesy of the Glasgow–Barren County Chamber of Commerce.)

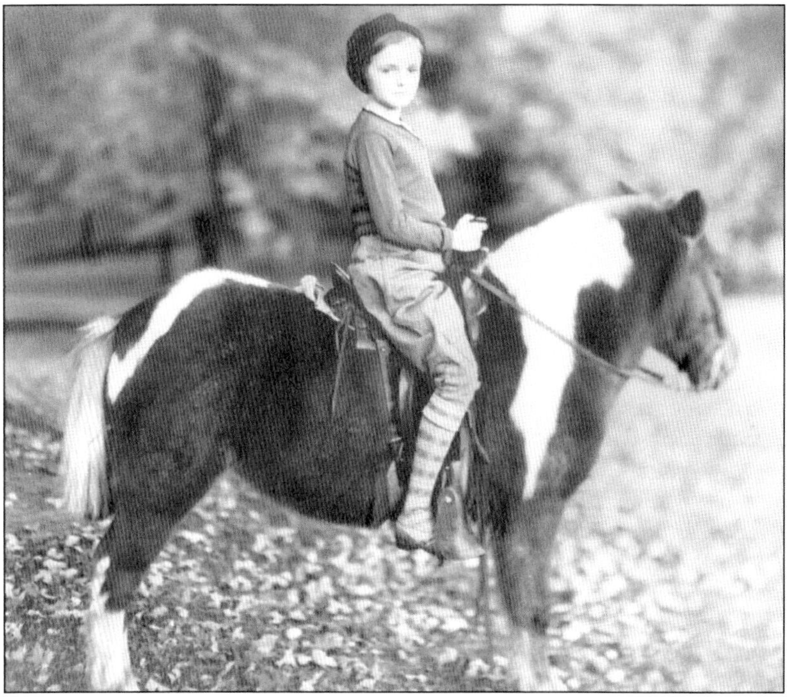

A Special Pet. Many children like to dream of the fun that they could have, if they only had a pony. For Sarah Rogers Coffman, that dream came true. Sarah sits proudly atop Topsy as she poses for her picture on North Race Street in 1930. (Courtesy of Perry Brantley.)

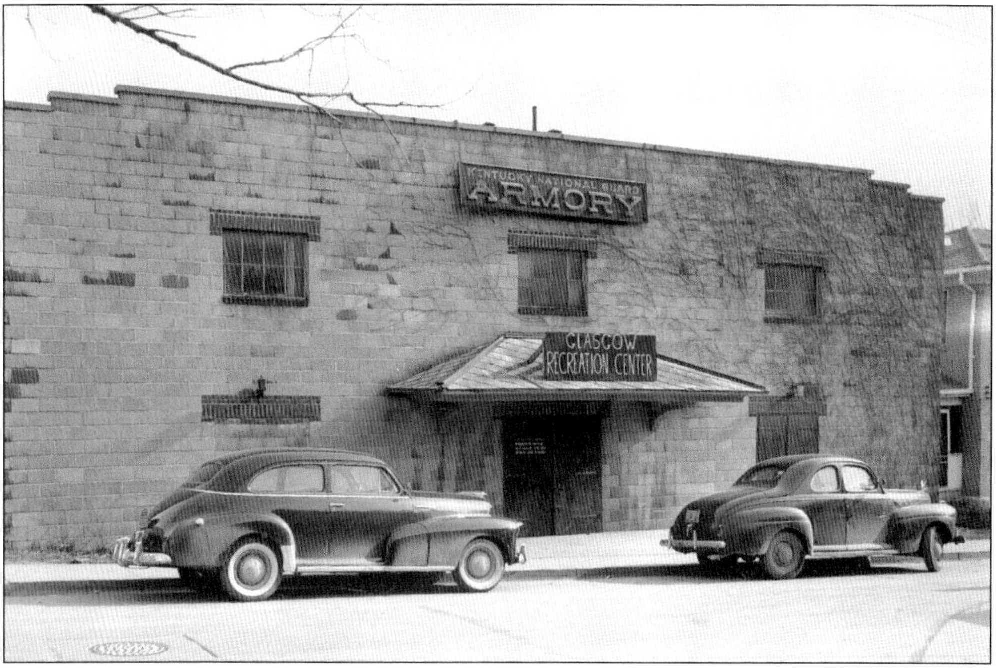

Dual Purpose. The Kentucky National Guard Armory on South Race Street served dual purposes, as have many of the buildings in Glasgow. The building, constructed in 1928, was one of the only places in town where larger functions could be held, and since it included a stage and dressing room, it was used for weekly wrestling matches. The National Guard used the building until 1964, when a new building was constructed on Cavalry Drive. (Courtesy of the Glasgow–Barren County Chamber of Commerce.)

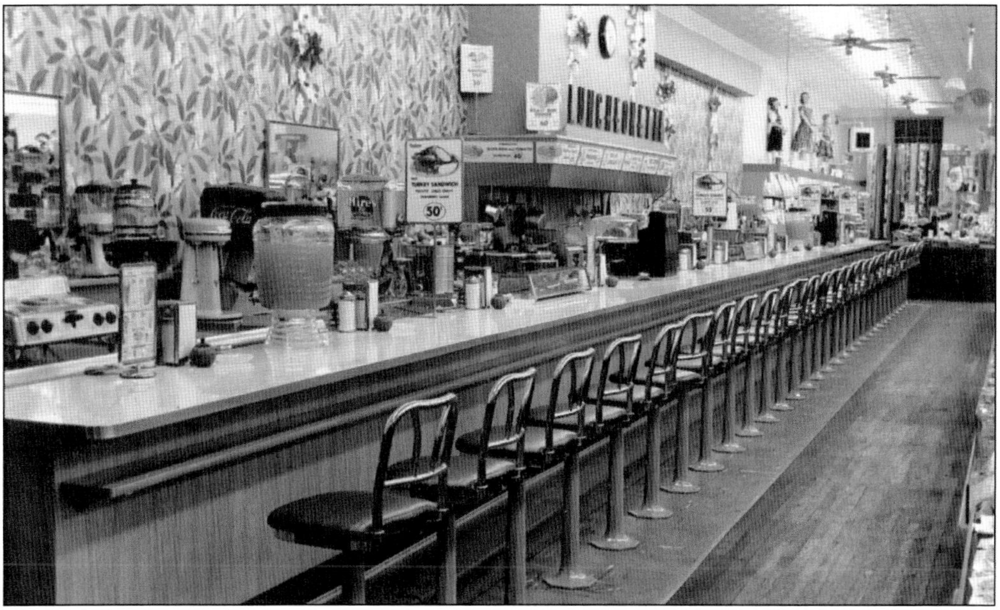

LUNCH TIME. Newberry's lunch counter in 1952 was one of the most popular spots in town to have a quick, but tasty meal. Many fondly remember the "Mexican" hamburgers and coleslaw. The store had two levels, and the stairs were well traveled, because at this time the toy department was in the basement. Note the mixture of merchandise juxtaposed with the hardware and toy departments and the five-and-dime store prices. Newspaper advertisements of the day, listed the following prices: cereal bowls and coffee mugs, three for 25¢; men's short sleeve shirt at 88¢; chenille bedspreads, $2.77; and extra-large woolen blankets at $2.80. The building housing the Newberry's store was torn down in 1999 for the construction of county government offices. (Both, courtesy of the Glasgow–Barren County Chamber of Commerce.)

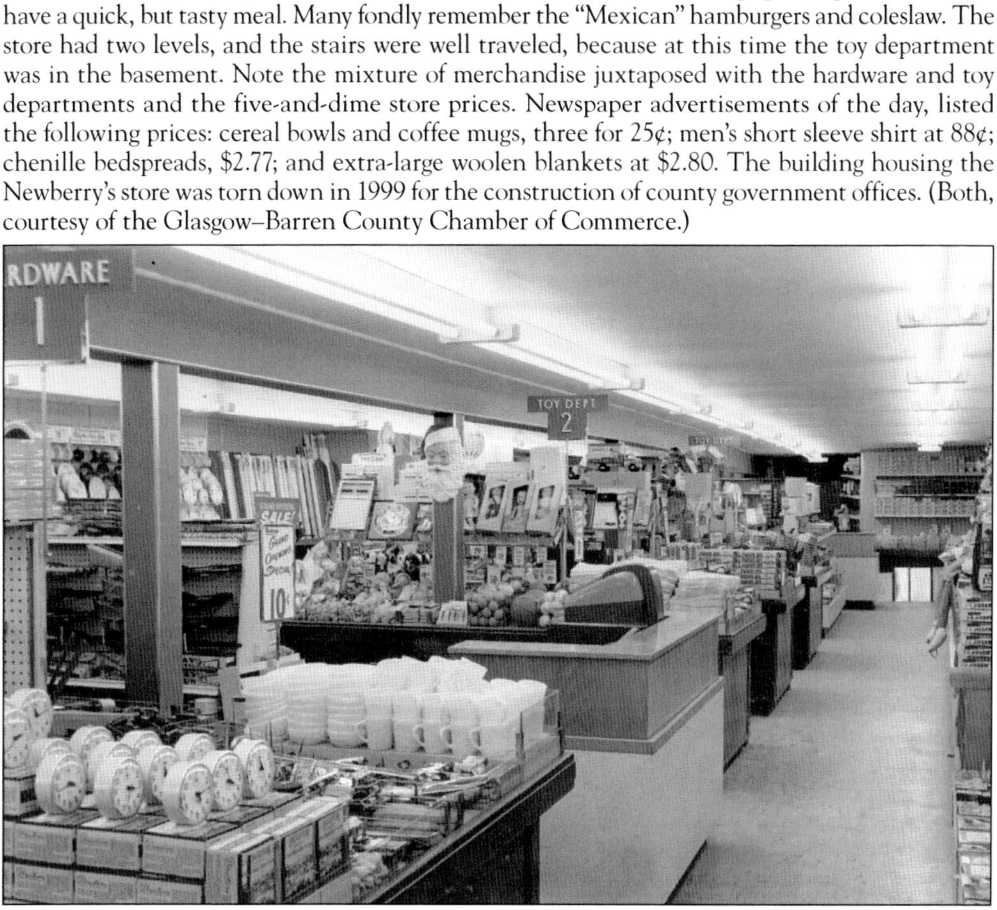

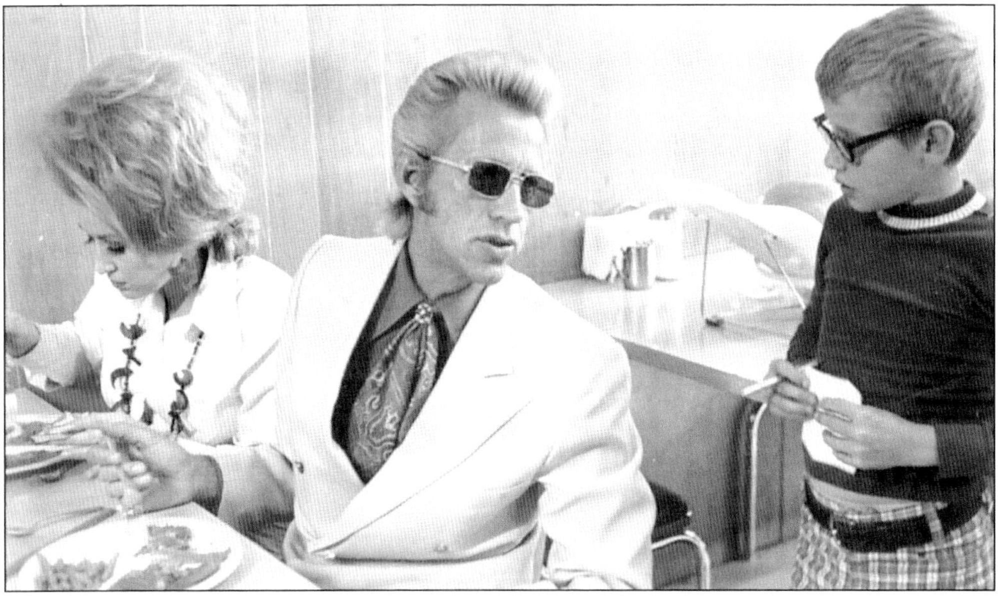

Dining with Dolly. Barren County has produced its share of celebrities, and as can be seen in this photograph, they have visited as well. A young Dolly Parton and her singing partner, Porter Wagoner, are enjoying a meal at Montgomery's restaurant on the Glasgow Square but are interrupted by an eager autograph seeker. (Courtesy of Jimmy Lowe.)

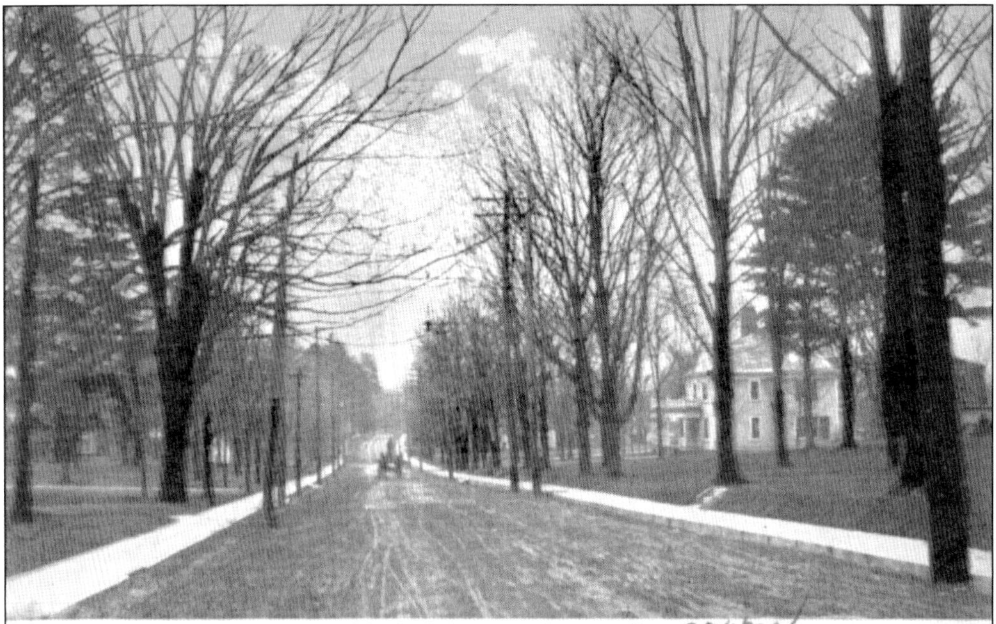

Scenic Street. There are many picturesque streets and scenic roads in Glasgow and Barren County. One of the most familiar to residents is shown in this postcard from 1900. Though it was known as Maple Driveway, the street is now called South Green Street. The beautiful well-kept homes are in stark contrast to the muddy unpaved streets in the image.

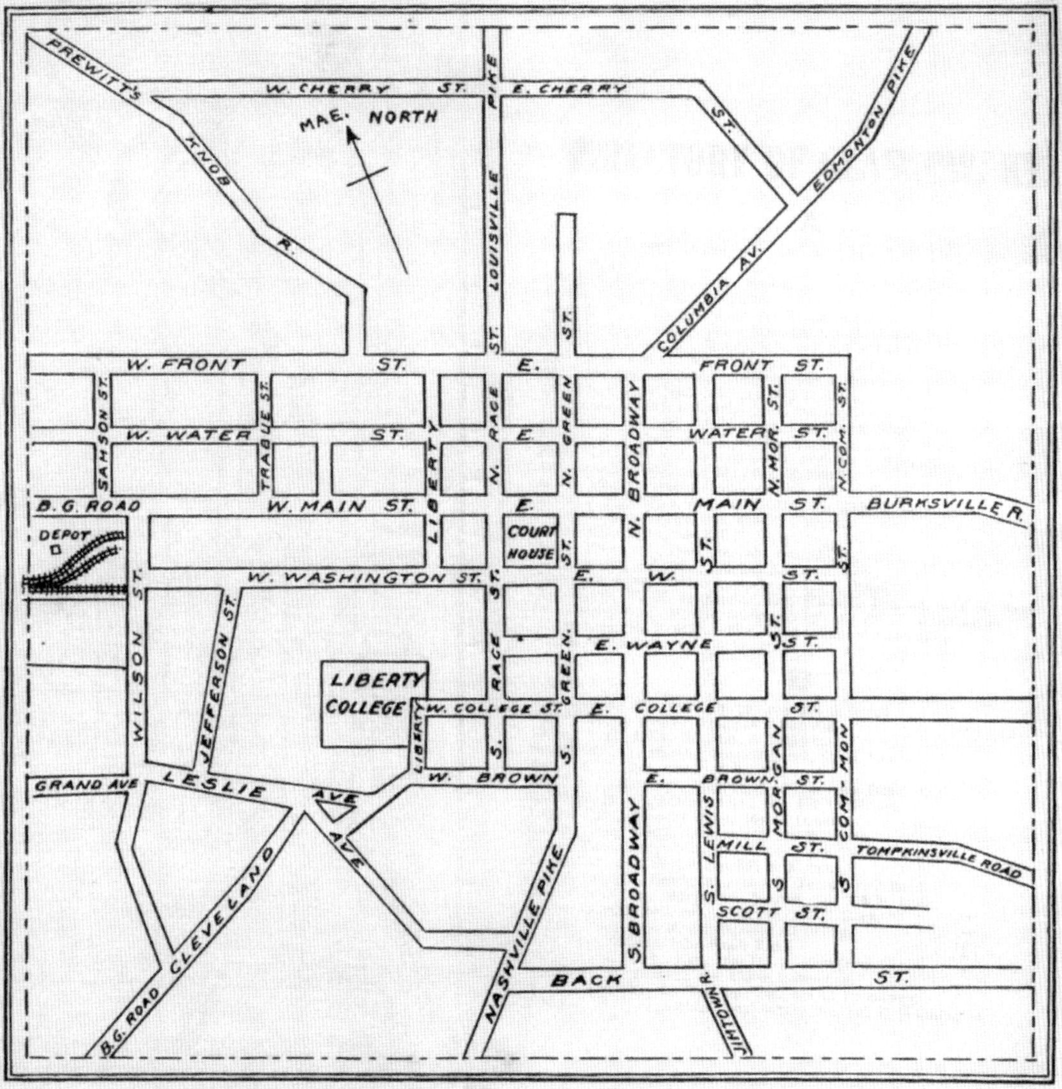

Streets are numbered East from N. Race and S. Green Sts. Streets are numbered North and South from Main St.

MAPPING GLASGOW. This map of Glasgow from the beginning of the 20th century shows the main streets, roads, railroad, and depot. The map would still be usable today, as most of the street names remained unchanged.

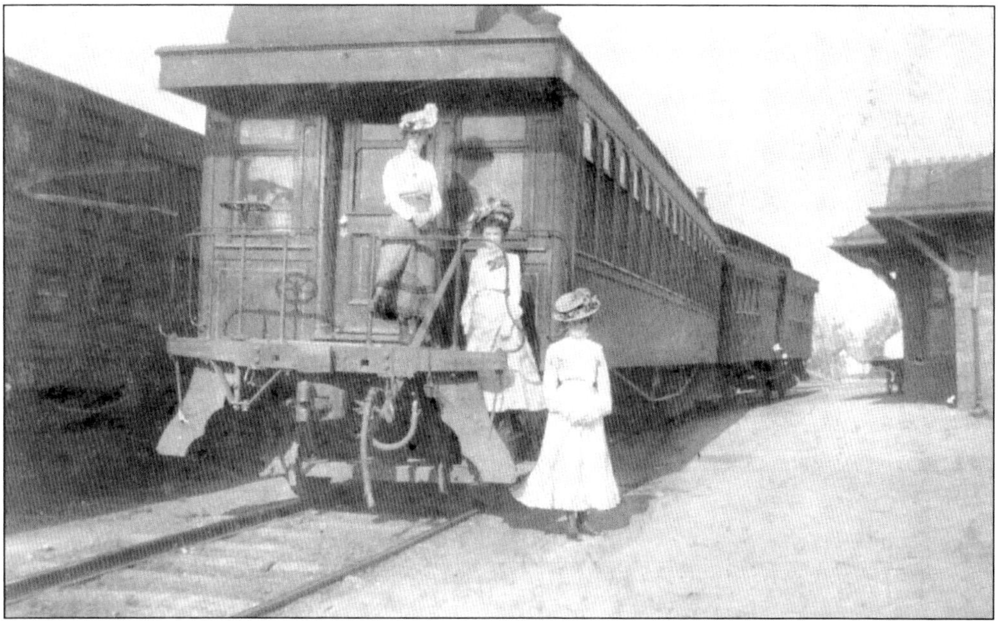

All Aboard! These young ladies are dressed in their best as they wait at the Glasgow Depot. Glasgow lost out to other communities for a main railroad line but built its own spur line to connect with the Louisville and Nashville Railroad at Glasgow Junction (Park City). The style of the depot was similar to many that were built in Kentucky following the Civil War. (Courtesy of Perry Brantley.)

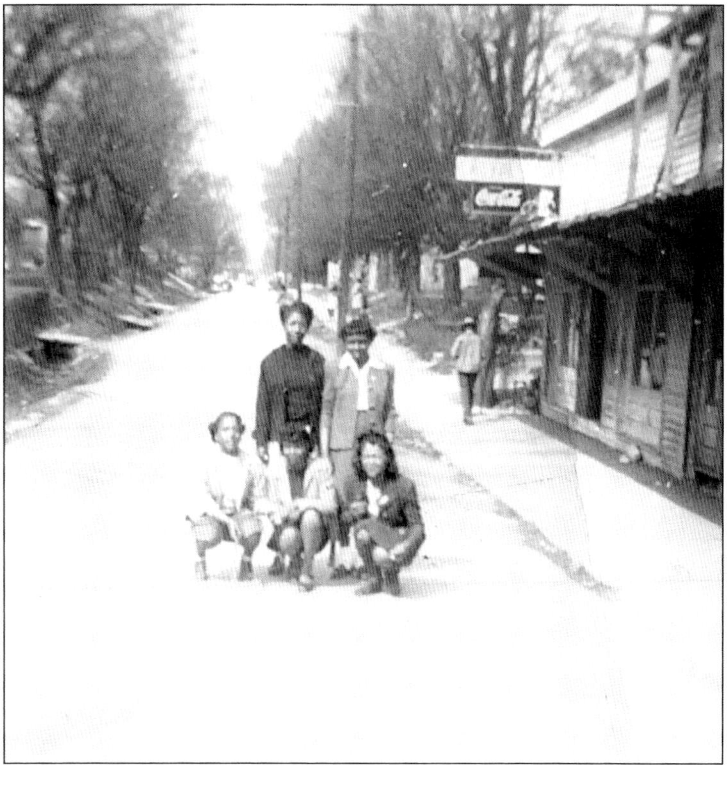

Proudly Posing. This group of young ladies happily poses for the camera on Lewis Street in front of the Royal Café. The sign can be seen in the background with its Coca-Cola advertisement. Many in the county still fondly remember the café and its wonderful food and fellowship. (Courtesy of Alma Glover.)

LOST TO FIRE. Moran's, a local Ford dealer, lost its business to a fire in the 1940s. The company was located at the intersection of Wayne and South Green Streets. Glasgow has suffered several devastating fires during the last century. In 1900, most of the east side of the square was destroyed when Raubold's Confectionery and Restaurant burned. (Courtesy of Winston Nunn.)

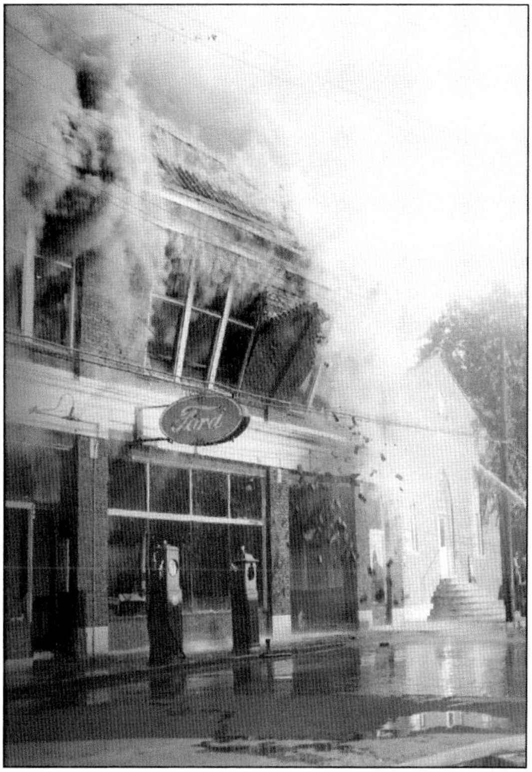

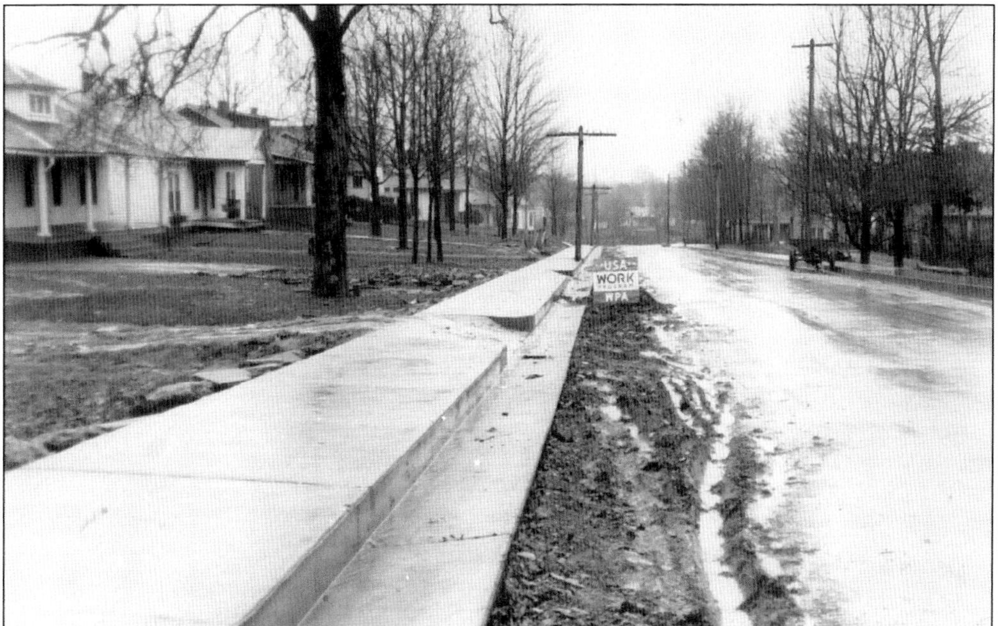

NEW AND IMPROVED. Barren County and Glasgow benefited greatly from the Work Projects Administration (WPA), as did the whole nation. It was, at one time, the largest employer in the country. Many men worked in public projects such as road building and the sidewalk, curb, and gutter reconstruction shown on this Glasgow Street in 1935.

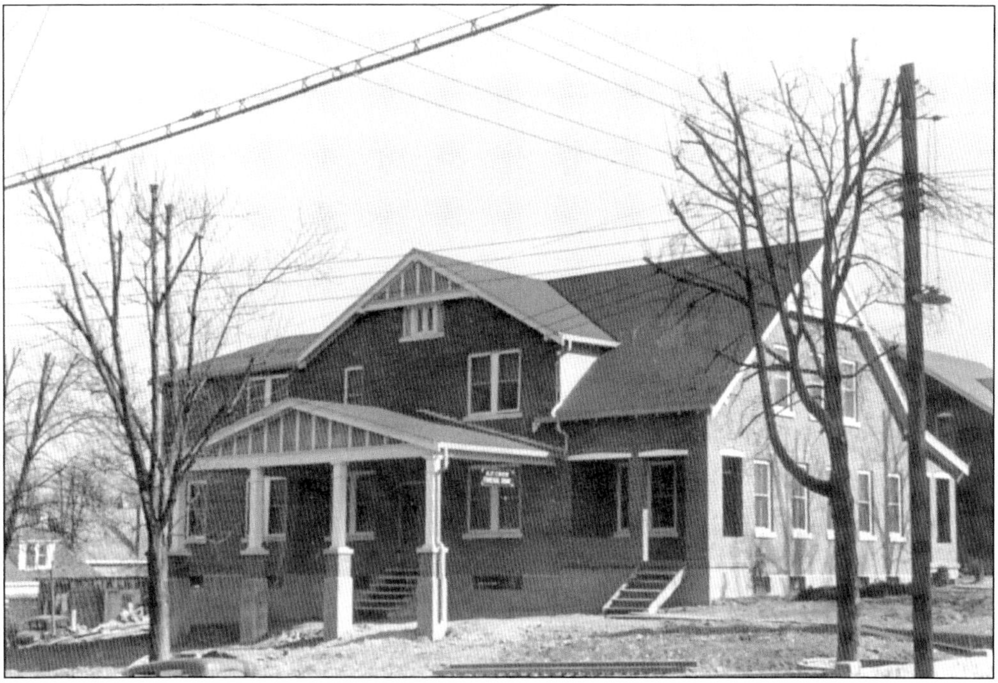

FAMILY BUSINESS. Aubrey F. Crow Sr. opened the Crow funeral home in 1928. A third generation of the family, Aubrey "Follis" Crow III continues as president and manager of the firm. The building facade has changed through the years, but its location is a landmark of Glasgow.

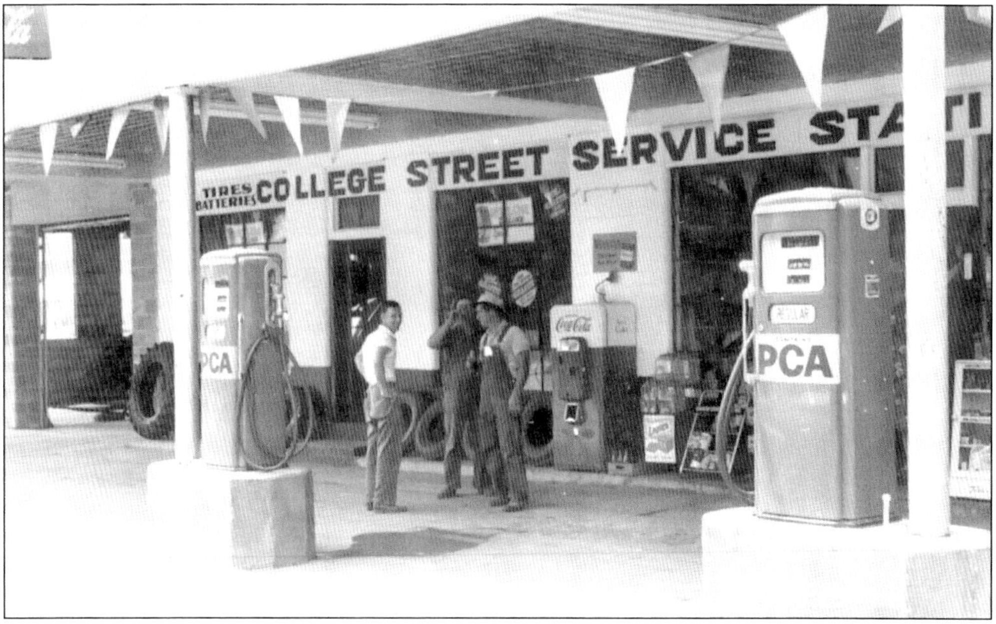

COLLEGE STREET SERVICE. The College Street service station is another Barren County and Glasgow landmark. Although the gas pumps have been removed, the exterior of the station remains virtually unchanged from the time of this photograph, and the station still offers quick and friendly service. (Courtesy of Billy Pritchard.)

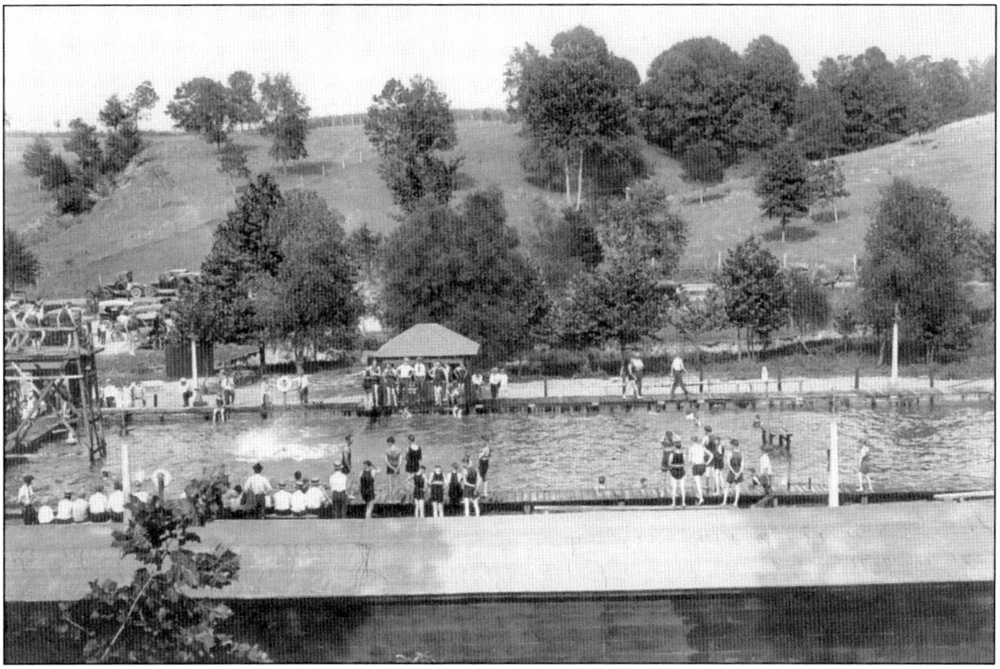

OLD SWIMMING HOLE. There was nothing old about this wonderful swimming pool that was once located on North 31-E. It was the first swimming pool in the county. The beautiful setting and large modern pool attracted many area-wide visitors for a day of fun in the water. Note the absence of young ladies in the pool and the Budweiser advertisement. (Courtesy of Perry Brantley.)

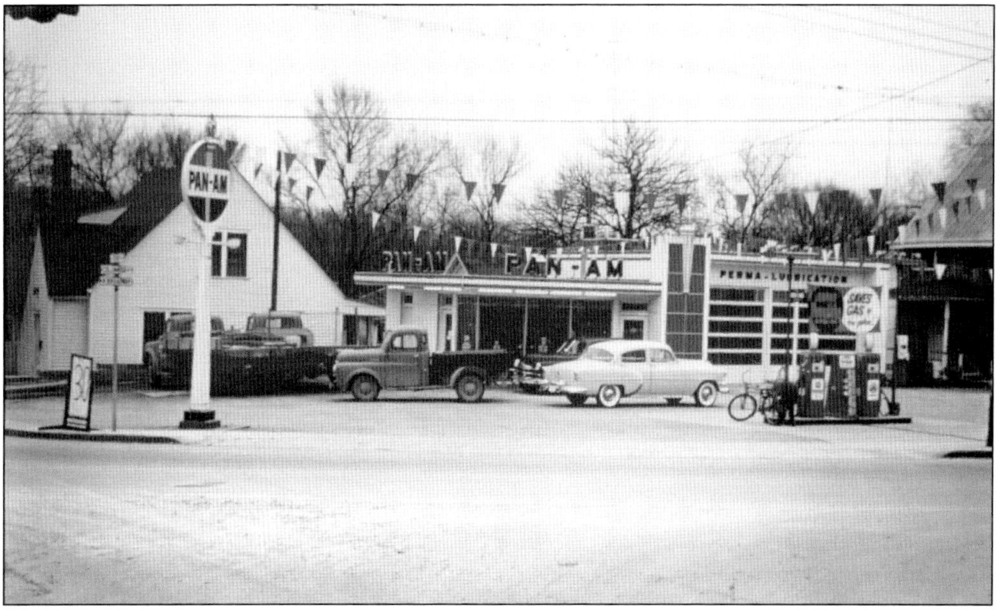

AT YOUR SERVICE. The advent of the car brought with it a service station building boom. There seemed to be one on every corner. The photograph shows a PAN-AM (Pan American Petroleum) station, with its familiar signage at the intersection of Broadway and Columbia Avenue. The station made it easy for customers to pull right in from the street. The price of gas at 30¢ per gallon would be a welcome sight today. (Courtesy of the Glasgow–Barren County Chamber of Commerce.)

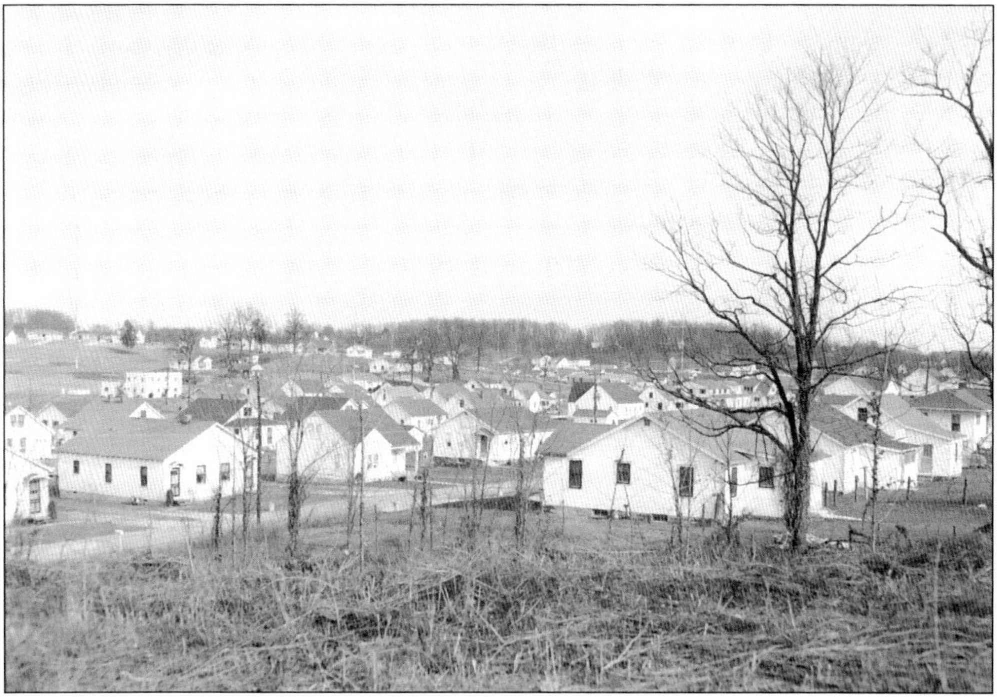

Radio Court. This new subdivision, typical of the 1950s, with its cookie-cutter homes, was nicknamed Radio Court because of its proximity to the WKAY radio tower, which can be seen in the background. This view shows Radio Court looking across Cedar and Walnut Streets. (Courtesy of the Glasgow–Barren County Chamber of Commerce.)

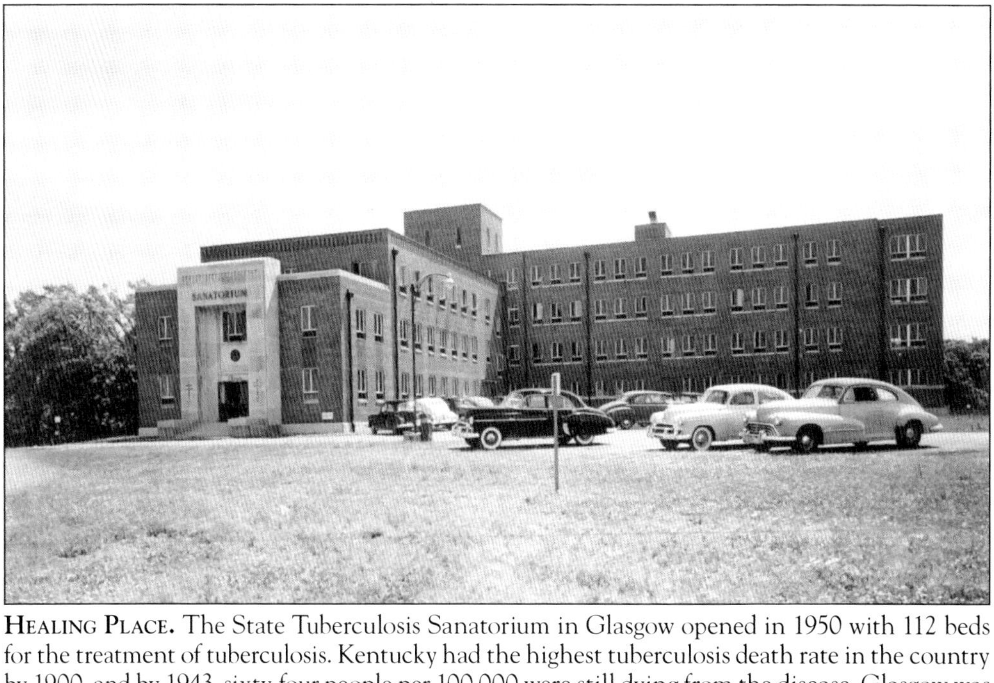

Healing Place. The State Tuberculosis Sanatorium in Glasgow opened in 1950 with 112 beds for the treatment of tuberculosis. Kentucky had the highest tuberculosis death rate in the country by 1900, and by 1943, sixty-four people per 100,000 were still dying from the disease. Glasgow was chosen as the location of one of five hospitals built for the treatment of the disease.

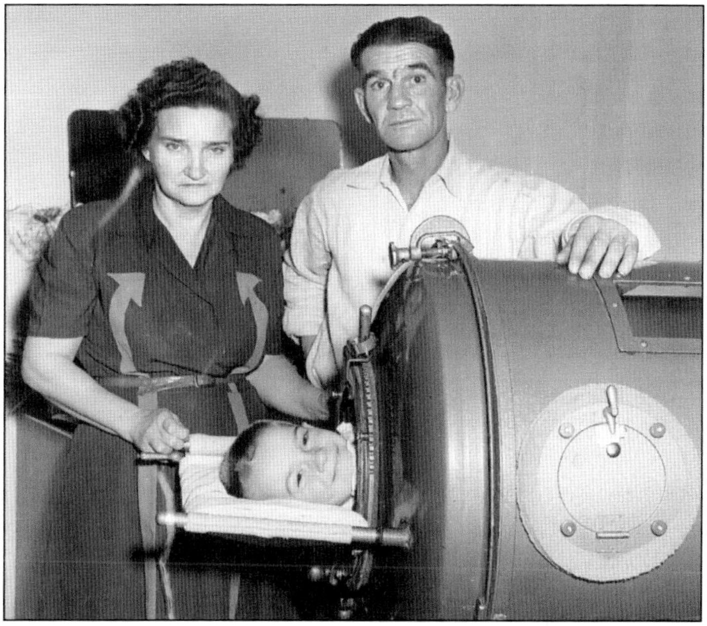

Ever Hopeful. Six-year-old polio victim Murrell Horn brightens the room with his sweet smile though he is enclosed in an iron lung. T. J. Sampson Hospital included a polio center that served the population of south central Kentucky and central Tennessee. The hospital opened in 1929. Arthur T. McCormick, Kentucky's chief health officer, stated, "Glasgow is fast becoming the health center of the state." (Courtesy of the Glasgow–Barren County Chamber of Commerce.)

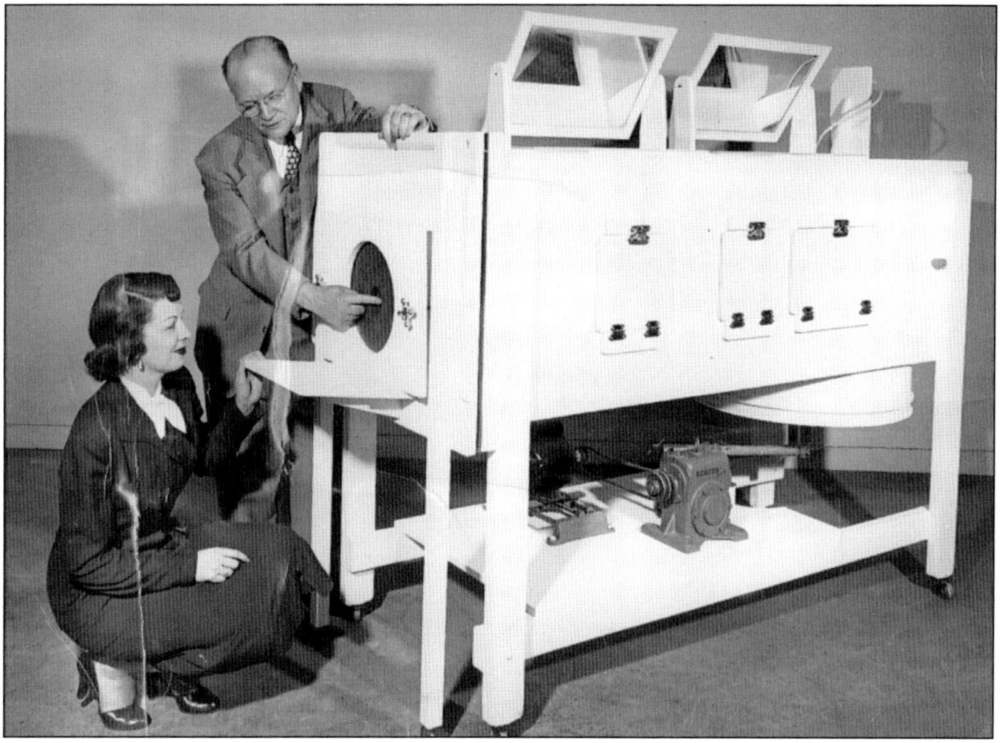

Junk to Machine. The Jaycees and the Glasgow Junior Chamber of Commerce gathered materials from automobile dealers, hardware and plumbing stores, and even junk dealers to construct this iron lung. They used blueprints found in *Popular Mechanics Magazine* to create this working machine, which was used in emergency situations. The wooden lung was constructed at a cost of $300, as compared with its $2,500 counterpart. (Courtesy of the Glasgow–Barren County Chamber of Commerce.)

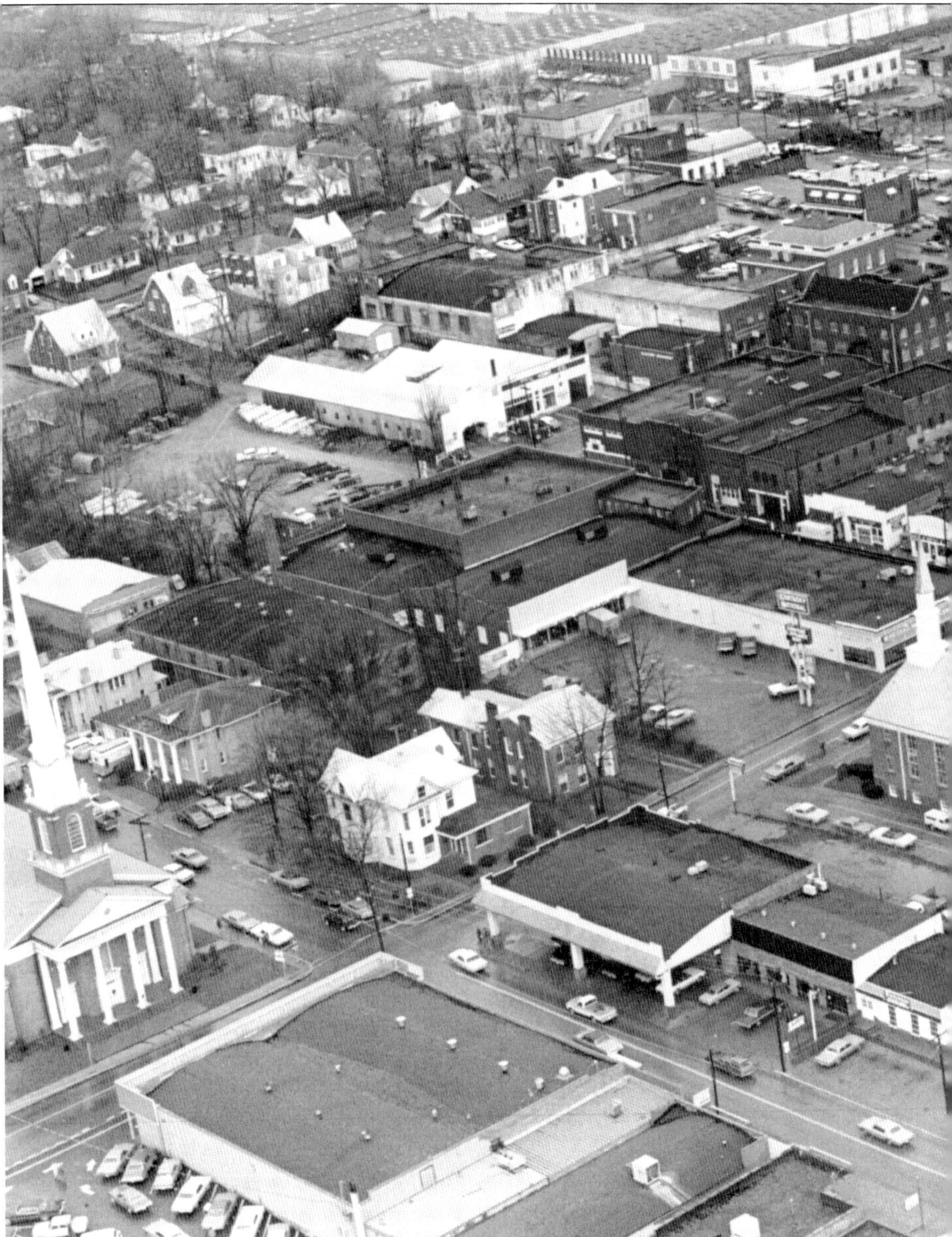

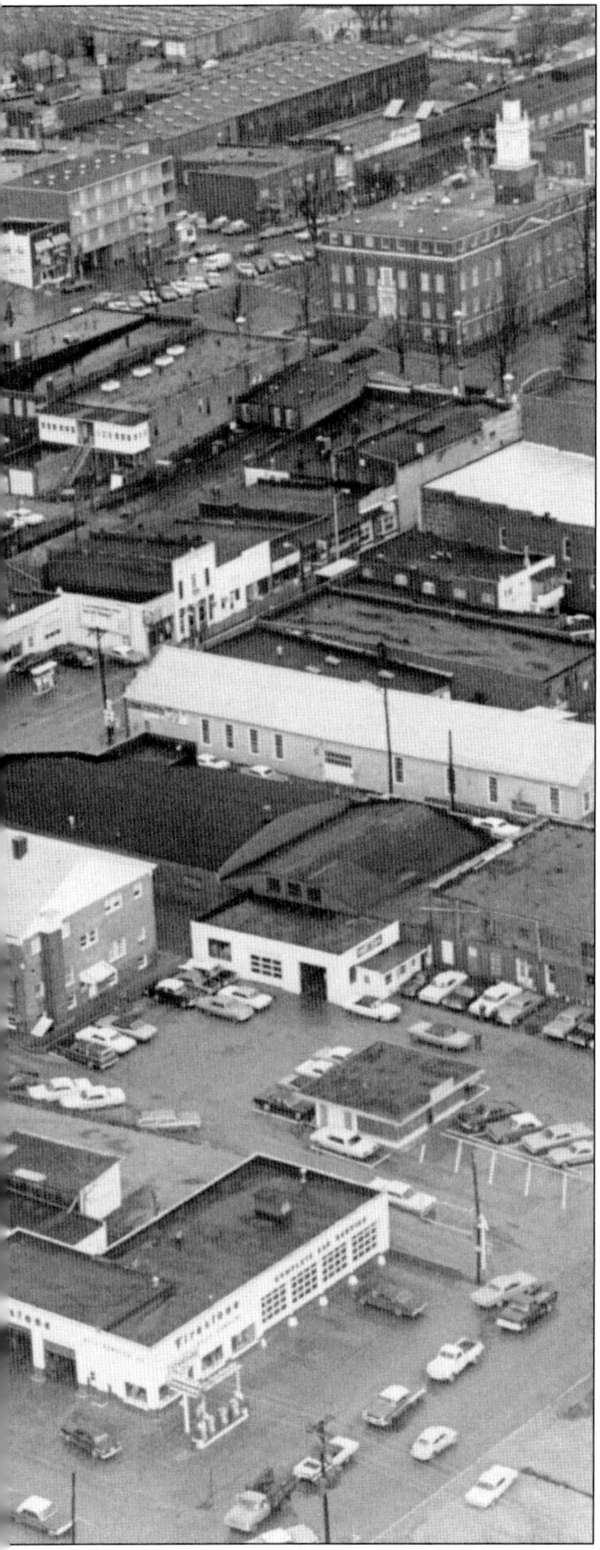

Disappearing Downtown. Many will remember the Glasgow as shown in this aerial shot of the town. However, some of the businesses have completely disappeared, and many buildings have been torn down. The tobacco warehouses in the top of the photograph are all gone except for their foundations. Other buildings remain but have been so remodeled that they are hardly recognizable. The anchor of the square, the courthouse, First Baptist Church, the Mary Wood Weldon Memorial Library building, the home of politician John A. "Old Reb" Murray, the Houchens building, South Green Street Church of Christ, and the post office building remain the same and are easily located in the image. (Courtesy of Jimmy Lowe.)

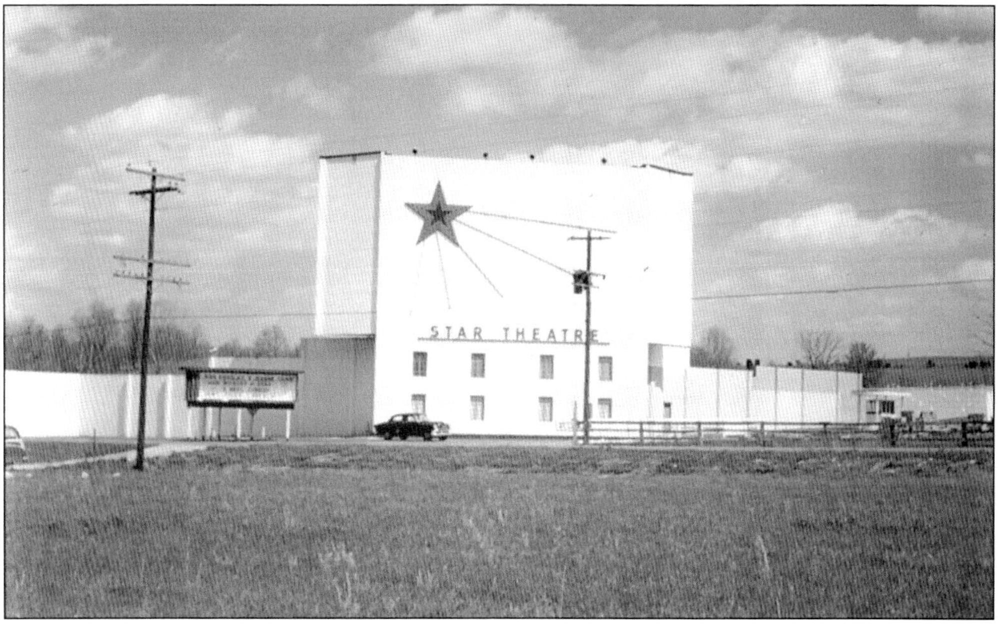

Drive-In Dreams. Below, Walter Duane "Jigger" Aspley stands with some happy children as they celebrate a birthday at the Star Drive-In. The drive-in opened in 1949 with a land capacity of 600 cars and was located on North U.S. 31-E. There was also a playground and picnic areas, and many children looked forward to the treat and novelty of going to the outdoor drive-in. Television and air-conditioned indoor theaters tolled the death knell for most of these drive-ins. The Gentry Equipment Company bought the Star Theater in 1986 after it closed. Out of the 116 drive-ins that were at one time in operation in Kentucky, there are now only 12 drive-ins still in existence. (Above, courtesy of the Glasgow–Barren County Chamber of Commerce; below, courtesy of Winston Nunn.)

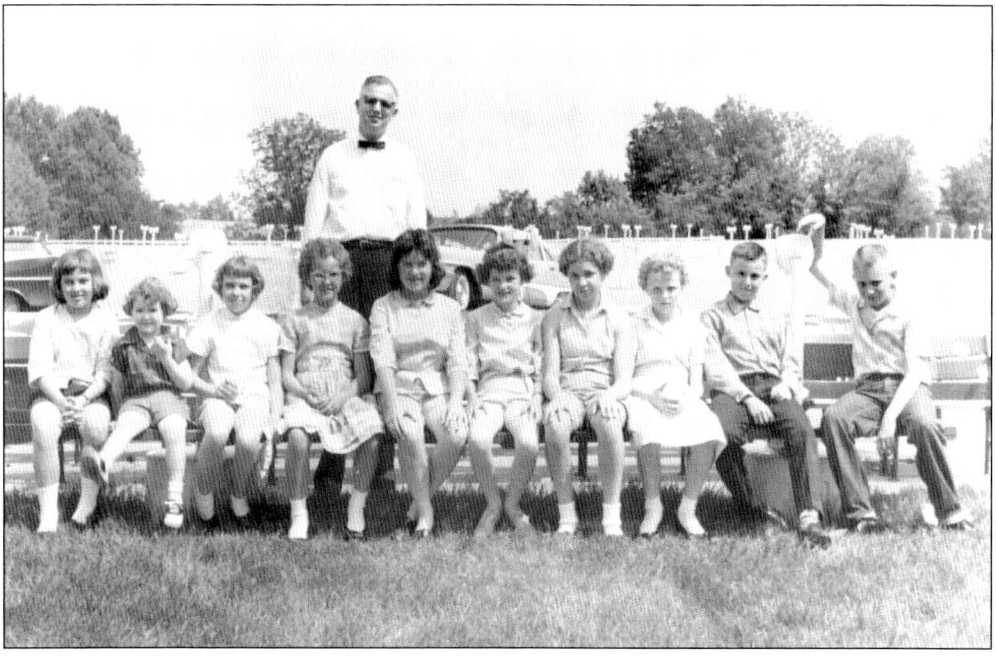

Two

People of Barren County

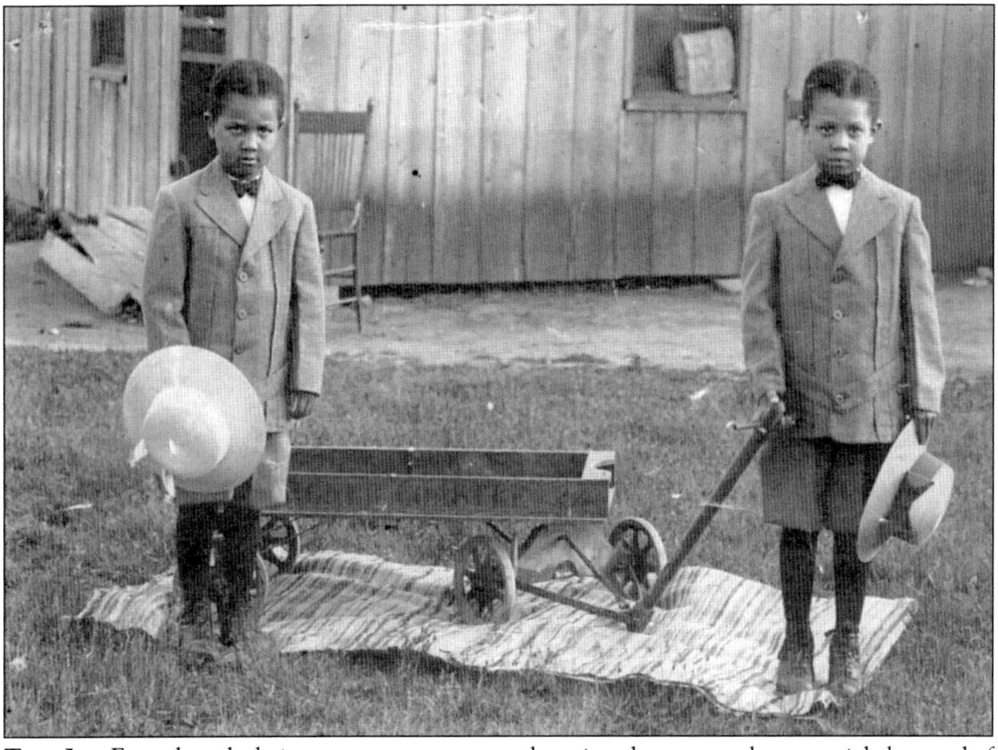

Twin Joy. Even though their appearance may say otherwise, these young boys are rightly proud of their new suits, hats, and wagon. Their gloomy expressions may be accounted for by the fact that their recreation must be delayed because Sunday school comes first. (Courtesy of Alma Glover.)

PROCLAMATION.

GLASGOW, Ky., July 10, 1862.

KENTUCKIANS.

I am once more among you! Confiding in your patriotism and strong attachment to our Southern cause, I have at the head of my gallant band raised once more our CONFEDERATE FLAG so long trampled upon by the Northern Tyrants, but never yet disgraced.

Let every true patriot respond to my appeal. RISE AND ARM! Fight against the DESPOILER! Fight for your Families, your homes, for those you love best, your consciences, and for the free exercise of your political rights, never again to be placed in jeopardy by the Hessian invader.

Let the stirring scenes of the late Richmond fight be constantly before you. Our brave army there is everywhere victorious.

McClellan and his foreign hordes are grovelling in the dust!

Our INDEPENDENCE is an ACHIEVED FACT. We have bought it with privation and suffering, and sealed the contract with the seal of blood!

Be not timorous; but rise, one and and all, for the good cause, to clear our dear Kentucky's soil of its detested invader!

KENTUCKIANS! Fellow-Countrymen! you know you can rely upon me.

JOHN H. MORGAN,

Acting Brig. Gen., C. S. A.

R. A. ALSTON, A. A. G.

WATCH OUT! In 1862, John Hunt Morgan's warning to Barren County residents was issued on one of his three raids into the county. This broadside proclaimed his presence once more among its residents. Kentucky's official stance was one of neutrality, but Morgan, who had been commander of a pro-Southern militia, the Lexington Rifles, joined the Confederacy. On September 4, 1864, while sleeping in Greeneville, Tennessee, Morgan was killed at the home of Catherine Williams. He was buried first in Richmond, Virginia, and then reinterred at the Lexington Cemetery on April 17, 1868. The Kentucky Library and Museum owns one of Morgan's saddles. Another well-known Confederate officer, Brig. Gen. Joseph H. Lewis was born in Barren County and is buried in the Glasgow Cemetery.

REBEL RAIDER. Gen. John Hunt Morgan was striking in appearance, with long curly hair covered with a stylish hat with an upturned brim. The dashing Morgan made three incursions into Barren County, on May 11, July 10, and December 25, 1862. On May 11, 1862, Morgan appeared at Cave City and destroyed freight and passenger cars. Wherever Morgan appeared he spread panic as he approached. His method of surprise caught most counties' hastily convened militias off guard, and they could only offer weak resistance.

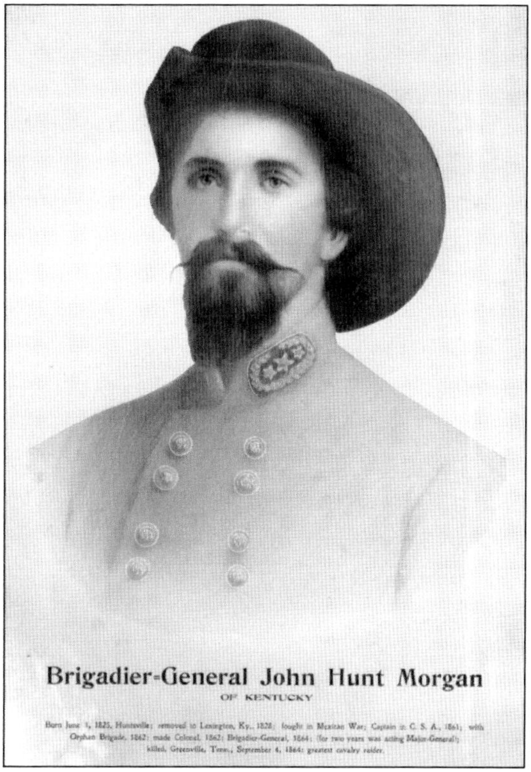

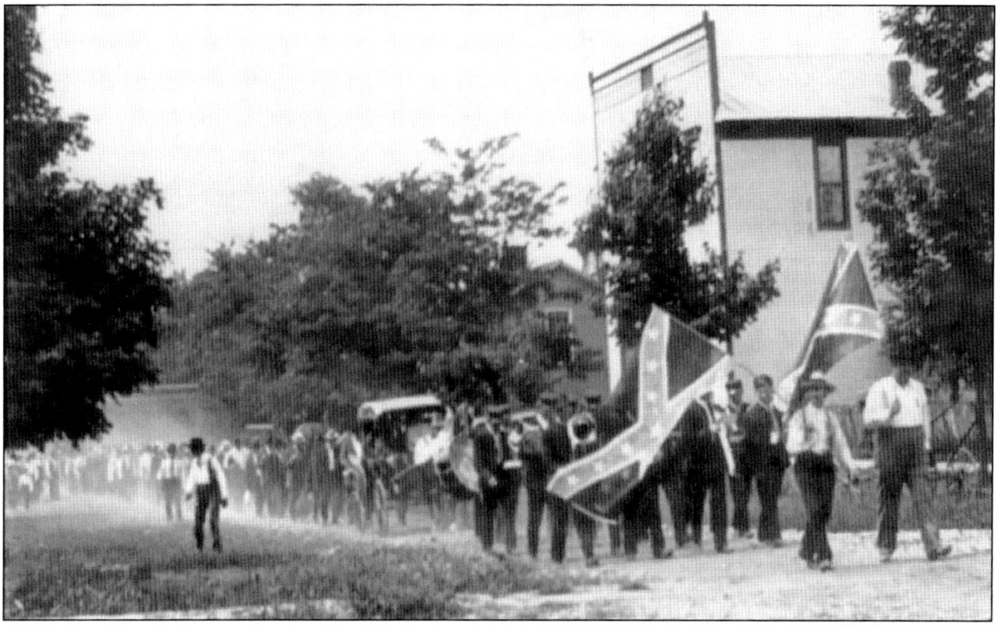

GONE WITH THE WIND. The First Kentucky Brigade of the Confederate army, the "Orphan Brigade" numbered about 4,000, but only about 500 survived the conflict. Reunions were common for these men, such as this one held in Cave City in August 1909. Newspaper accounts are filled with drama as they record, "Their hearts filled with emotion, their eyes with tears, but they remain undimmed by the smoke of many a battle." (Courtesy of Linda Hunt.)

PENSIONS.

All soldiers of the late war are entitled to pensions, if they incurred any disability in the service, whether wounds, injuries, rupture, falling of mumps or measels, sunstroke, rheumatism, diarrhea, hemorrhoids or piles, loss of sight, impaired hearing, fever and ague, disease of heart, liver or kidneys, weak back, enlarged veins, disease of throat or lungs, asthma, bronchitis, catarrh, dropsy, scurvy, or any other disability, provided it disables to any extent for the performance of manual labor. Any disibility that is the result of another, which was incurred in the service is pensionable.

The widows or heirs of soldiers who died of disease, wounds, incurred while in the service, are entitled to pensions. If the soldier left no widow or heirs the mother is entitled, if dependent at the date of soldier's death, or if she be dead the father is entitled. If the soldier left no other heirs, brothers and sisters who were dependent on him for support and under 16 years of age at his death are entitled.

If you have never applied for pension, you should do so at once. Remember the longer you delay the more difficult your case may become. If you apply now I can render you invaluable service as an attorney.

Arrears of pensions for widows under the act of Congress approved June 7 1888, widows' pensions now commence from date of death of husband.

Arrears for remarried widows, under the act of June 7, 1888, a widow who has remarried can apply for and obtain pension from date of soldier's death to date of her remarriage, provided soldier died of disease or wounds contracted while in the service of the United States and in line of duty.

Increased rating can be obtained for many diseases resulting from the disability for which pensioned. No direct connection between these disabilities need be proved, if the resulting disability can be shown to be reasonably due to the condition caused by the disability orignating in service.

Charges of desertion on the records against soldiers and sailors during the late war can now be removed under certain circumstances.

Officers or soldiers who lost horses or equipments in the late war can get pay for same, if they file their claim by the 13th of August 1891.

Increase of pension on account of increase of disability is one of my special claims for prosecution. Many more claims are being filed for increase than original.

Address me at Glasgow Ky., and your claim shall have prompt attention.

If you have no use for these papers please hand them to some comrade that would probably use them.

Respectfully,
W. D. TOLLE, Glasgow, Ky.

BANNER JOB PRINT, Glasgow, Ky.

APPLY TODAY! Barren County's Union army soldiers, widows, and minor children could apply for a pension. Many who survived the war were unable to continue farming or other employment, as their wounds or disabilities affected them for the rest of their lives. W. D. Tolle was a well-known correspondent for the local newspaper and a general pension attorney and legal advisor.

SEEDBED. Shown at right in 1912, world-renowned evangelist and founder of Asbury Theological Seminary, Henry Clay Morrison was reared in his grandfather's home. From this childhood cabin, located on Highway 63, Morrison would see the world go by and would write later of a continual parade of Civil War soldiers during the war years. The troops would bring news, which kept all in the house in a continual state of fear. "Yankees are coming into Glasgow as thick as pigeons." William Jennings Bryan described Morrison as "the greatest pulpit orator on the American continent." Among Morrison's other accomplishments were those of educator, college president, and founder and editor of the *Pentecostal Herald*. Morrison returned regularly to the county to preach in the camp meeting park, which he established near his old home. (Both, courtesy of Asbury Theological Seminary Archives.)

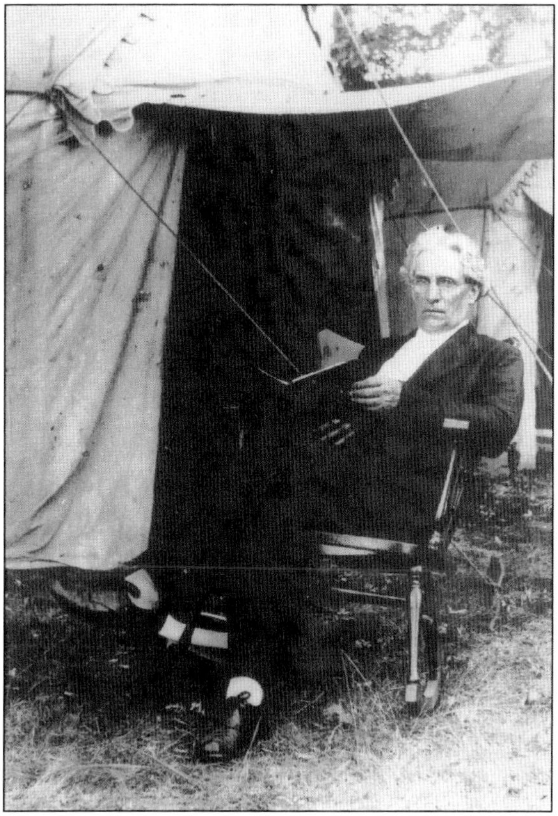

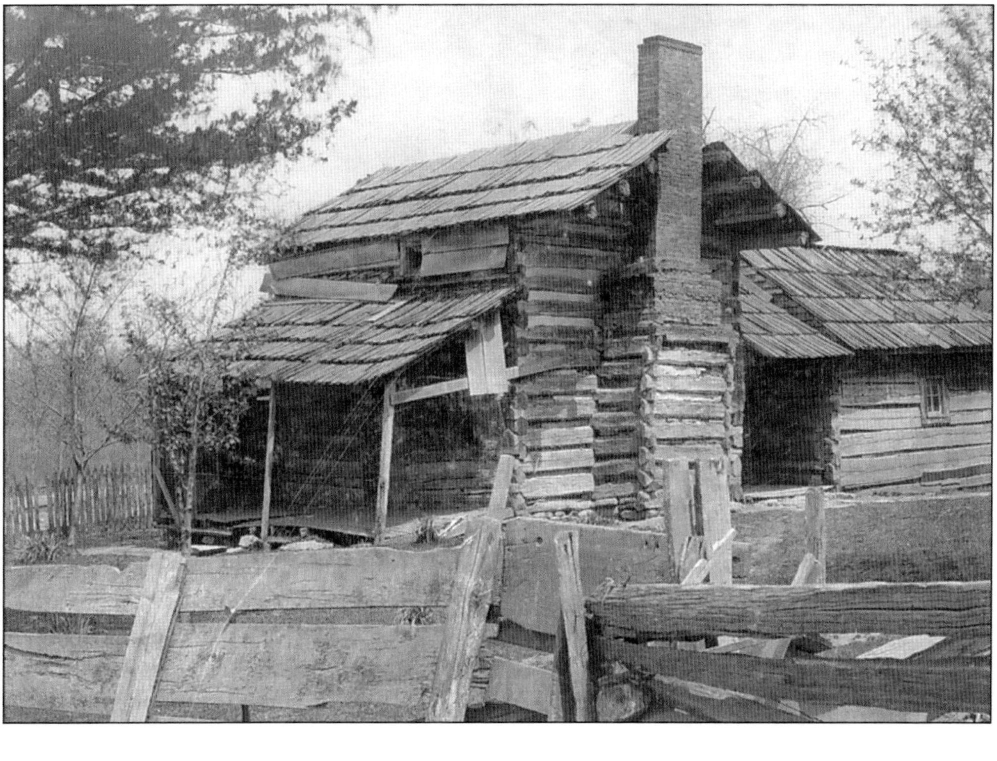

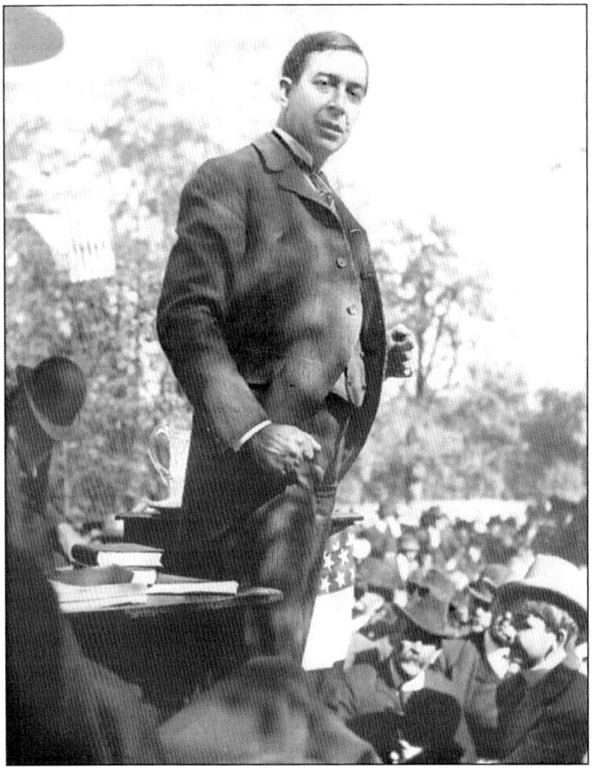

GOEBEL SHOT. In 1900, William Goebel was declared the victor in the hotly debated gubernatorial election, but soon after, on the capitol grounds, an unknown assailant shot him. His death is still controversial and debated. There was not a lack of accusations all over the state, even reaching into Barren County. J. M. Davidson from the county was falsely accused and so distraught he committed suicide. Goebel remains the only governor to die while in office by an assassin's hand.

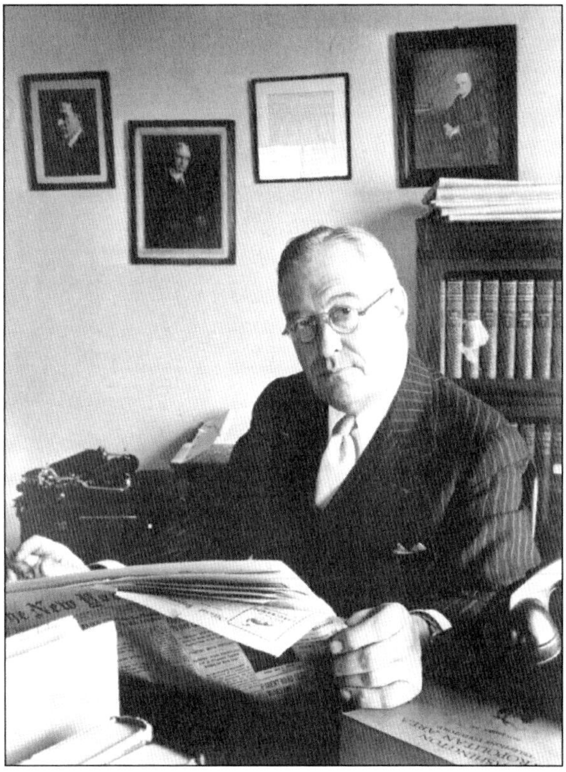

NOTED NEWSMAN. Arthur Krock was born in Glasgow in 1886. Krock won four Pulitzer Prizes and wrote the column, "In the Nation," which was published in the *New York Times* for 33 years. In a letter to a Barren County admirer, he wrote, "Someday, I am coming back to Glasgow again and it will be pleasant, even though the dimensions have shrunk, to walk the streets and the hilly turf again." (Courtesy of Princeton University Library.)

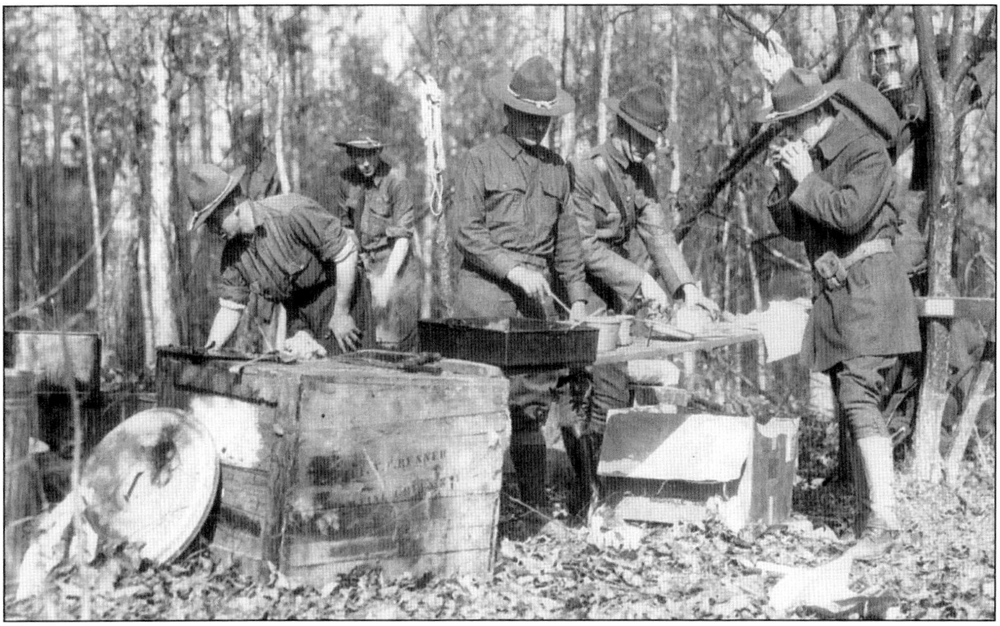

Trapped. William Floyd Collins became a national folk hero with his entrapment in Sand Cave on January 30, 1925. The subsequent efforts to free him captured national attention and riveted the world's gaze on Barren County. The story is listed as the third-largest news event of the 20th century, which follows Charles Lindbergh's crossing of the Atlantic, the kidnapping of Lindbergh's child, and the World Wars. The sensationalism and hysteria were unmatched, as well as the unprecedented efforts to save him. This group of Kentucky Militia men, shown above, was among the many who tried to rescue Collins. Though Collins died on February 13, 1925, his body was not removed until April. His casket and pallbearers are shown in the photograph below. In 1989, Collins's body was moved again and was reinterred at the Mammoth Cave Baptist Church Cemetery.

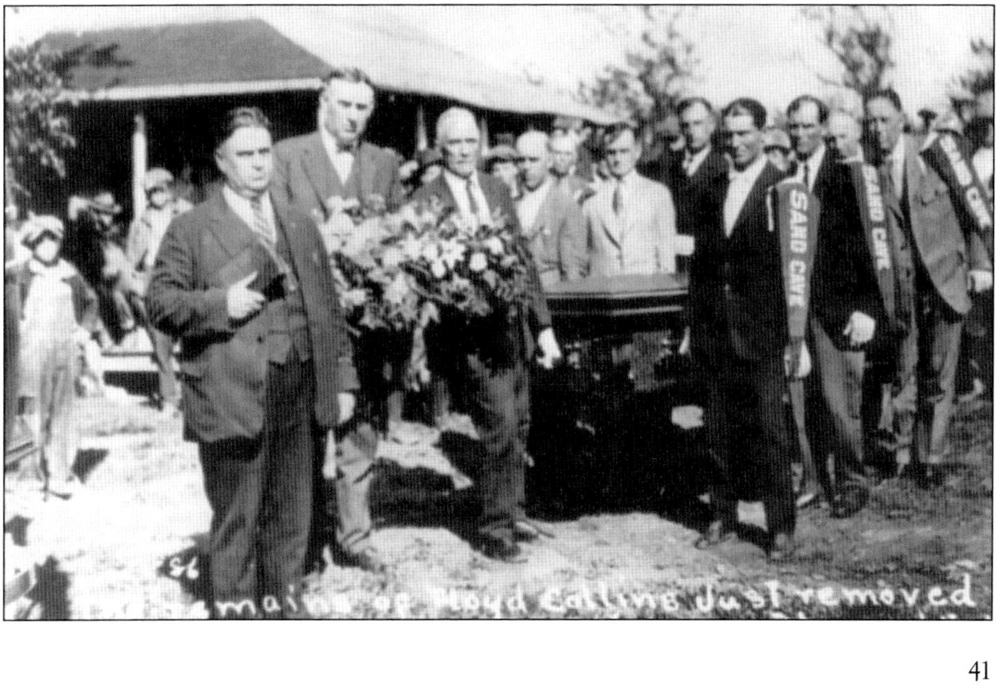

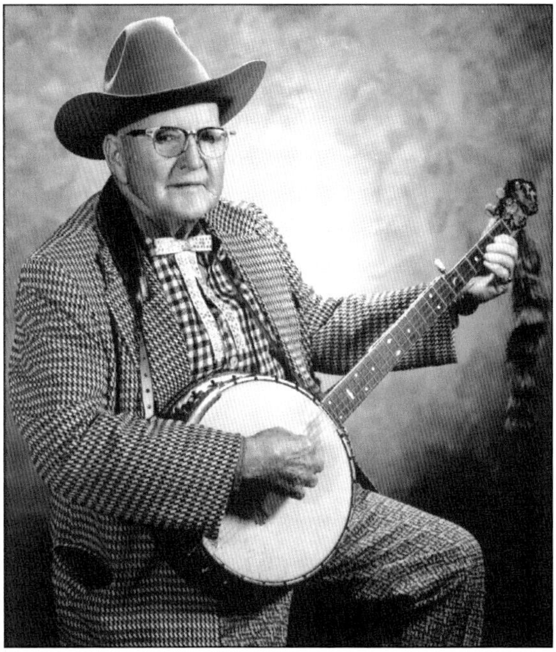

Showman. Noble "Uncle Bozo" Carver was part of a talented family whose first members began performing in the area in the 1880s. Carver and his brother, Warner, made several recordings for Paramount in 1929. They were the first from this area to have a record contract. Carver became a member of the Grand Ole Opry in 1932. Even Uncle Bozo's outfits caught the eye and would not let go!

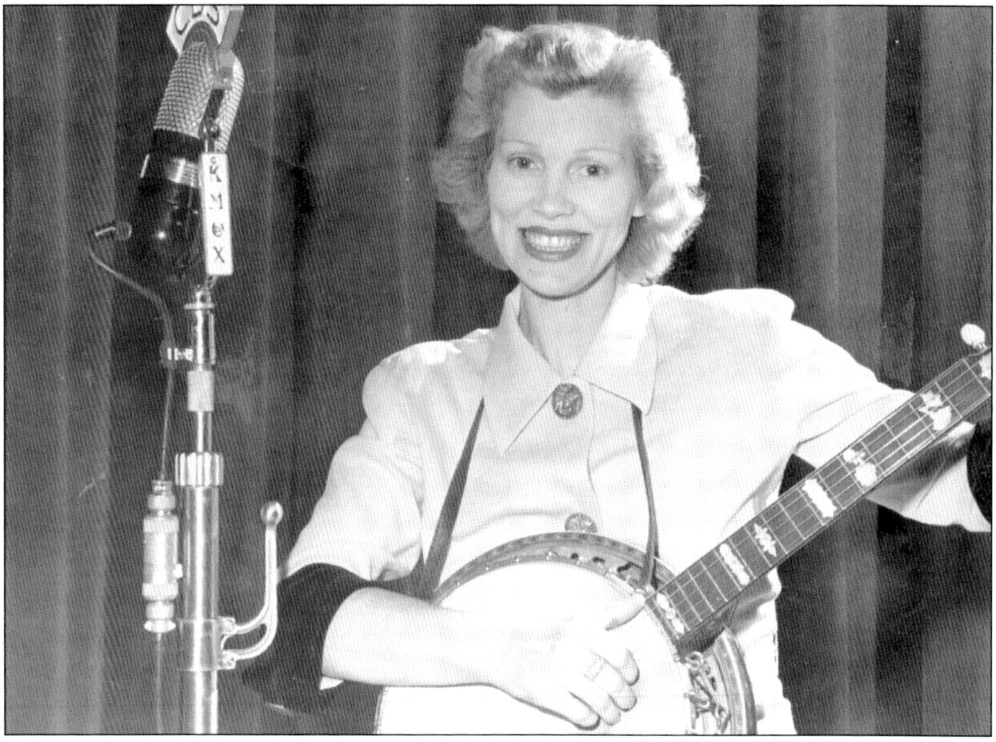

One-Girl Band. Cynthia May Carver was born in Barren County in 1903. Though no longer a household name, Carver, who performed as "Cousin Emmy," is still highly regarded by folk music historians. She was the first woman to win the National Old Time Fiddlers Contest and had a popular radio show, *Cousin Emmy and her Kinfolks*, during the 1930s. She was also the writer of the Bluegrass classic "Ruby."

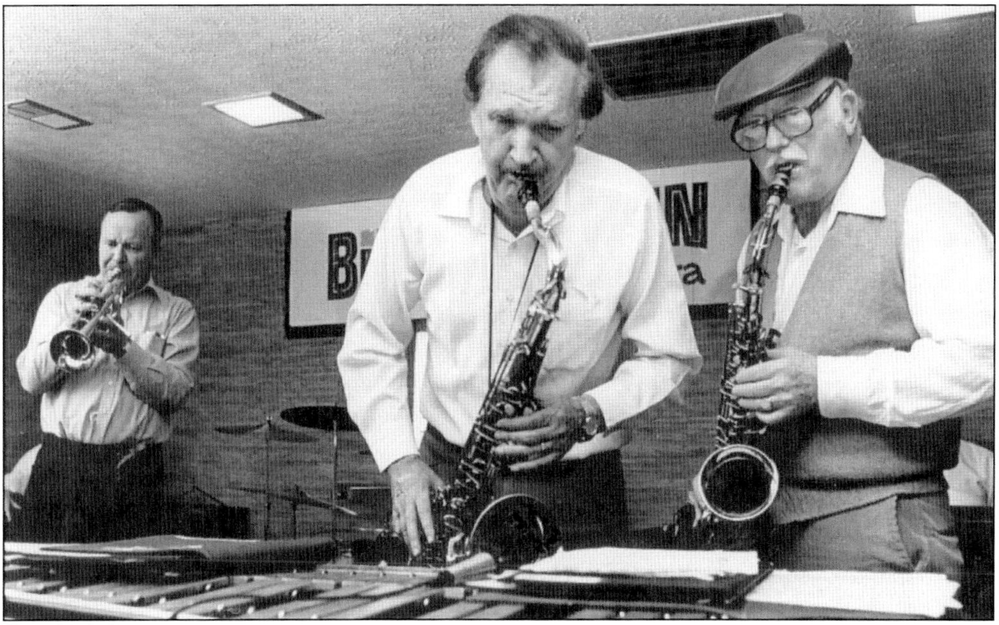

Beautiful Sounds. Billy Vaughn, born in 1919, became one of the most popular orchestra leaders and arrangers of the 1950s and 1960s. His style was described as clean and non-offensive. His career began in 1952 with the vocal quartet "The Hilltoppers." He continued recording his own instrumental records through the 1960s, producing a string of easy-listening hit singles. Vaughn is pictured on the right with David "Doc" Livingston. (Courtesy of WKU Archives.)

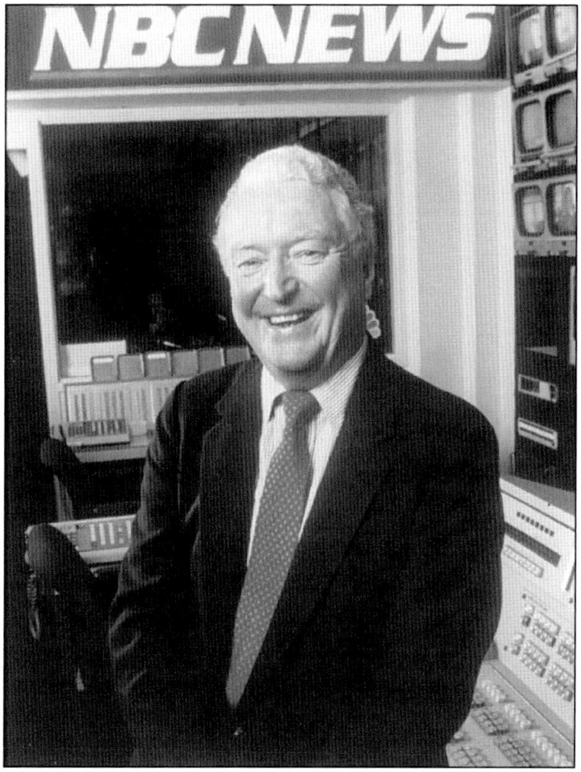

Chairman of the Board. Julian Goodman was born in Barren County and graduated from Western Kentucky University. He rose quickly up the corporate ladder at NBC and held the positions of broadcast journalist and editor, president, and chairman of the board in his 34-year career. He was called "a champion for freedom in broadcasting," for his efforts to gain full First Amendment rights for radio and television news reporters.

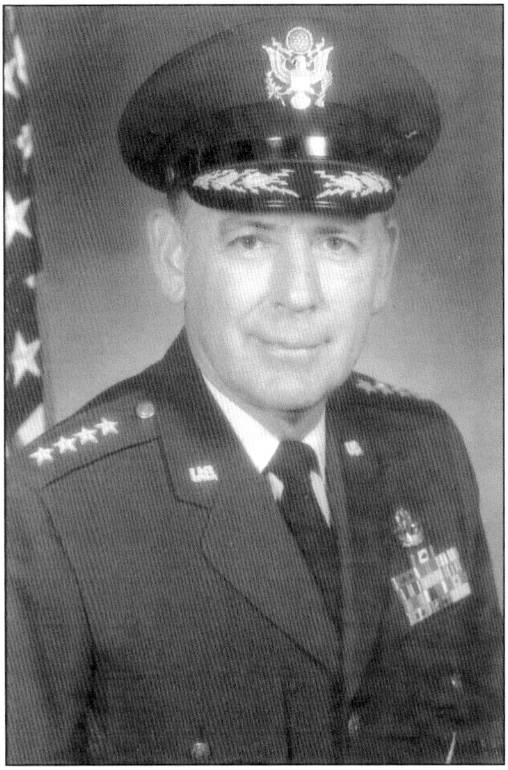

Decorated Commander (AFA). Russell Dougherty wanted a career in law because in his early life he was influenced by the trials he attended at the Barren County Courthouse. However, his law career took a back seat as World War II started. He would rise through the ranks, during the height of the cold war to become a four-star general and head of the Strategic Air Command. Dougherty remembered and praised the county residents' eagerness to serve by saying, "If Tennessee is the Volunteer state, then Barren is the Volunteer County."

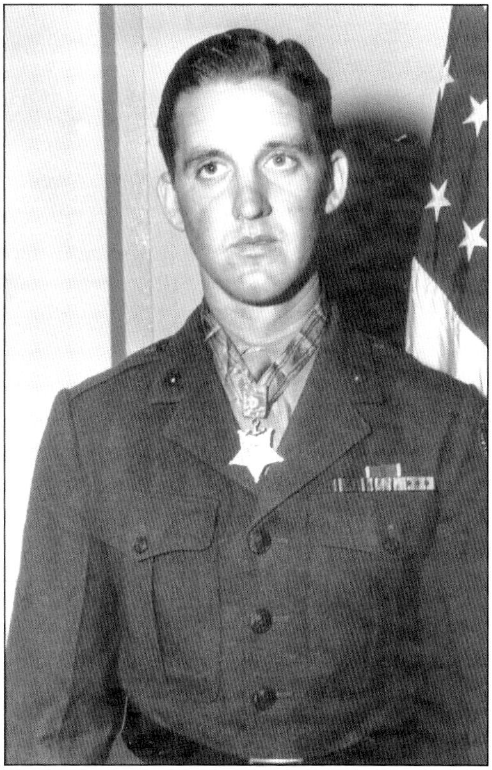

Honor Roll. Kentucky has sent service people to every conflict and is on record for having the only woman in history to be awarded the Medal of Honor. Barren County also has two Medal of Honor winners, Richard Bush and William L. Day. Bush, pictured in 1945, threw himself on a grenade and saved the lives of many personnel. Day, of the U.S. Cavalry, was cited for bravery during the Native American conflicts.

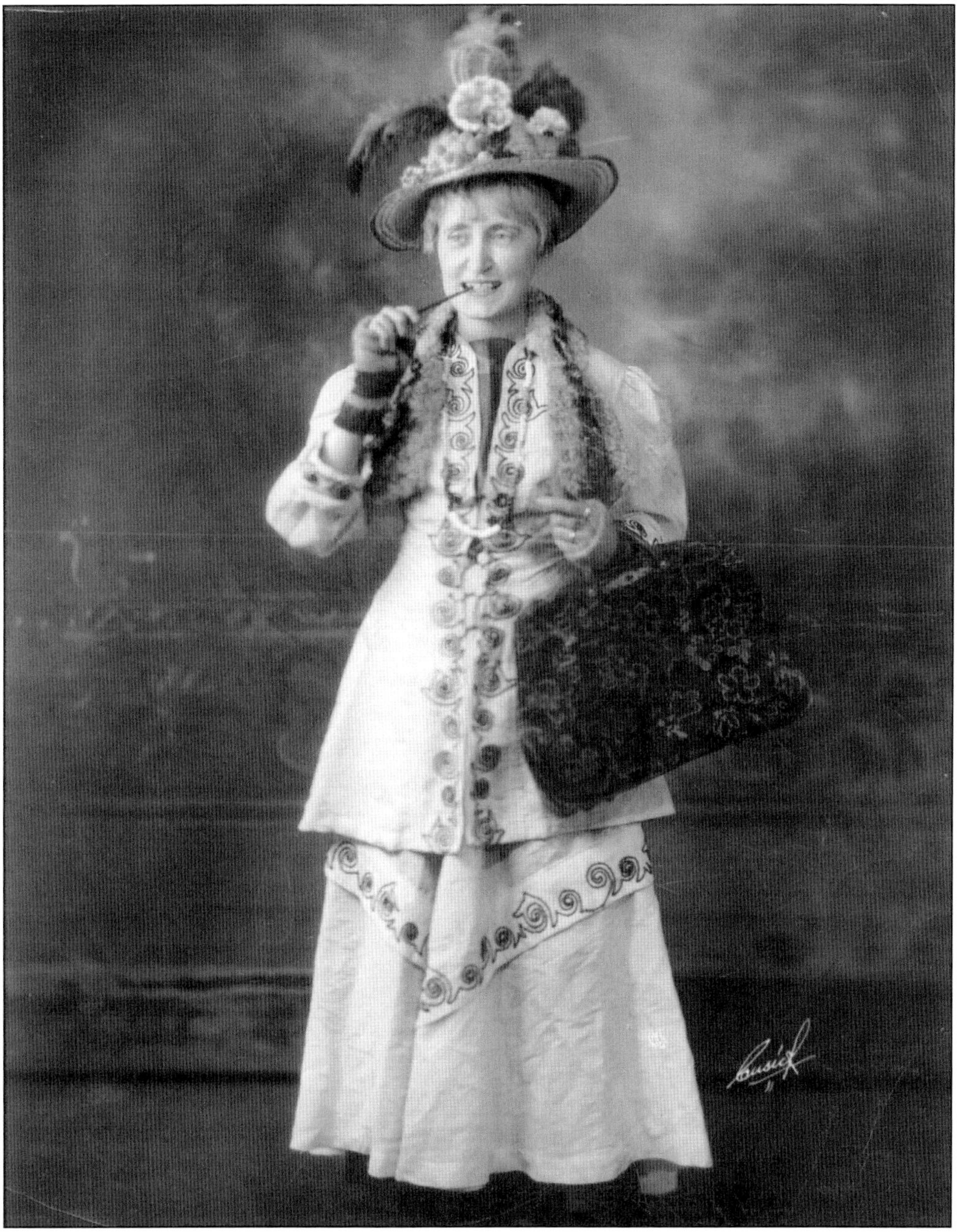

KENTUCKY WRITER. Gordia Greer Petrie was born in the Merry Oaks community in 1872. She began her professional career in 1904 with a collaborative short story, "When the Bees Got Busy." This was the first development for what would be her most remembered works, the Angeline Keaton series. The novels were about Angeline and her backwoods family and were set in Bear Wallow (Holler), Barren County. The novels sold well through the early 1940s, and as shown in the photograph, Petrie appeared all over the country in costume as her beloved Angeline. In this role, Petrie poked fun at the snobs that looked down on the "plain uneducated folks" of the countryside. There were also many references to her home county throughout the novels. She died in Louisville in 1964. (Courtesy of the Filson Historical Society, Louisville, Kentucky.)

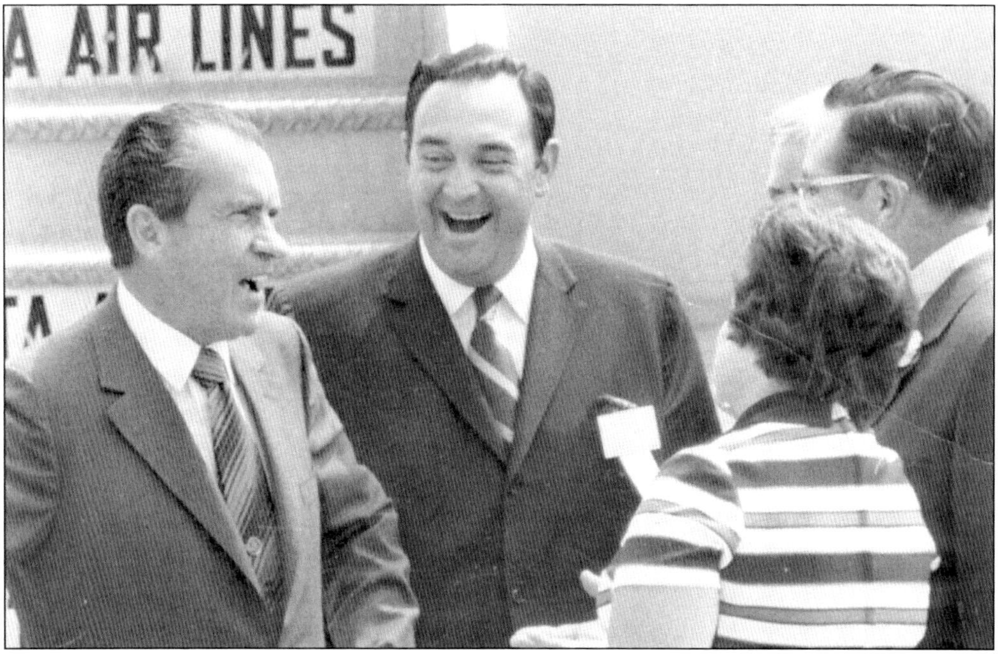

Glasgow Goes to Frankfort. The county was home to two governors of Kentucky, Preston H. Leslie and Louie Broady Nunn. Nunn was elected in 1967, the first Republican in 24 years. He was criticized for raising the sales tax from 3 to 5 percent (Nunn's Nickel), but he is also credited with the development of Barren River State Park and the improvement of many roads in the county.

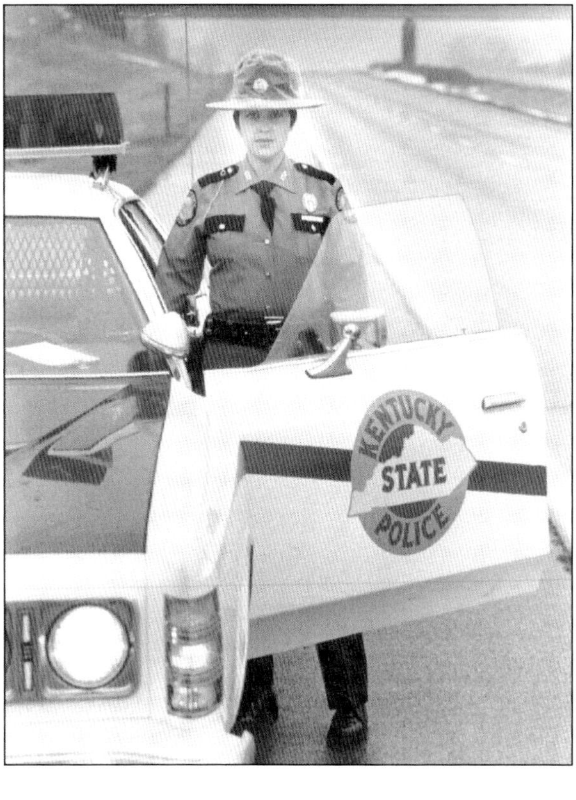

Opening Doors. Linda Bewley Mayberry was the first female police officer in Glasgow and Barren County and one of the first female state troopers in Kentucky. A career law enforcement officer, Mayberry retired after having served as deputy commissioner of the Kentucky State Police, directing operations for all divisions. Colonel Mayberry is now an assistant federal security director for the U.S. Department of Homeland Security and is currently assigned at Blue Grass Airport. (Photograph by Donnie Beauchamp.)

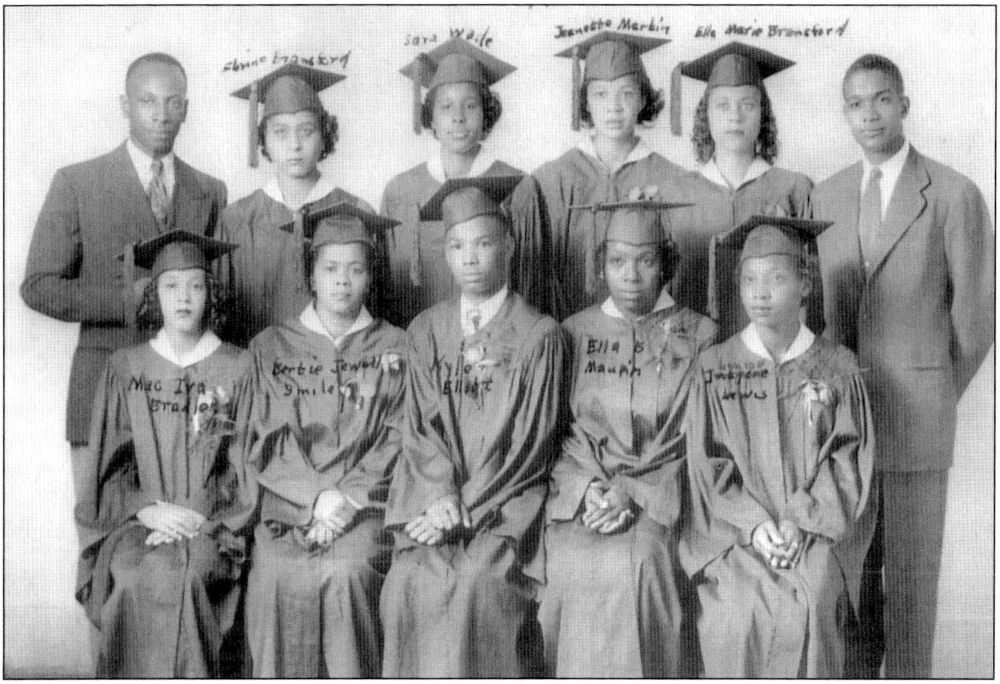

Kentucky Pioneer. The 1947 Glasgow Training School class is shown with their principal, Luska J. Twyman (standing, far left). He was born in Hiseville and was the first African American to become an elected official in Barren County and Kentucky's first African American mayor. Kentucky Highway Historical Marker No. 2019, located on the square in Glasgow, is dedicated to this civil rights pioneer. (Courtesy of Alma Glover.)

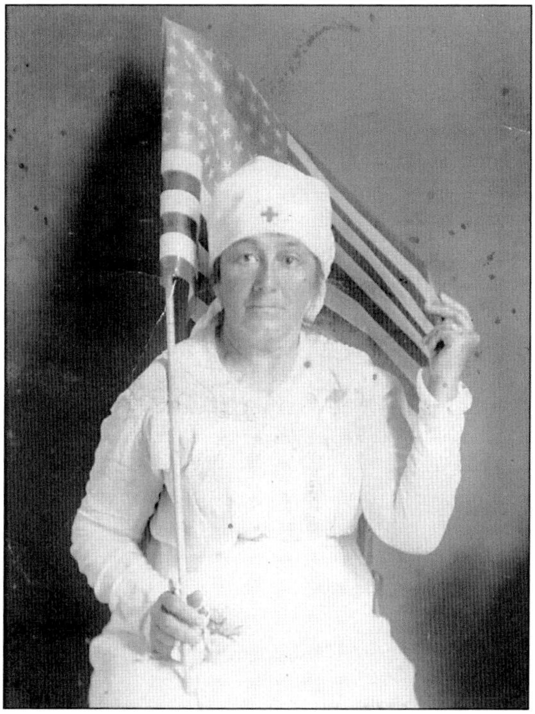

In Service to her Country. In World War I, the American Red Cross served as a nursing reserve for the army and navy, and added its own touch to the changing uniforms of the field. Elizabeth Post Dugard is shown in the starched white uniform that heralded the professionalism shown by the women, as it was worn as a badge of honor. African American Maggie Sproul of the county also bravely served in the Women's Army Corps during World War II. (Courtesy of Kuristen Jones.)

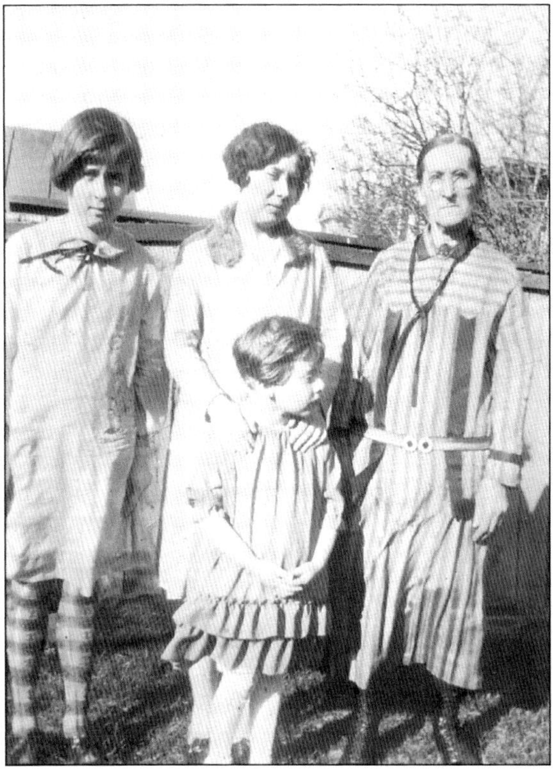

The Height of Fashion. This three-generation family photograph from 1920 shows off the close-knit bonds of the family and their best fashions. Notice the grandmother's stylish stripes and her high-top laced boots and the young lady's diamond-pattern stockings. (Courtesy of Jardy Bewley.)

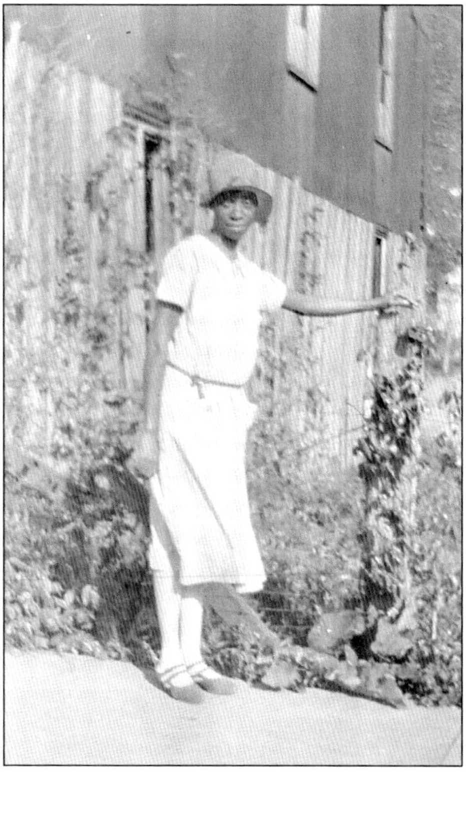

Standing By. Margaret Anderson Davidson from Cave City shows off the latest fashions from 1900 and proudly poses for her photograph. Davidson was a schoolteacher and was well known in the community for her assistance to many citizens of the area. (Courtesy of Karen Phillips.)

WEDDING GOWN. Nelle Terry Ellis can still wear her wedding gown 10 years after the ceremony. She was married in 1927 at the First Christian Church. She is pictured in her home on Leslie Avenue in Glasgow. The stately house was built in 1867 by James G. Thompson and remains one of Glasgow's most beautiful. The wedding gown was later given to the Kentucky Library and Museum.

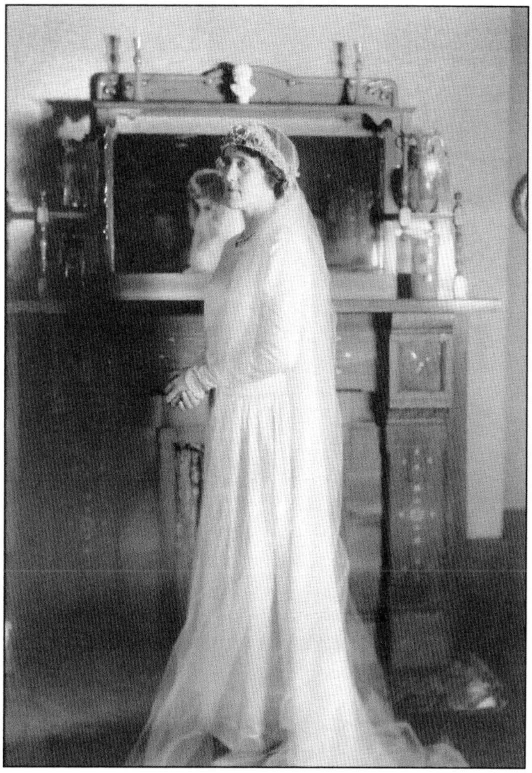

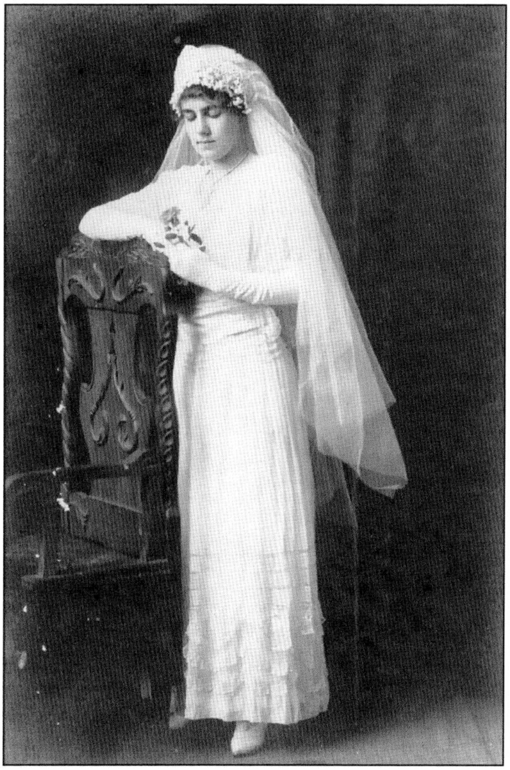

WEDDING BEAUTY. Mary Richardson Coffman is wearing a beautiful gown for her wedding day on June 2, 1915. The gown was the latest fashion, with its de rigueur cap-style veil that fit closely over the forehead and fell gracefully at the back. It was made from silk tulle, starched and pleated; of the finest Lyon or Brussels lace; and hand-decorated embroidery floss, ribbon, or metallic gimp. (Courtesy of Perry Brantley.)

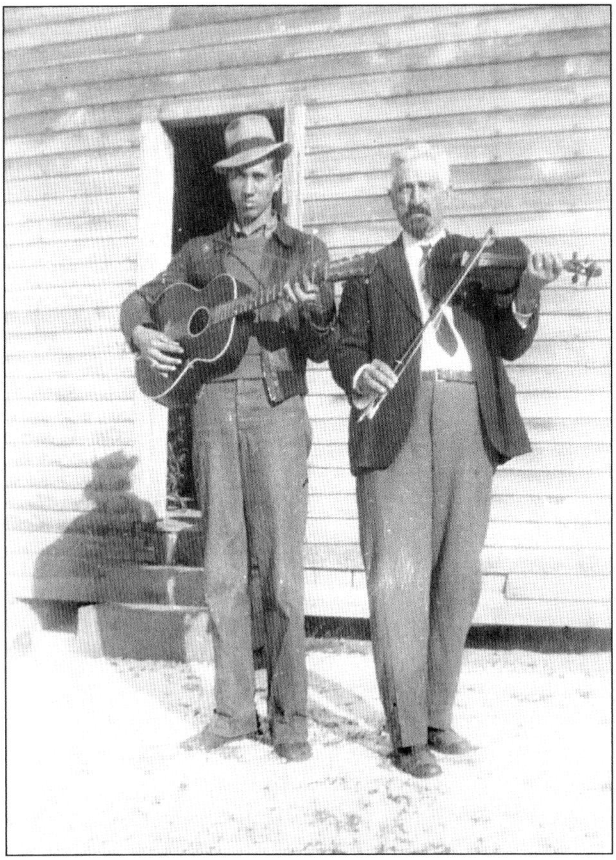

Following Tradition. Musical ability and talent was fostered in many families and passed along generational lines. The Wyatt family illustrates this love of music, as grandfather and grandson are shown posed with their prized instruments. They would have listened to and performed in a limited social sphere, mainly in their homes, neighborhoods, and workplaces. Traditional ballads and hymns would have been commonplace, but with the advent of radio, popular songs of the times would have been copied and performed. The love of music and its influence continues today throughout the county. There are many groups and bands that still regularly perform in such local venues as shown in the photograph below. The group pictured is Robbie Jones and the Kentucky Gentlemen. (Left, courtesy of Danny and Carolyn Wyatt.)

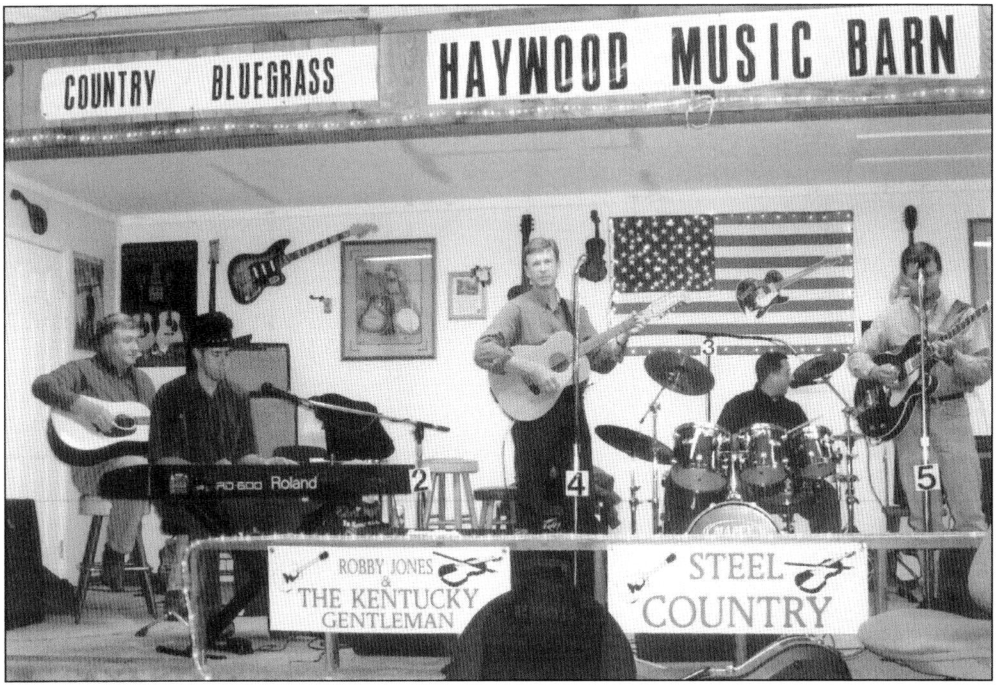

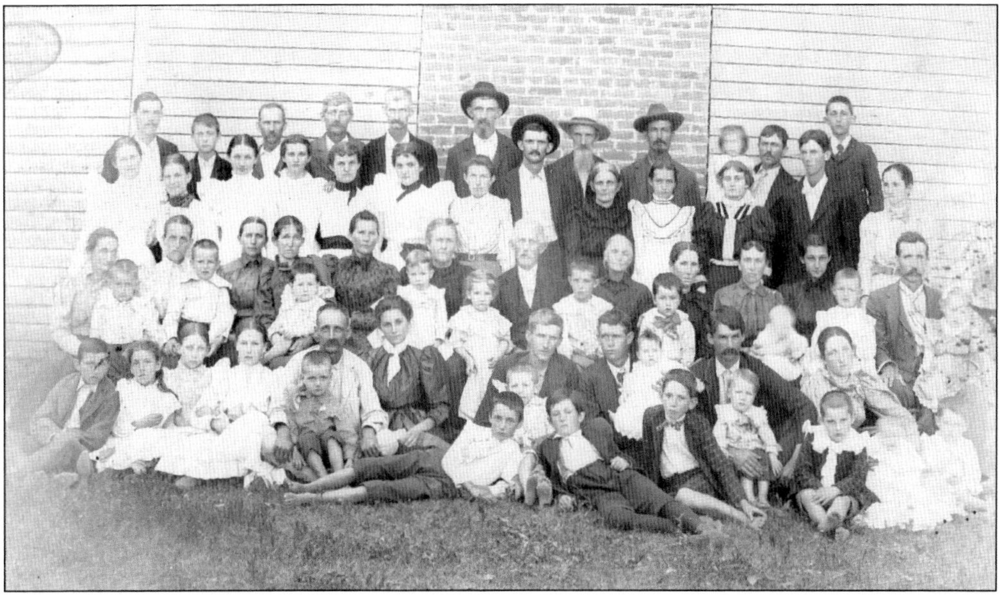

Family Patriarch. Members of the Bowles family, their spouses, and children proudly pose with their patriarch, and papa, Henry Holman Bowles to celebrate his 73rd birthday on July 19, 1899. These were occasions for much celebration and gave the family a chance to once again unite. Other surnames included in the photograph are Harlow, Wright, Meadows, Tolle, Green, Gray, Barrick, Mansfield, and Anderson. (Courtesy of Perry Brantley.)

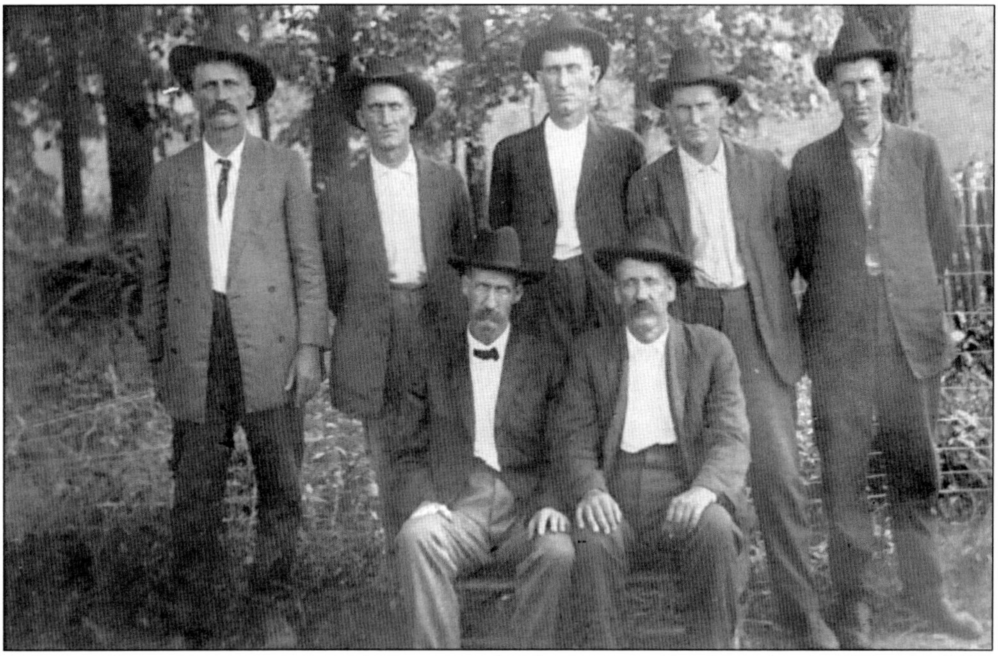

All in the Family. The seven, stalwart Wyatt brothers are gathered on the church grounds for an associational church meeting in 1916. From left to right are (seated) John and Jim; (standing) Luther, Ruben, Ernest, Riley, and Hardin. They were the children of Radford M. and Matilda Adeline Steenburgen Wyatt and the progenitors of many families in the Austin area. (Courtesy of Amy Coomer.)

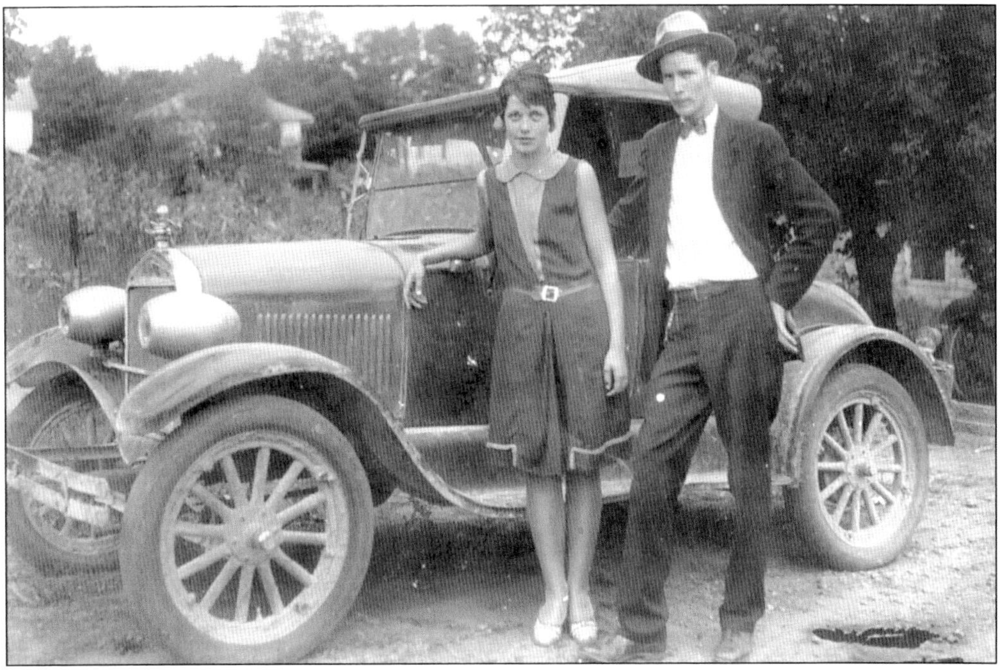

Out for a Ride. Fidel Chapman Sr. stops and poses with his bride-to-be, Jessie Lee Estes, in the 1928 photograph. He is justly proud of both his new car and his pretty girl. She is dressed in the finery of the day and has the requisite bobbed hairstyle of the new modern age. The hairstyle, along with shorter skirts and rolled stockings, signaled a changing world. (Courtesy of Geraldine Denison.)

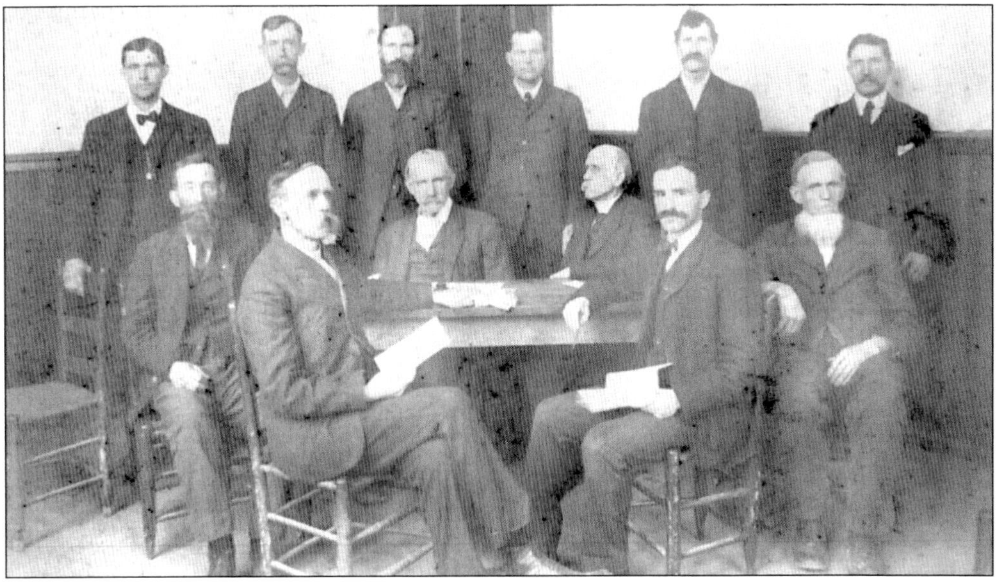

Justice Prevails. This photograph by Adolph Rapp was taken in 1910 and shows members of the Barren County Circuit Court Grand Jury. From left to right are (seated) H. L. Johnson, Louis Rogers, J. H. Dearing, T. S. Puckett, Louis Morris, and John Vaughn; (standing) Lewis Harlow, T. F. Monday, F. M. Chapman, Trigg Ennis, R. S. Martin, and D. C. Renfro. (Courtesy of Geraldine Denison.)

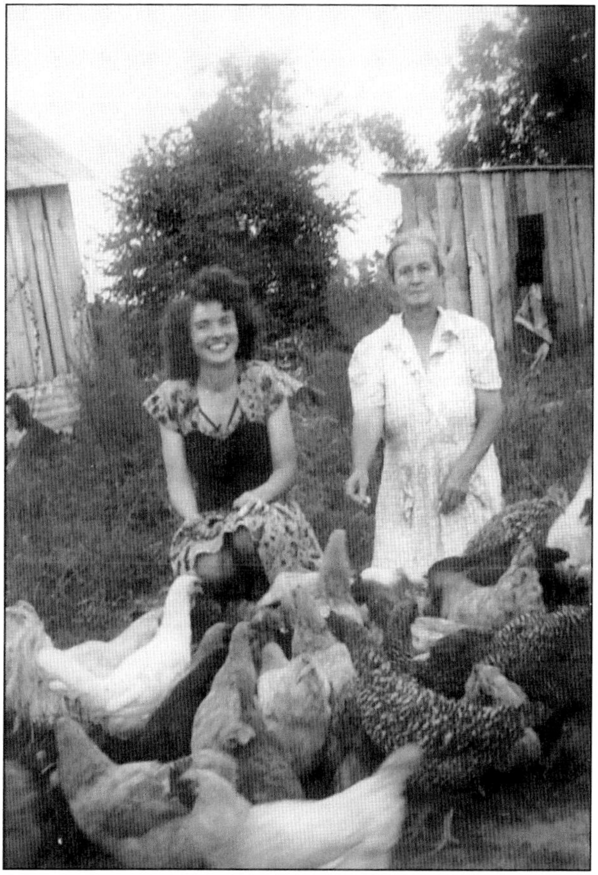

Butter and Eggs. The family farm produced almost everything that the family needed to survive, but for extra things there was the "butter and egg" money. Women contributed to the household income with this and bought things for themselves and others by selling the eggs the chickens produced. Shown here in 1940 are Gertrude "Gertie" (left) and Eva Mae Post Bunch on their Kino farm. (Courtesy of Charles Borders.)

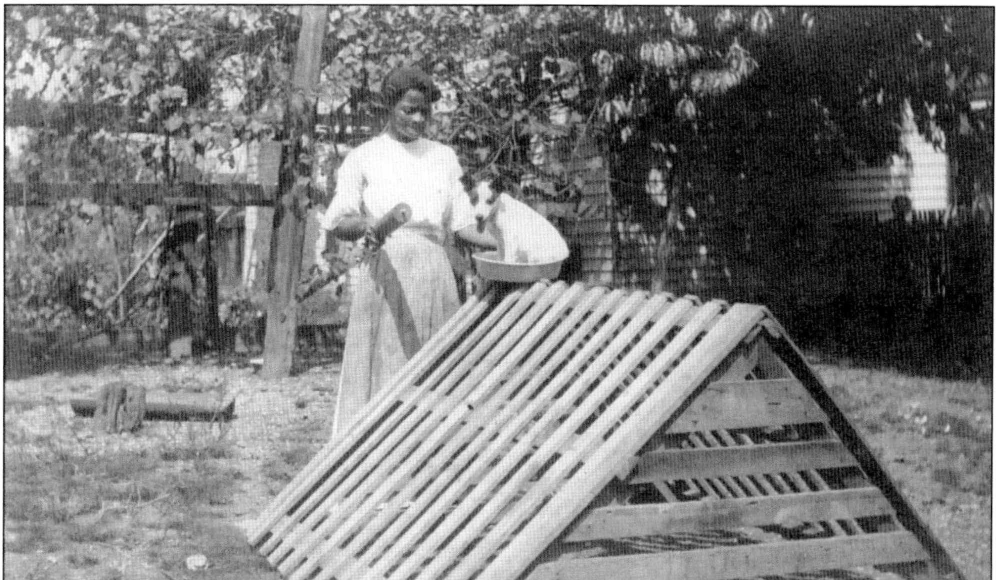

Be Good! This is a wonderfully fun photograph of a wayward dog who seems unwilling to obey or to take a bath. He will surely reform or be placed in the cage with the chickens.

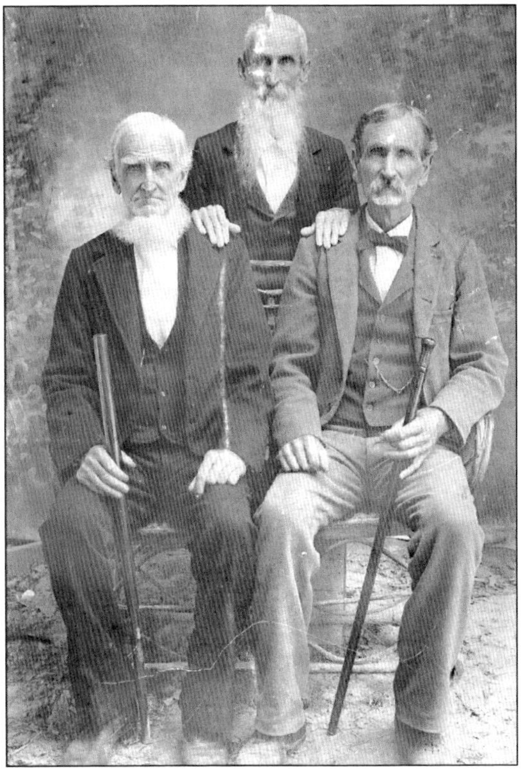

Guns and Glory. The Bradshaw family produced one of Barren County's pioneer preachers, Seth Bradshaw. It was said of Preacher Bradshaw before his conversion that he would rather fight than eat anytime! He led the flocks of Concord, also known as Trace Creek, Poplar Log, Glovers Creek, and Puncheon Camp. His sons, shown here, are (left to right) Madison, Tom, and William Bradshaw. (Courtesy of Danny and Carolyn Wyatt.)

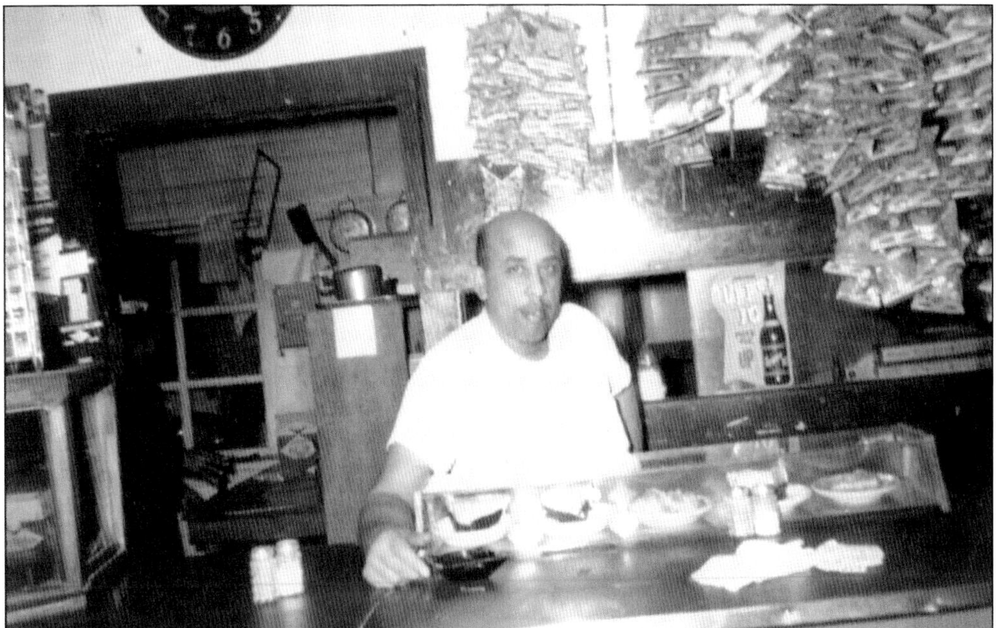

May I Help You? Otha Curd was the owner of the Royal Café, which was one of the most popular eateries in Glasgow. Before McDonald's and other fast food restaurants, these neighborhood businesses provided a good income for the owners and an outlet for socialization in the community. The Royal Café was located on Lewis Street. (Courtesy of Alma Glover.)

Off to Town. Bernard Wyatt (left) and Charlie Britt of the Austin Community have stopped long enough to have their photograph taken. The buggy would have made a trip to town quite an adventure. Physicians used these types of buggies for house calls, and they continued to be used by rural mail carriers. H. M. "Buck" Pedigo was listed as having the first top buggy in the county in 1878. (Courtesy of Danny and Carolyn Wyatt.)

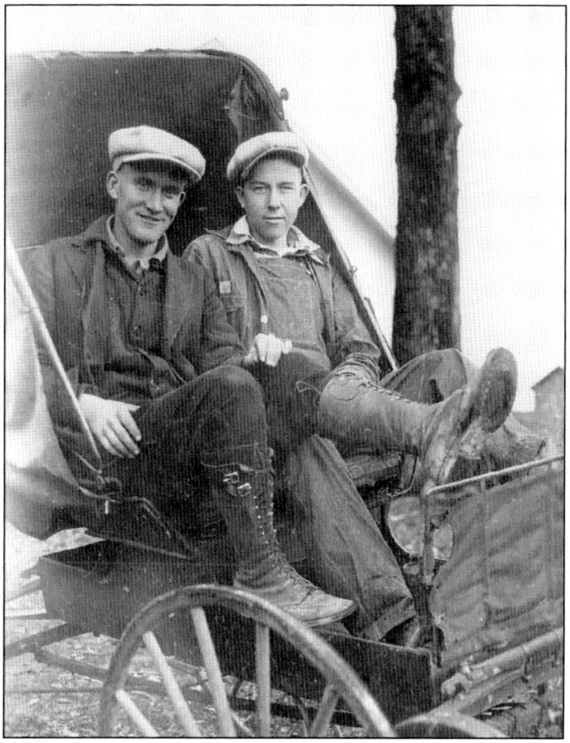

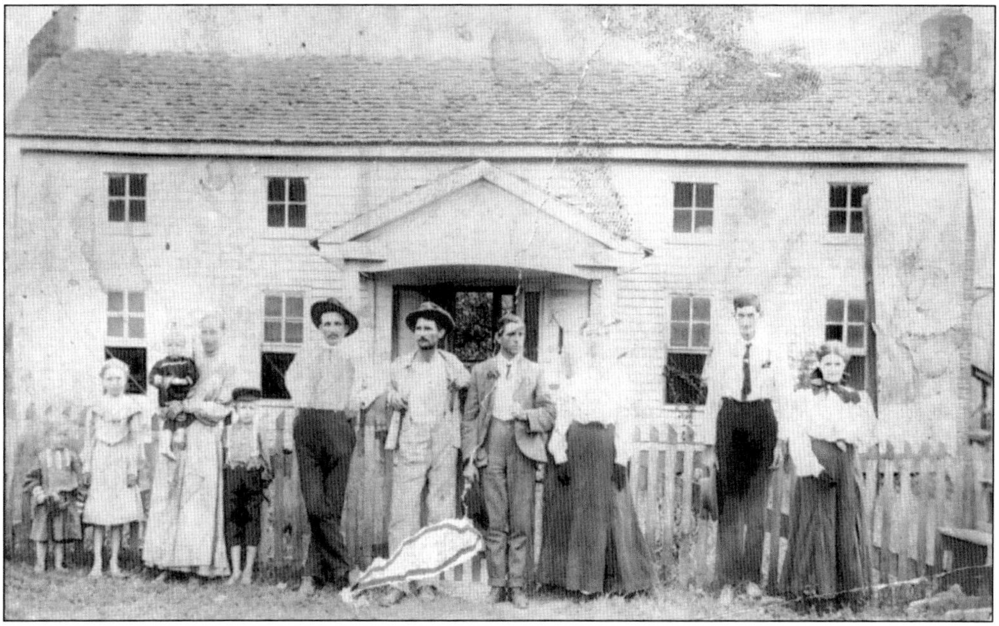

In the Neighborhood. A traveling photographer took this shot of the James H. Richey family in 1906. The family lived in the Freedom (Black Walnut) area of Barren County on what is now Lyons School Road. Shown in the photograph are, from left to right, Maggie Richey Elmore, Mary Richey Cooksey, Ish Richey, Nellie Tibbs Richey, Joe Richey, Johnny Jones, Sam Richey, Henry Soards, Florence Richey Soards, Charlie Gillan, and Maude Richey Gillan. (Courtesy of James and Olene Richey.)

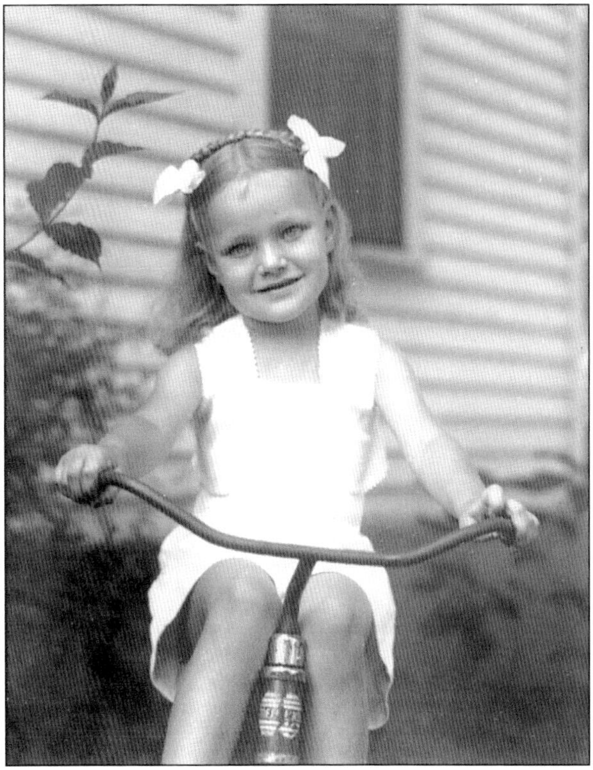

BARREN BEAUTY. Barren County is well known for the beauty of its land and natural resources. The beauty of its people is also recognized, which is visible in this youngster, Shelba Jean Underwood Lyons, as she enjoys a ride on her new tricycle. (Courtesy of Jardy Bewley.)

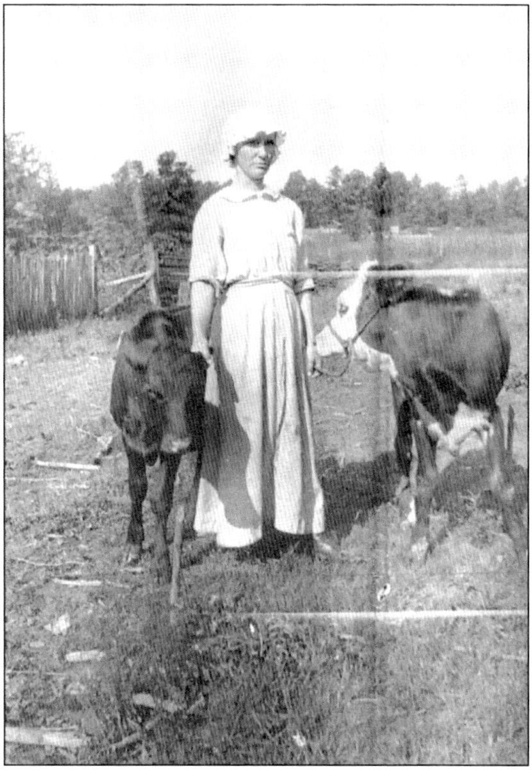

MILKMAID. Alva Hunt Logsdon of Cave City looks very much like a traditional milkmaid in her summer bonnet. These head coverings were functional for both farm chores and special occasions. They were not purely decorative in nature. The bonnet kept a person's head warm in winter and protected it from the sun in summer. It also came in handy for chasing down errant calves such as these. (Courtesy of Doug Aronson.)

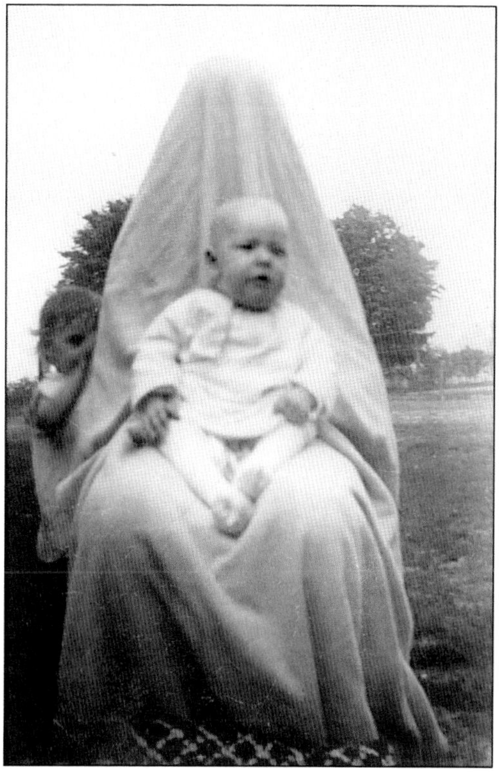

Spooktacular Photograph. This mother, wanting the focus of the photographer to be on her child, creates a ghostly scene that proves to be far more distracting than if she had been in the photograph herself. (Courtesy of Jardy Bewley.)

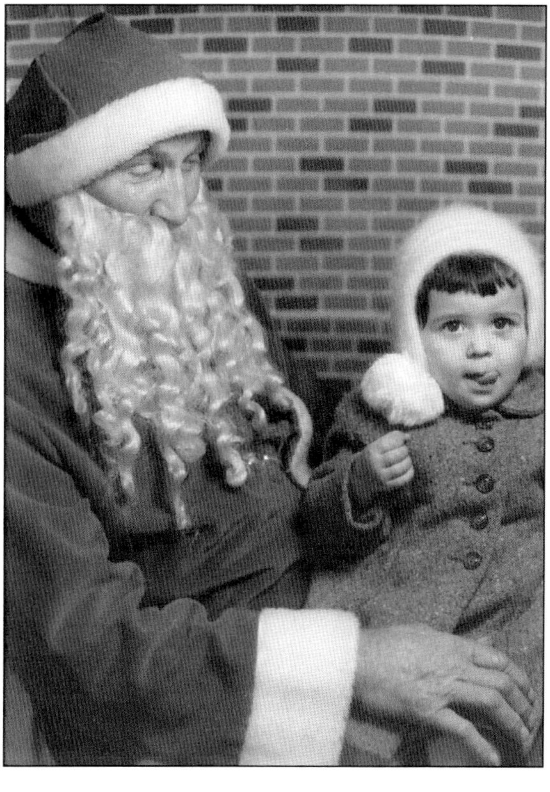

Santa Came to Town. The arrival of Santa in Glasgow every year was a much-anticipated event and was proclaimed one of the largest events of its kind in the state. The chamber of commerce sponsored "Santa Claus Day." It featured bands, lighted decorations, and gifts for all who stopped by to visit with St. Nick. Linda Bewley is shown here having her picture made with Santa. (Courtesy of Linda Bewley Mayberry.)

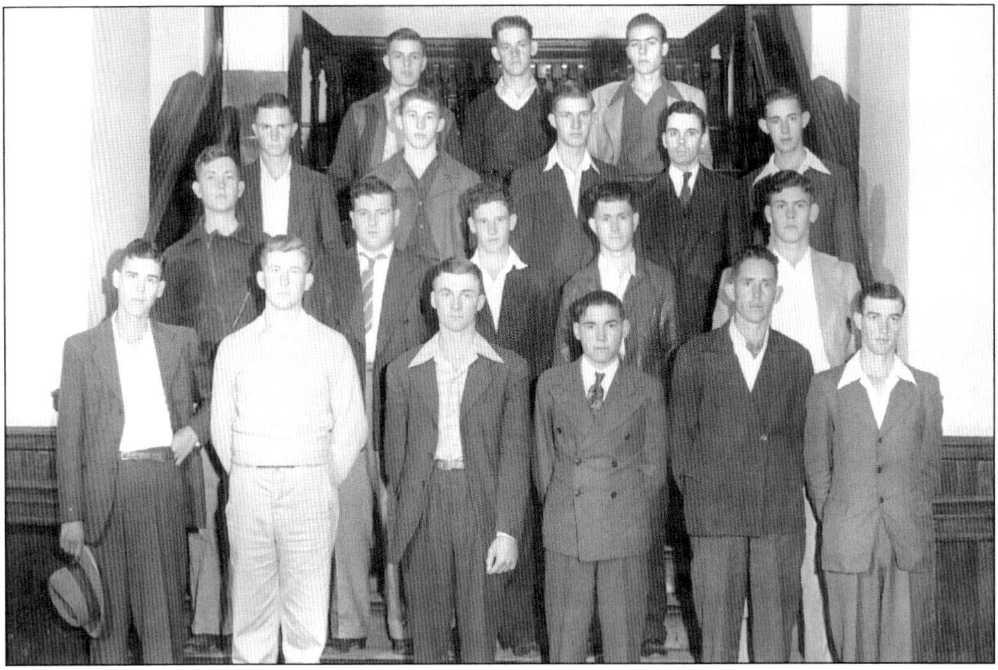

Answering the Call. These young men pose for their picture inside the courthouse on November 7, 1944. Among those pictured here are Lee Raymond Bewley, Leroy Jones, and Winston Nunn. During World War I, 900 men went into service, and 35 lost their lives. During World War II, 31 local men were killed in action. (Courtesy of Gary Bewley.)

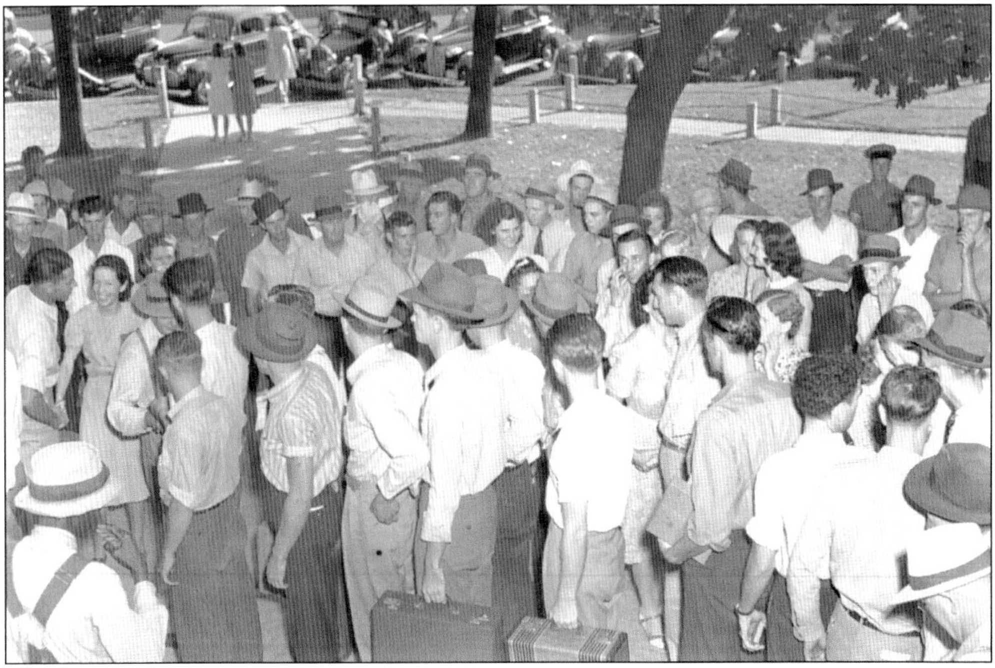

Ready to Go. Barren County sent 2,900 service people to serve in World War II, and 79 never returned. The county has always tried to offer support to its troops, whether they were going to fight or were returning home. Each Veteran's Day, a fine parade is held in their honor.

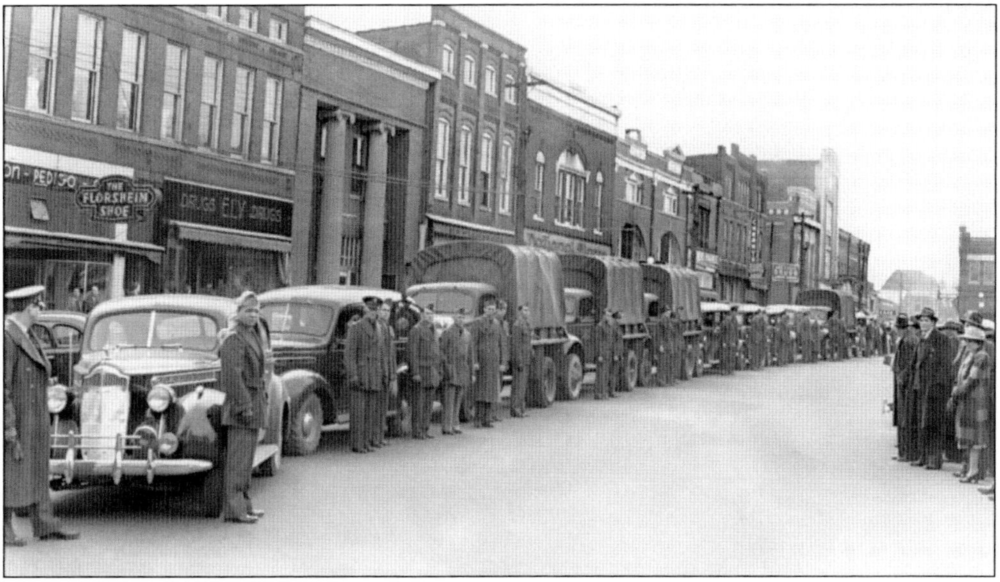

Saying Goodbye. As they leave the Glasgow Square, a motorcade of new recruits receives a big send-off and a long goodbye. Readiness for service is evident in this photograph of the young men who have been recruited or enlisted in the service for World War II. There was much fervor and dedication to the war effort for these Barren County men and the countless others. In 2009, the Glasgow and Barren County Veterans Association dedicated a Veterans Wall of Honor to all who have served from the county.

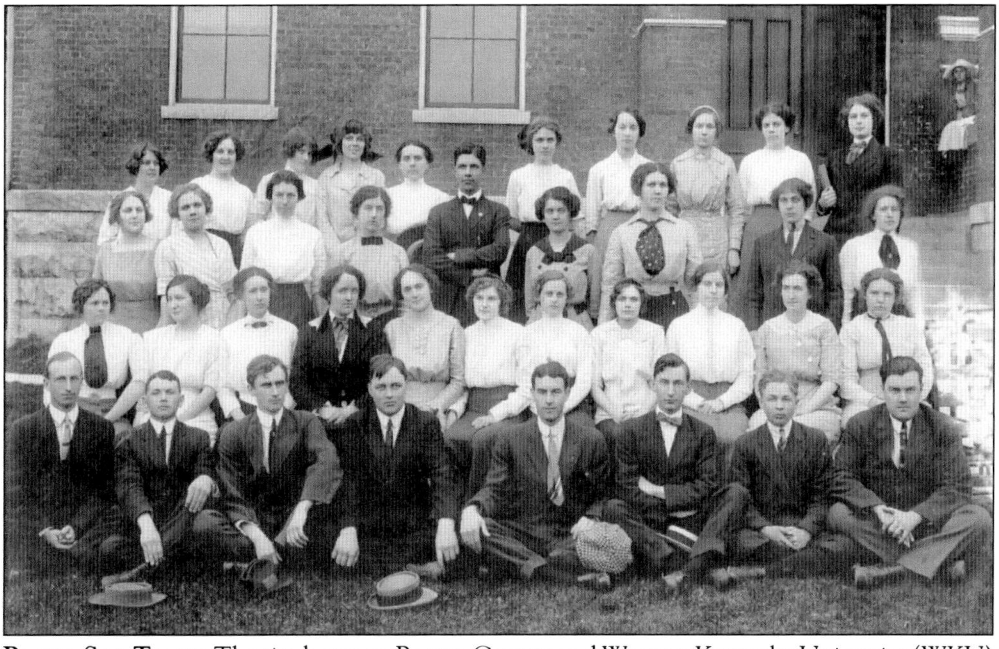

Ready, Set, Teach. The ties between Barren County and Western Kentucky University (WKU) are strong. The Glasgow Normal School started in 1874 but moved to Bowling Green, where it became known as the Southern Normal School. In 1911, the school moved to the "Hill." The photograph shows some of the first Barren County graduates in 1913. Today, coming full circle, WKU has an extended campus location in Glasgow. (Courtesy of WKU Archives.)

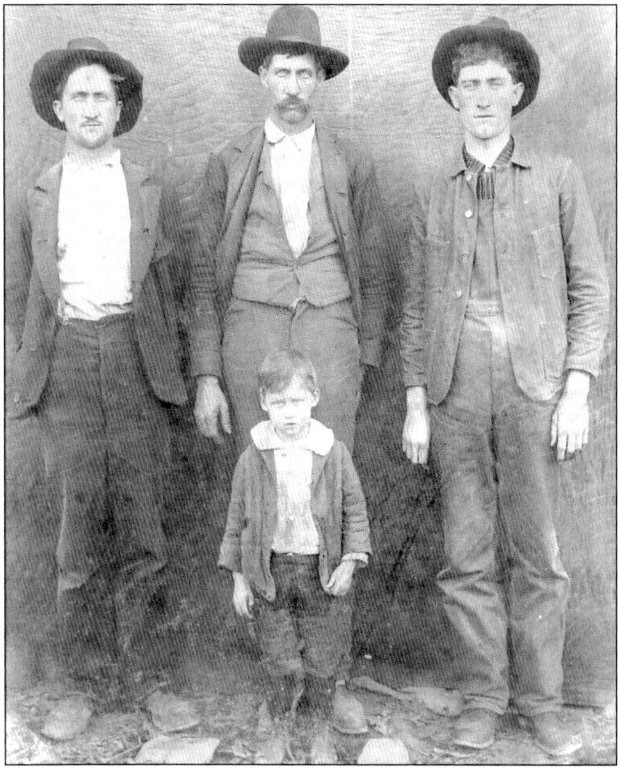

Smile, Please. Itinerant photographers traveled Barren County and Kentucky, and with impromptu backgrounds such as this quilt, set up shop. Many of the early photographs in this book and other publications came from the cameras of such traveling photographers. This cabinet card photograph was made around 1906 and was printed on heavy, brown, embossed card stock. By this year, Kentucky had more than 120 full-time photographers. (Courtesy of Danny and Carolyn Wyatt.)

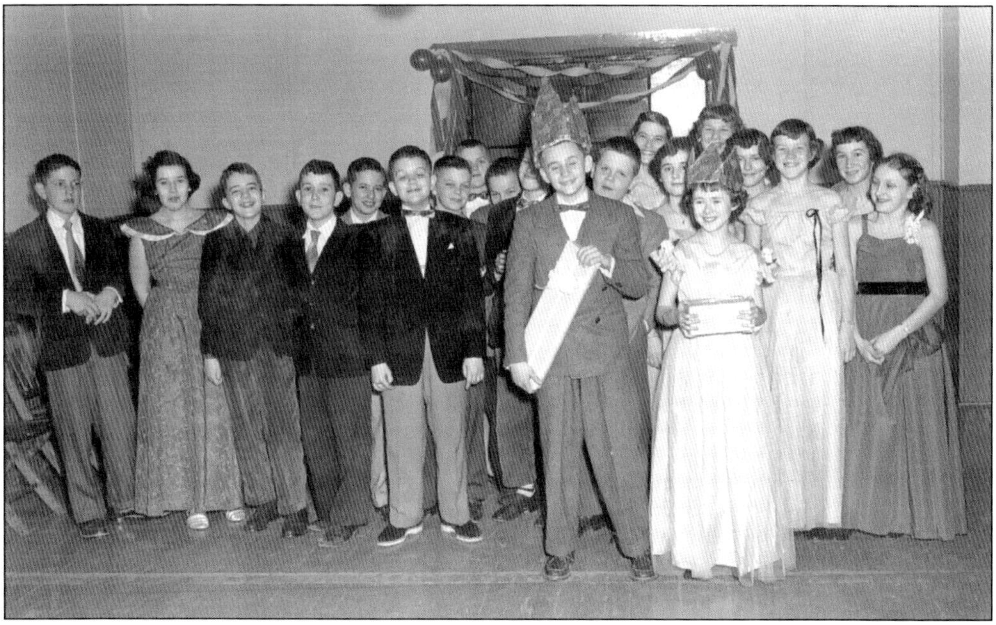

Small Royalty. Many free educational and social programs were offered by the Recreational Center so that everyone was able to participate in them. These children, as noted by their wide smiles, were happy to be chosen as King and Queen of the Recreation Center in 1952. The event was the highlight of the dance program. (Courtesy of the Glasgow–Barren County Chamber of Commerce.)

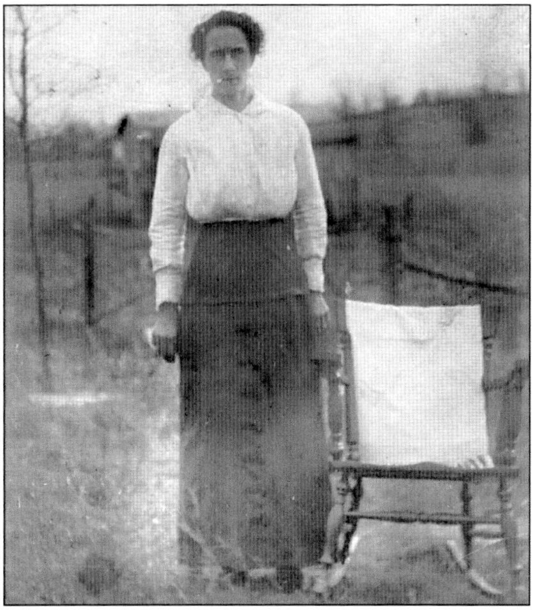

Cherished Piece. In this striking image, Lula Page of Barren County poses next to an empty rocking chair. The chair had been a favorite of a deceased family member, and the photograph created a memorial to them. The image was also placed on a postcard so that Page could share the memory with others.

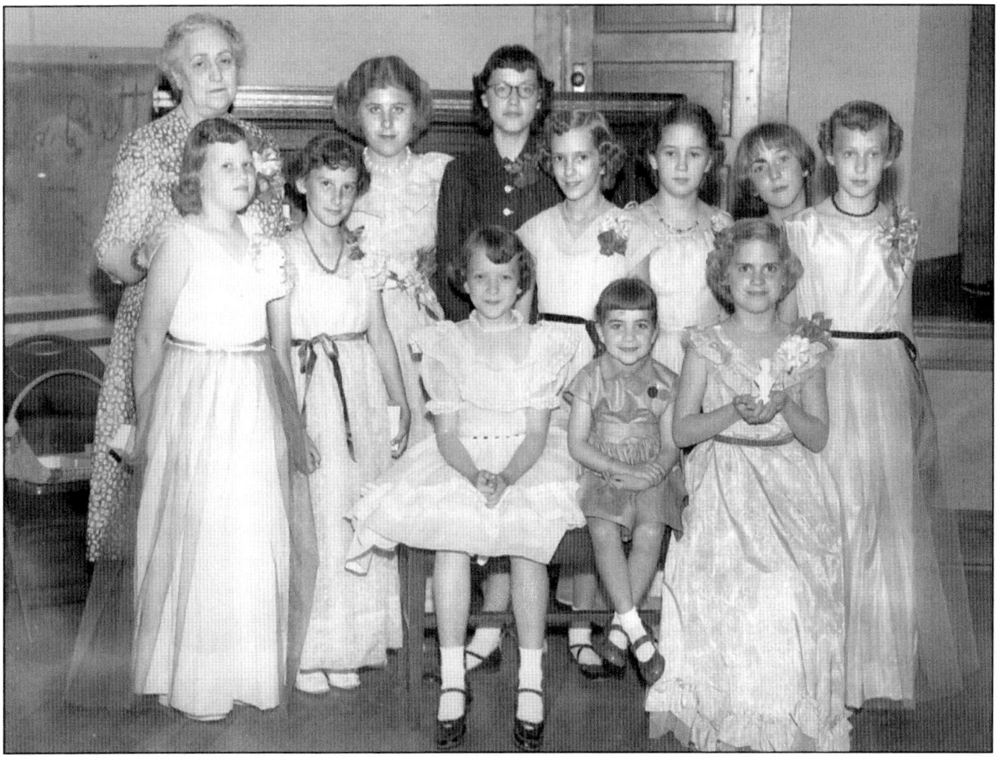

A Touch of Class. Elsie Dickson Trigg is shown with some of her piano students. They gave one of the first programs of a week's series of recitals. The students were Pauline Arnold, Joyce London, Linda Taylor, Carolyn Smith, Velma Christy, Barbara Davis, Anna Margaret Alexander, Betty Atnip, Betsy Dickinson, Bonnie Potts, Donna Quigley, Brenda Simmons, Judy Alexander, Anna Hamilton, Ann Dickinson, Janice Mosby, and Betty Holder. (Courtesy of the Glasgow–Barren County Chamber of Commerce.)

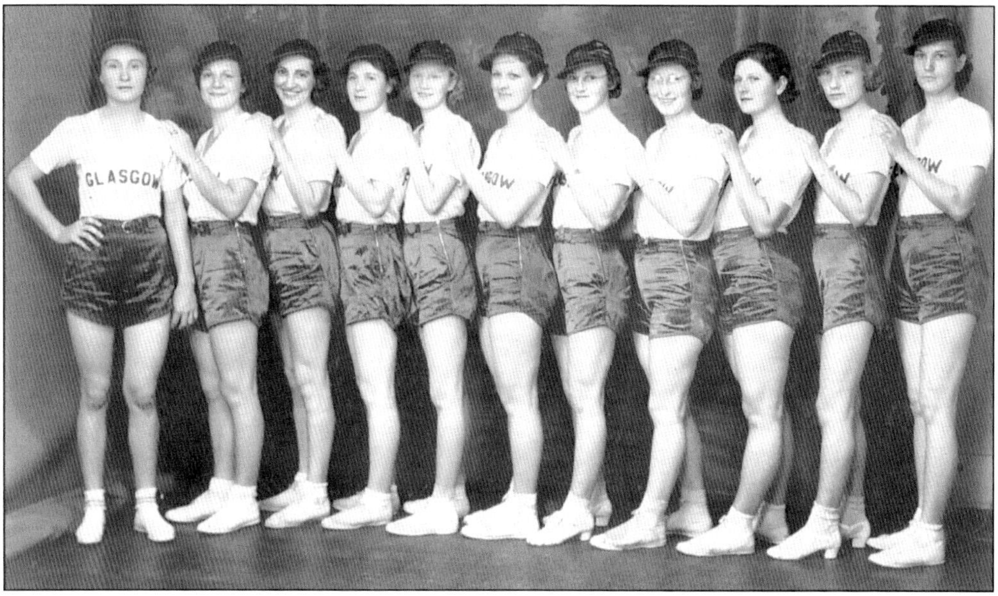

THAT WINNING SEASON. The talented young women shown above in 1935 were from Temple Hill School and enjoyed their time in the limelight as a team sponsored by Gerald's Furniture Company. The stylish belted uniforms and jaunty hats were unique and created a wonderful image. The team members are, from left to right, Gene Wells, Velma Wilkerson, Katherine Curd, Irene Gassaway, Irene Nuckols, Punk Rush Wheeler, Helen Gassaway, unidentified, Leona Poore, unidentified, and Loretta Smith. Barren County's female athletes continued the winning basketball tradition in the 1975–1976 school season, as the Trojanette's basketball team captured the Kentucky state runner-up title. Women's basketball leagues had been disbanded in the schools in the 1930s, so this was the first time in 40 years that a girls' basketball tournament had been played in Kentucky. Members of the Trojanette's team are shown below. (Above, courtesy of Jardy Bewley; below, courtesy of Debbie Bunch Jones.)

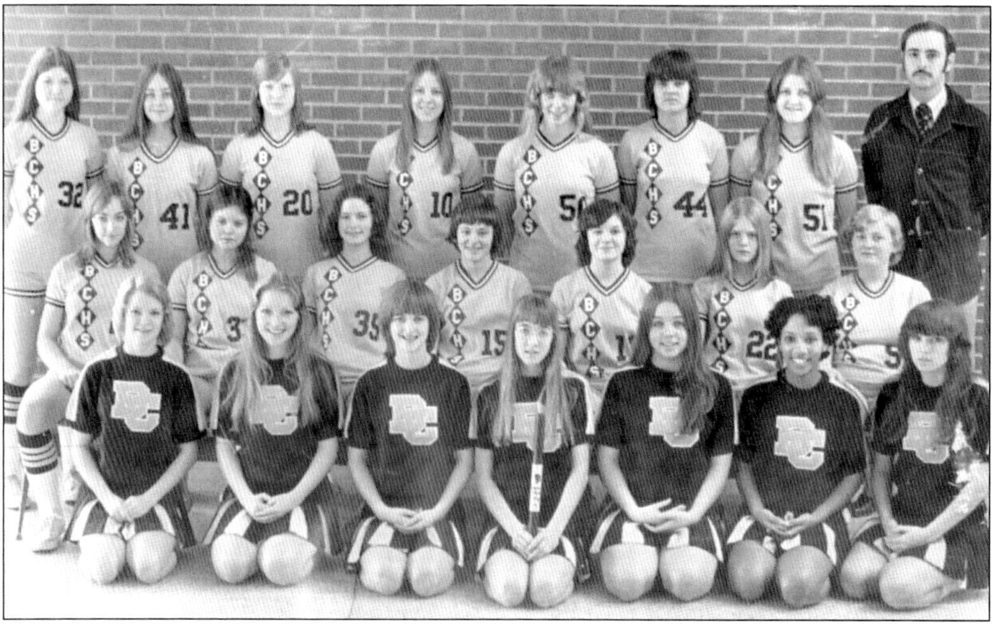

Tragic Loss. The sad loss of their tiny child is shown in the faces of this couple. They have chosen a beautiful white casket and draped its sewing machine bier with fine linen. The homemade bouquets and wayward chicken accentuate the rural starkness of the scene. The photograph is unusual in that most postmortem images focus on the deceased, but the casket takes central stage in this one. (Courtesy of Doug Aronson.)

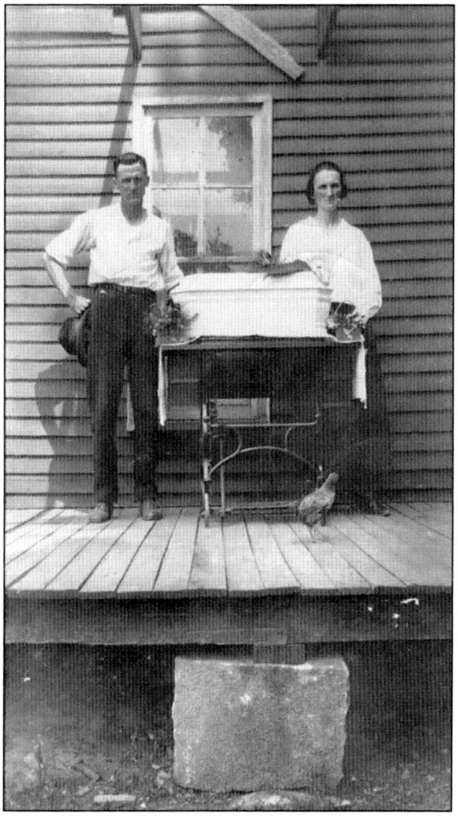

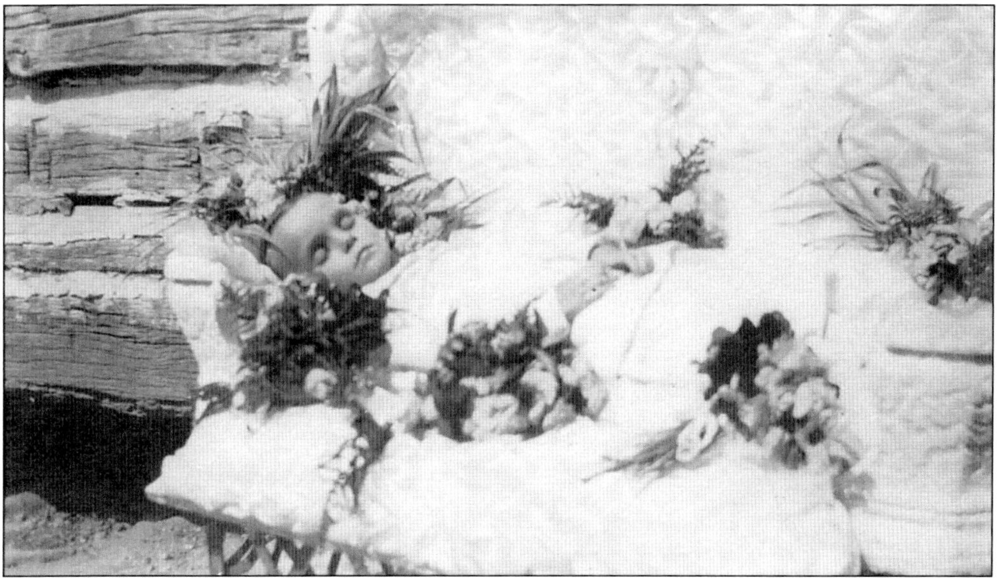

Sad Day. This child honored in death with the finest flowers, casket, and clothes was also, as tradition warranted, memorialized in this postmortem photograph from 1900. The photograph was placed in a prominent point in the home, and the image was added to postcards to be shared with those who could not attend the services. The rough-hewn cabin stands in striking contrast to the funeral finery. (Courtesy of Jardy Bewley.)

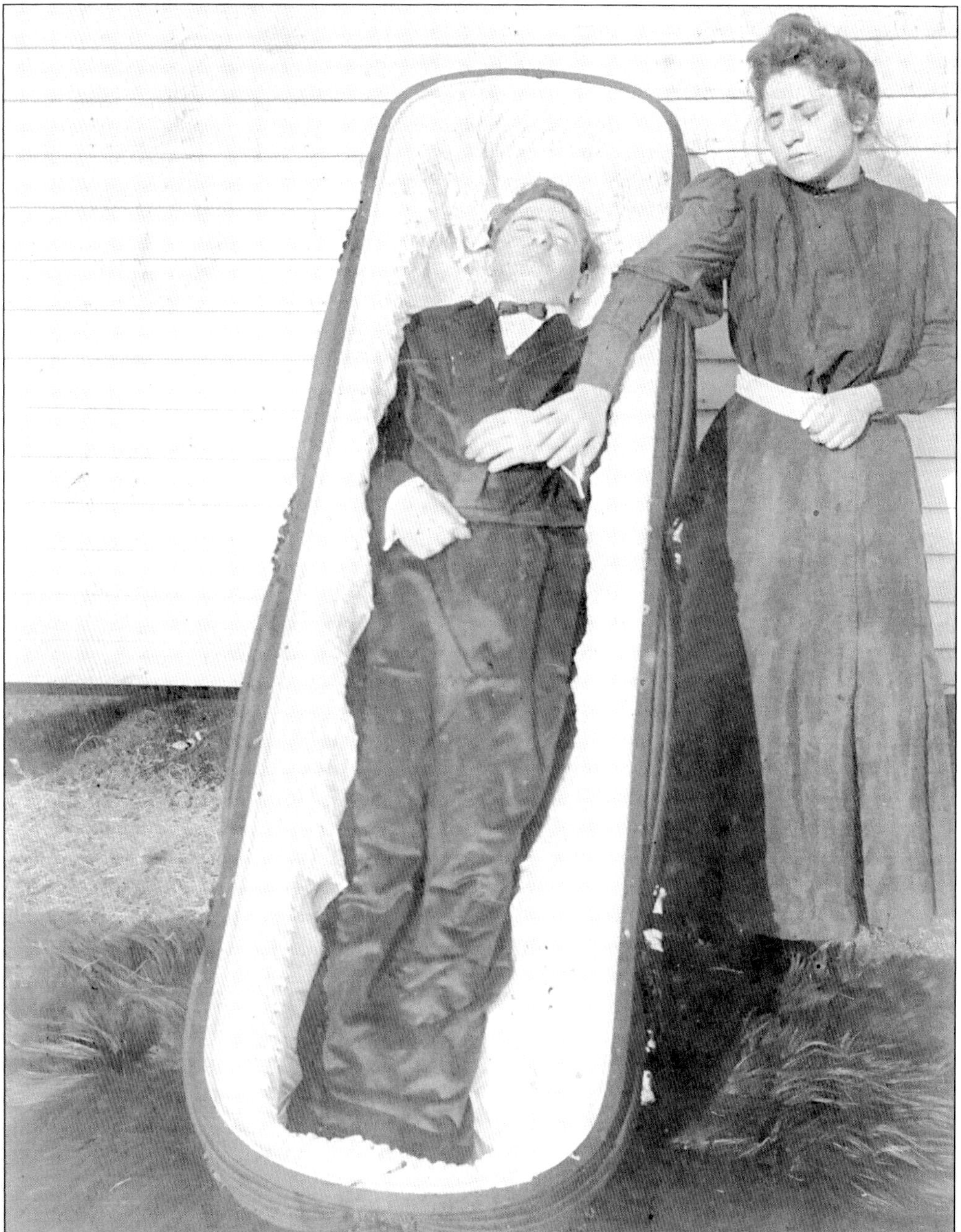

GONE BUT NOT FORGOTTEN. The tradition of taking postmortem photographs was one way that south central Kentuckians found to ease the grief experienced in the loss of a loved one and to capture a visual remembrance of the deceased. The photographs could be enlarged, framed, and hung on a wall or placed in an album. Taken on January 1, 1908, this photograph of Clarence Carver in death illustrates both the deceased and the mourner in attendance. It is unique in that the focus is as much on Myrtie Berry as it is on Clarence Carver. Poetry of the period added to the melancholy scene, "we will meet but we will miss him, there will be his vacant chair; we will linger to caress him, while we breathe our evening prayer." (Courtesy of Runell and Terry Houchen.)

Three

AROUND THE COUNTY

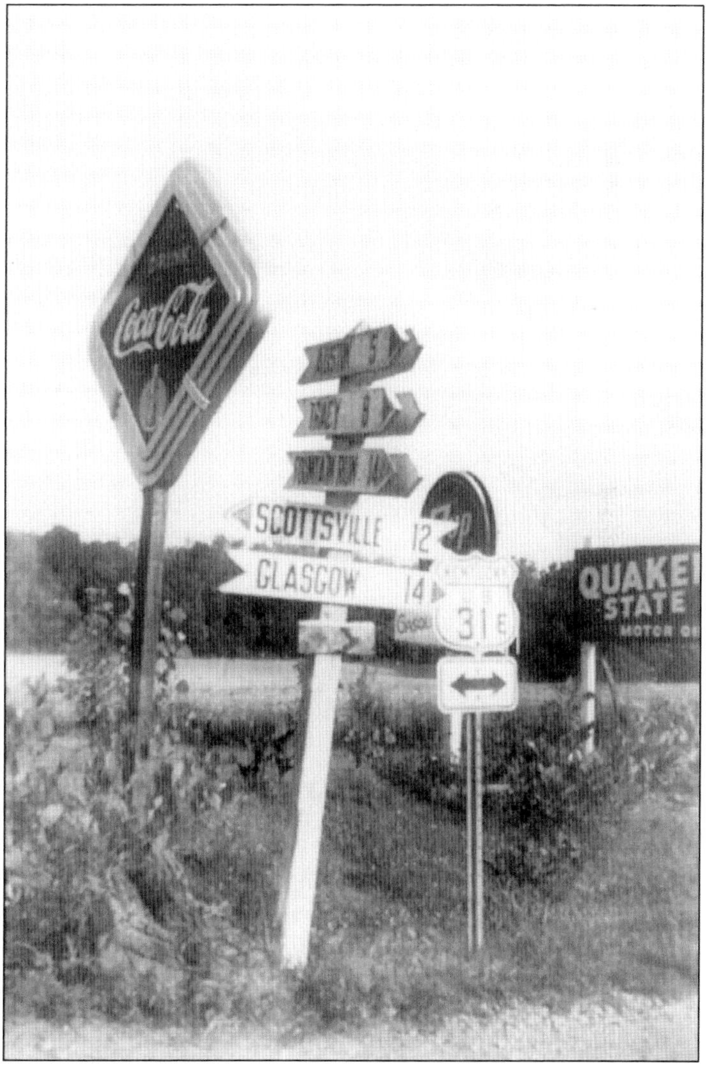

WHICH WAY TO GO? The signs posted near what is now the Barren River State Park direct travelers and visitors to nearby Glasgow, Scottsville, Fountain Run, Austin, and Tracy. It can also be seen that roadway advertising is not new. Quaker State Oil, 7UP, and Coca-Cola all wanted to be seen by travelers. (Courtesy of Martha Harrison.)

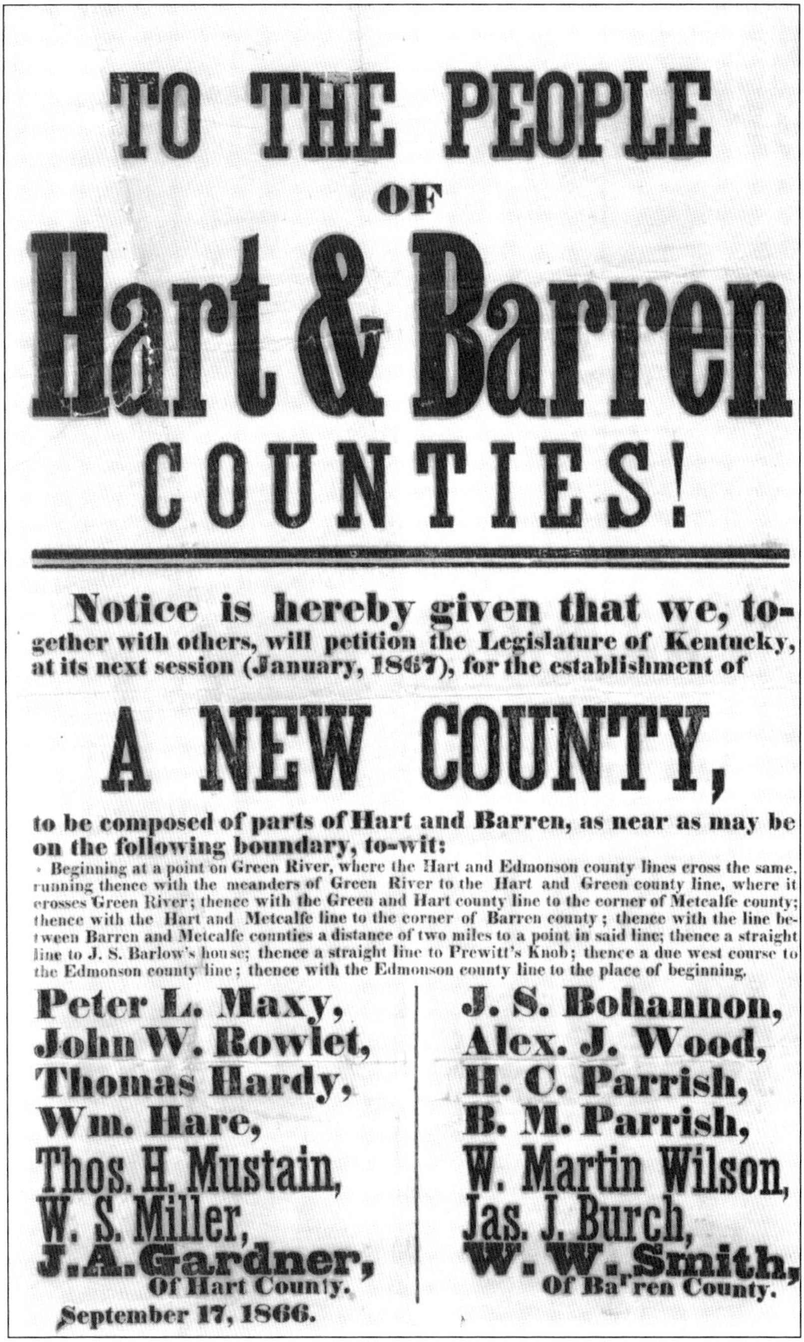

TO THE PEOPLE

OF

Hart & Barren

COUNTIES!

Notice is hereby given that we, together with others, will petition the Legislature of Kentucky, at its next session (January, 1867), for the establishment of

A NEW COUNTY,

to be composed of parts of Hart and Barren, as near as may be on the following boundary, to-wit:

Beginning at a point on Green River, where the Hart and Edmonson county lines cross the same, running thence with the meanders of Green River to the Hart and Green county line, where it crosses Green River; thence with the Green and Hart county line to the corner of Metcalfe county; thence with the Hart and Metcalfe line to the corner of Barren county; thence with the line between Barren and Metcalfe counties a distance of two miles to a point in said line; thence a straight line to J. S. Barlow's house; thence a straight line to Prewitt's Knob; thence a due west course to the Edmonson county line; thence with the Edmonson county line to the place of beginning.

Peter L. Maxy,
John W. Rowlet,
Thomas Hardy,
Wm. Hare,
Thos. H. Mustain,
W. S. Miller,
J. A. Gardner,
Of Hart County.

J. S. Bohannon,
Alex. J. Wood,
H. C. Parrish,
B. M. Parrish,
W. Martin Wilson,
Jas. J. Burch,
W. W. Smith,
Of Barren County.

September 17, 1866.

POSTING NOTICE. The county's power and influence as a unit is firmly entrenched in the political makeup of the commonwealth. This broadside from 1866 was giving notice that a request for a new county was going to be presented to the Kentucky Legislature in 1867. The creation of a new county was rejected this time but not for long—Kentucky holds the distinction of having the third highest number of counties in the United States. Barren would become the "mother county" for Allen County in 1815, Hart County in 1819, Monroe County in 1820, and Metcalfe County in 1860.

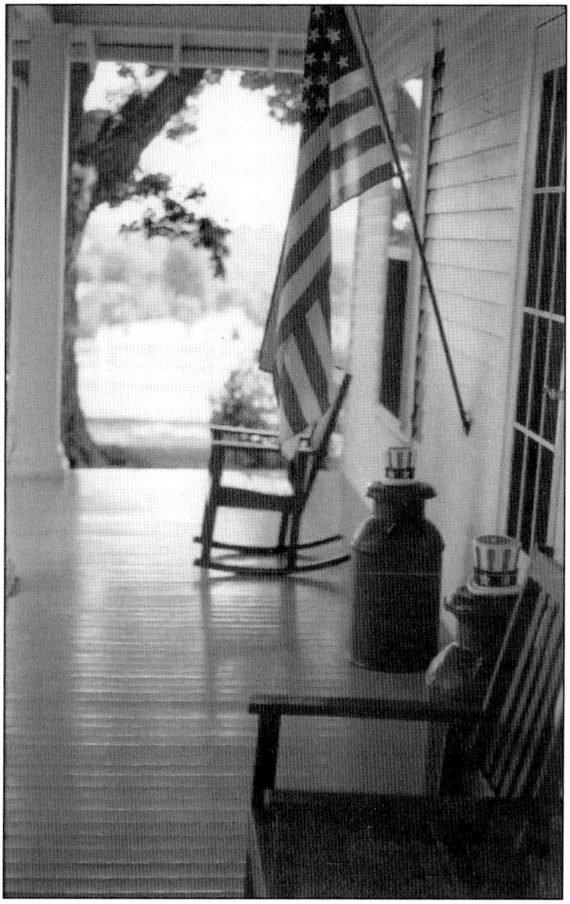

Pretty Porch. Barren County's beautiful, spacious pastoral areas still abound, along with its many country homes. Seen below, sights such as the open rolling hills, as well as the welcoming front porches, are still plentiful. The cherished porch and swing fostered a connection to this beautiful land and was a place for family and friends to stop, visit, and share news of their lives and the world. Sadly, with new construction trends in the county and elsewhere, the traditional American front porch is fast disappearing as an architectural design. (Both, courtesy of Gary Bewley.)

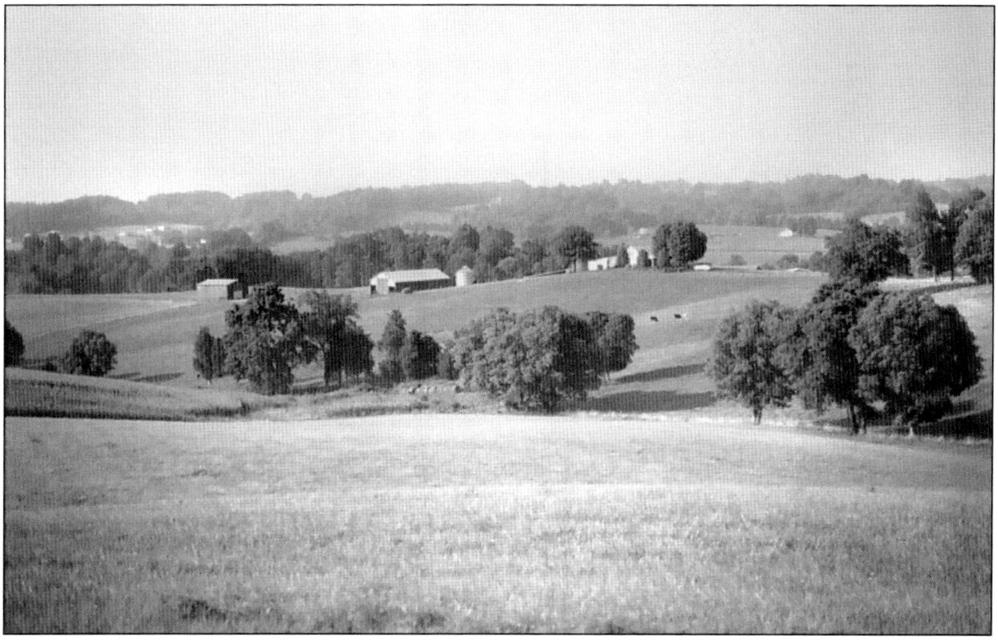

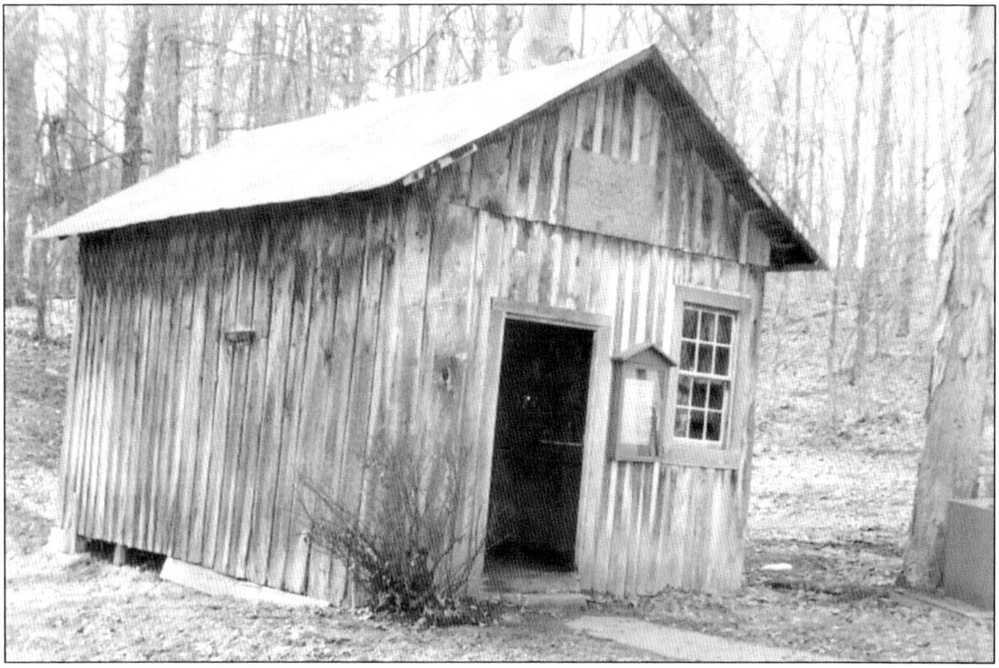

The Beginning. Ervin G. Houchens opened his first store a few miles south of Glasgow on his father's farm in 1917 at the age of 19. The store was housed in the 12-by-20-foot shed shown here. Houchens followed the new model of self-service in grocery stores. Houchens Industries is now the fourth-largest grocery store operator in Kentucky.

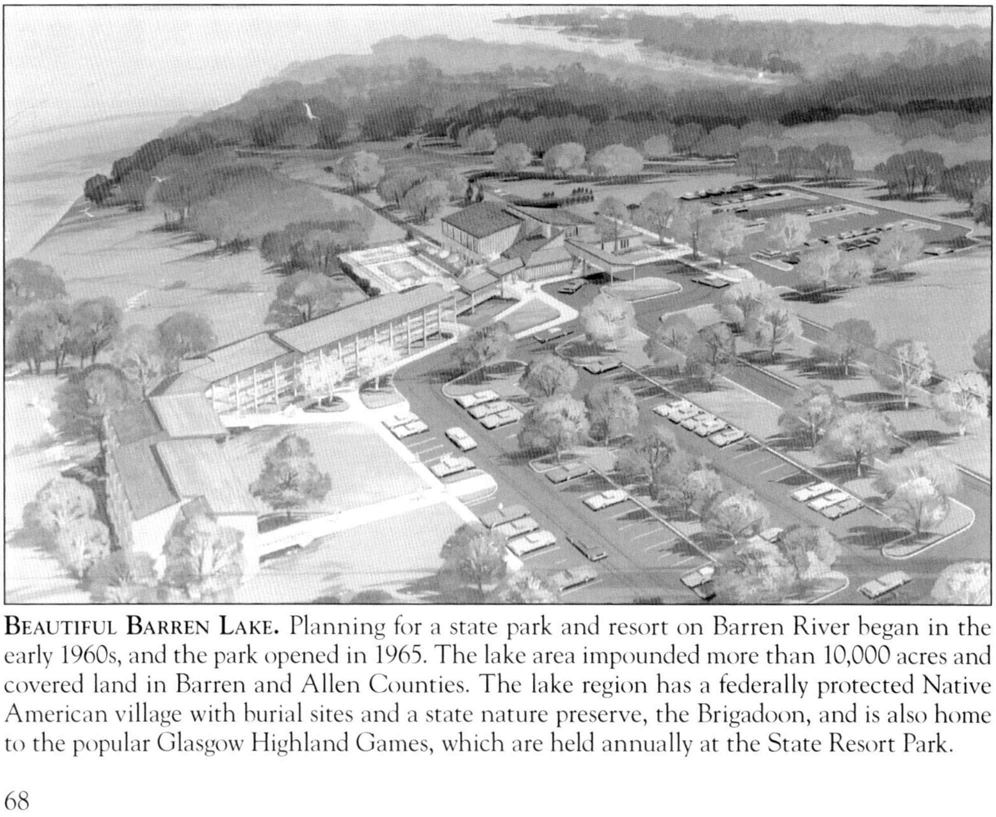

Beautiful Barren Lake. Planning for a state park and resort on Barren River began in the early 1960s, and the park opened in 1965. The lake area impounded more than 10,000 acres and covered land in Barren and Allen Counties. The lake region has a federally protected Native American village with burial sites and a state nature preserve, the Brigadoon, and is also home to the popular Glasgow Highland Games, which are held annually at the State Resort Park.

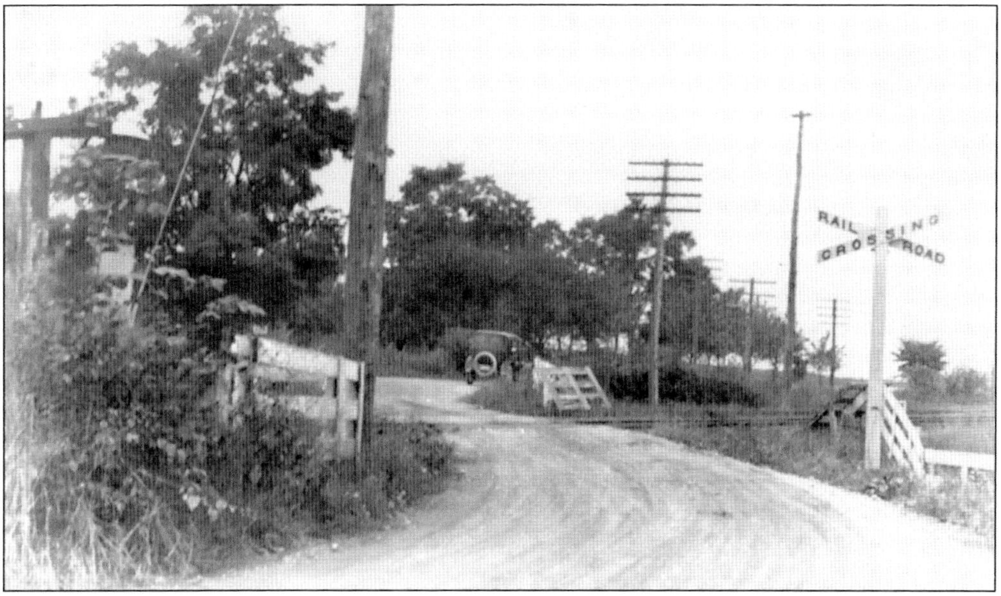

Making a Stop. With the arrival of the train came the ubiquitous railroad crossings, as seen above. The crossings were dangerous, and many deaths were caused by these lethal intersections. Pictured at right, the Louisville and Nashville train pulls into Cave City on its way to Bowling Green. The coming of the railroad to Cave City was the most important event in the development of the town. The first trains began passing through in 1858. At the time, the line was part of 26 miles of railroad that ran through the county. Cave City was not named because of its proximity to Mammoth Cave but for a small cave located in the east end of town, which was where the railroad had its pumping station. The cave was the source of the town's drinking water. (Right, courtesy of Karen Phillips.)

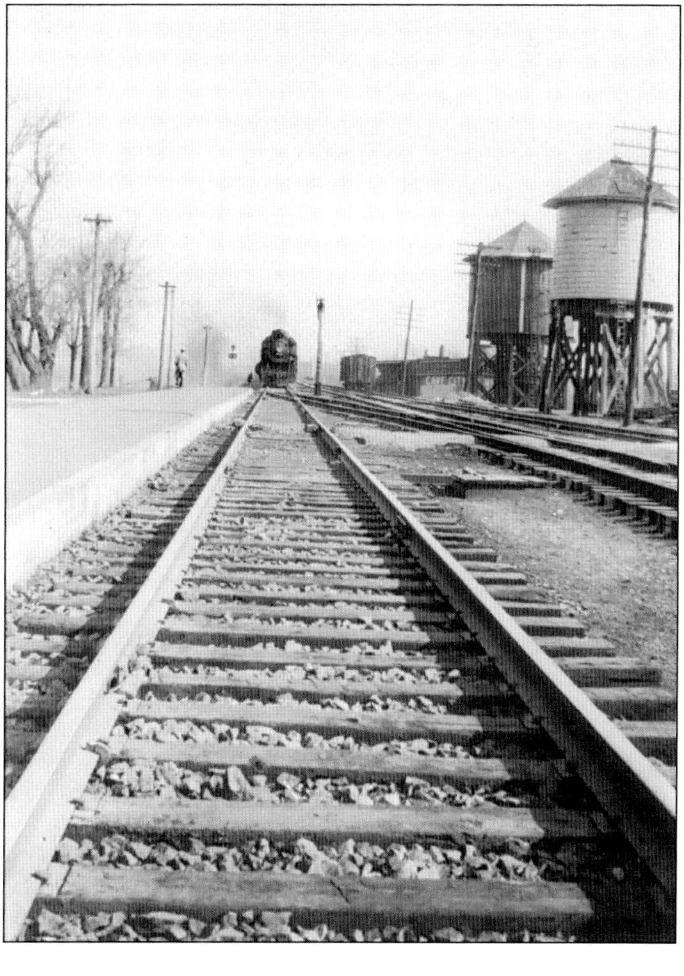

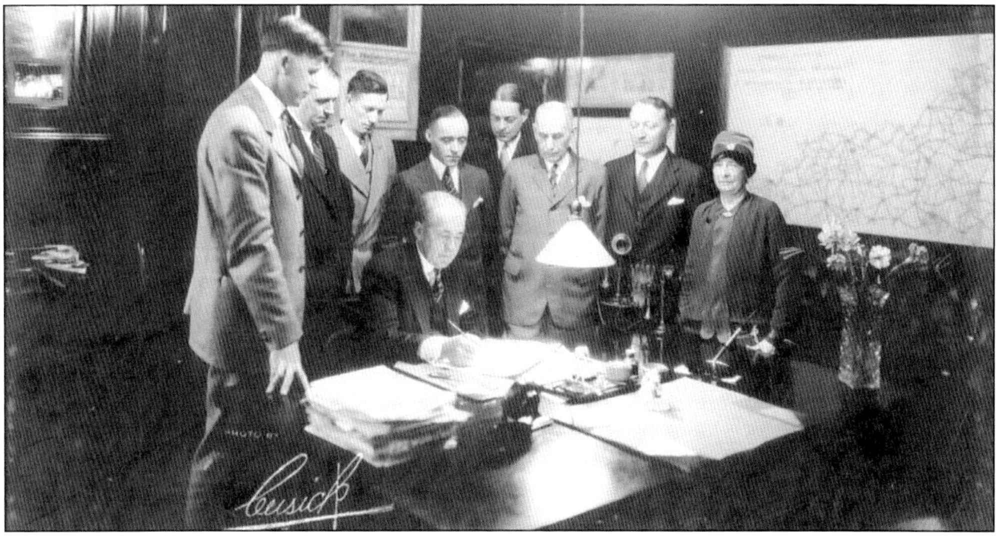

CREATING HISTORY. Flem D. Sampson, governor of Kentucky is shown signing the bill that would supply state funding to the Mammoth Cave National Park Association. With Governor Sampson in this 1926 photograph are, from left to right, Clarence Bartlett, J. S. Milliken, Walter Smith, James Breathitt Jr., Arch Quarles, Frank L. Strange, Harry G. Smith, and Emma Guy Cromwell. Governor Sampson had visited the county just a few months earlier to promote the park.

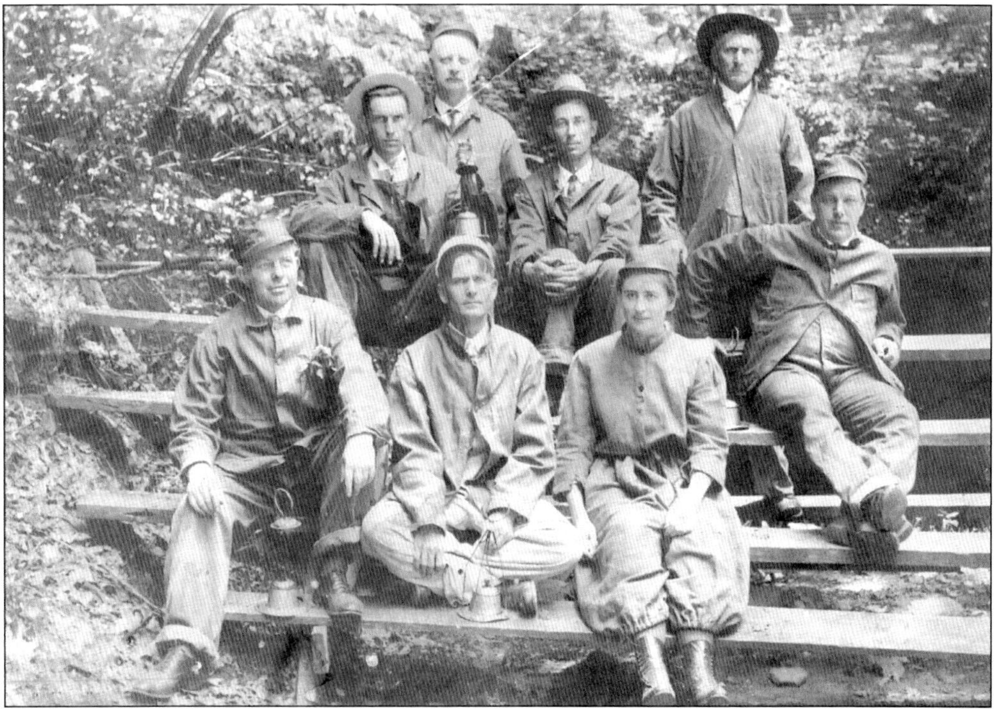

CAVING PIONEERS. Photographs such as this were taken in front of the historic entrance to Mammoth Cave at the beginning of the 20th century. The photographic souvenirs were ready for purchase after the tours. An inscription on the back of the photograph states that this is the first group to go through the cave when the historic entrance opened. The lone woman pictured wears her "bloomers" as she readies for exploring the cave and getting dirty.

HISTORIC HOTELS AND CABINS. Many Barren County residents, along with countless tourists, enjoyed staying at the Mammoth Cave Hotel and outlying cabins. It was considered one of the finest hotels in the state and was noted for its ballroom, log fires, and orchestral performances. The hotel is shown in the background of the photograph at right as (from left to right) Elizabeth Cox Hunt (standing), Dovie Morrison, Mary Miller Cox, and May Morrison pose for this generational shot. Below, the four unidentified ladies are also enjoying the area in front of more rustic cabin accommodations. The young ladies look quite pleased, but the donkey is not so sure about this situation. (Right, courtesy of Doug Aronson.)

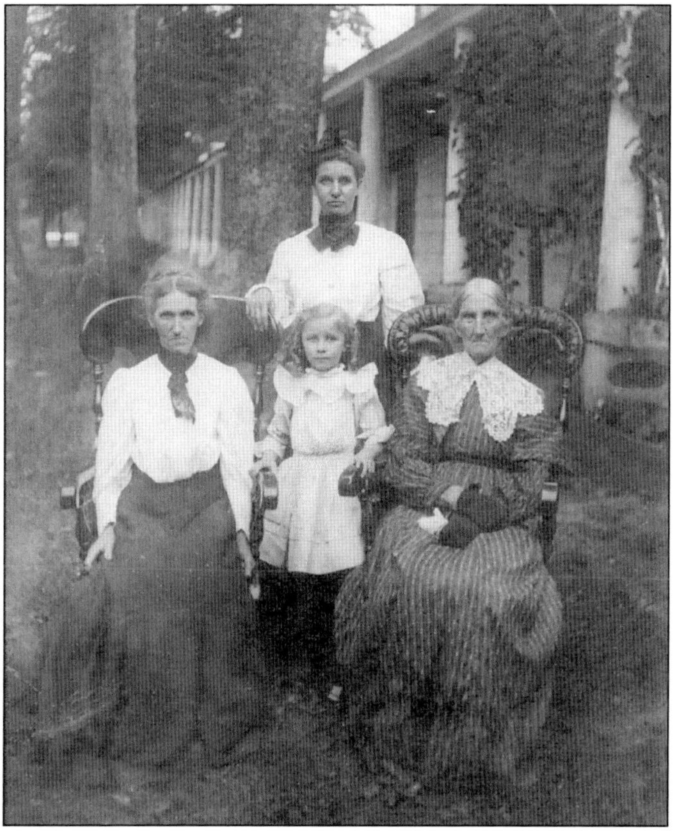

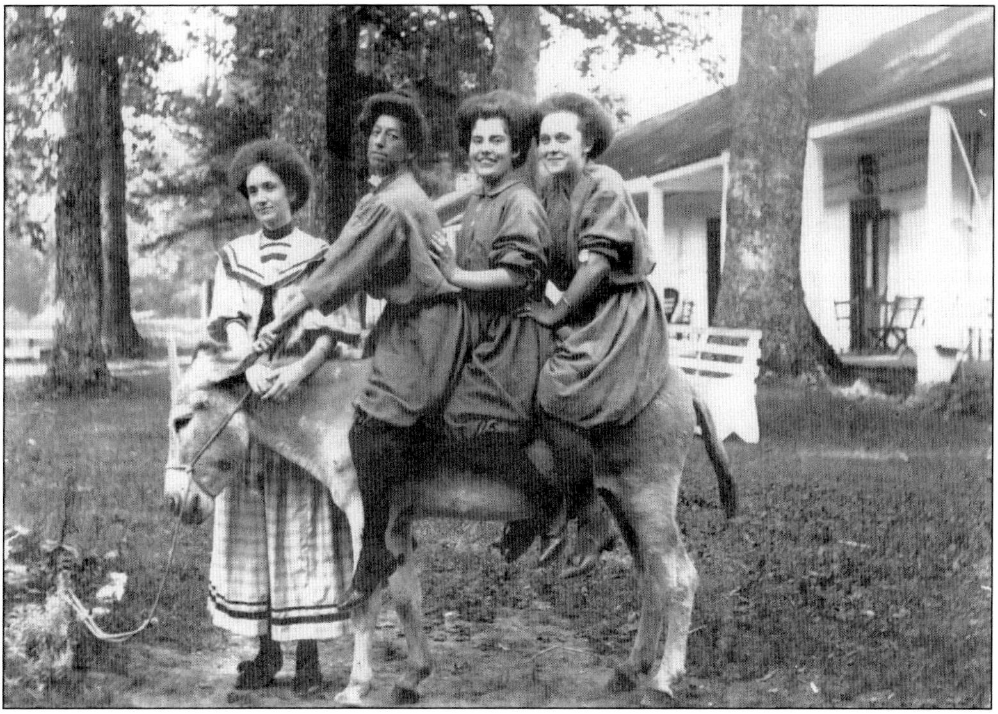

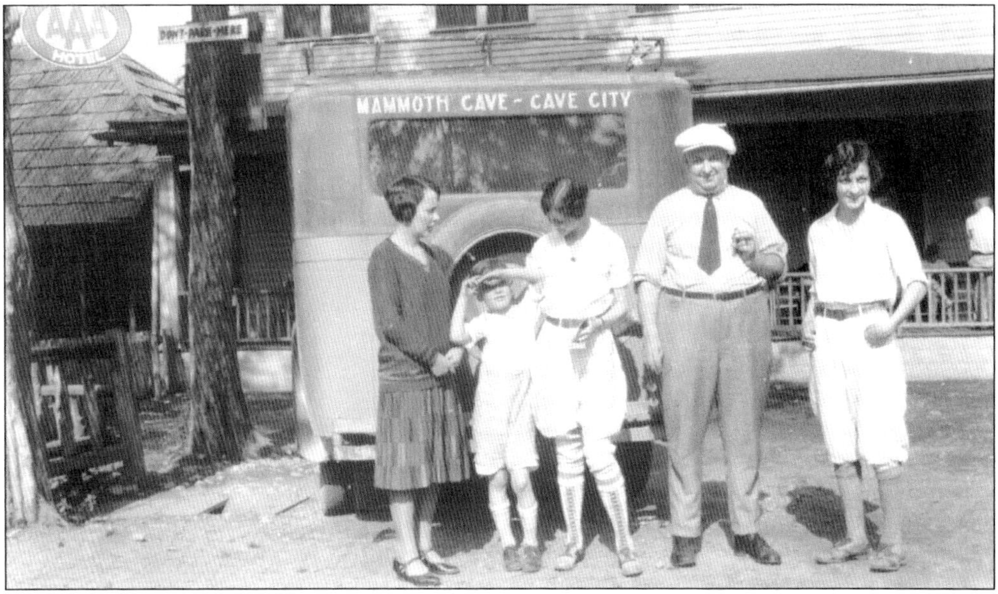

NEXT STOP: MAMMOTH CAVE. It is a bright, beautiful day as this group waits for the next bus trip to the cave. This type of bus service ran regularly between the cave area and Cave City and brought eager tourists for once-in-a-lifetime tours. Notice the dashing sporty pantaloons of the ladies, as they are dressed for the rigors of spelunking. (Courtesy of the National Park Service.)

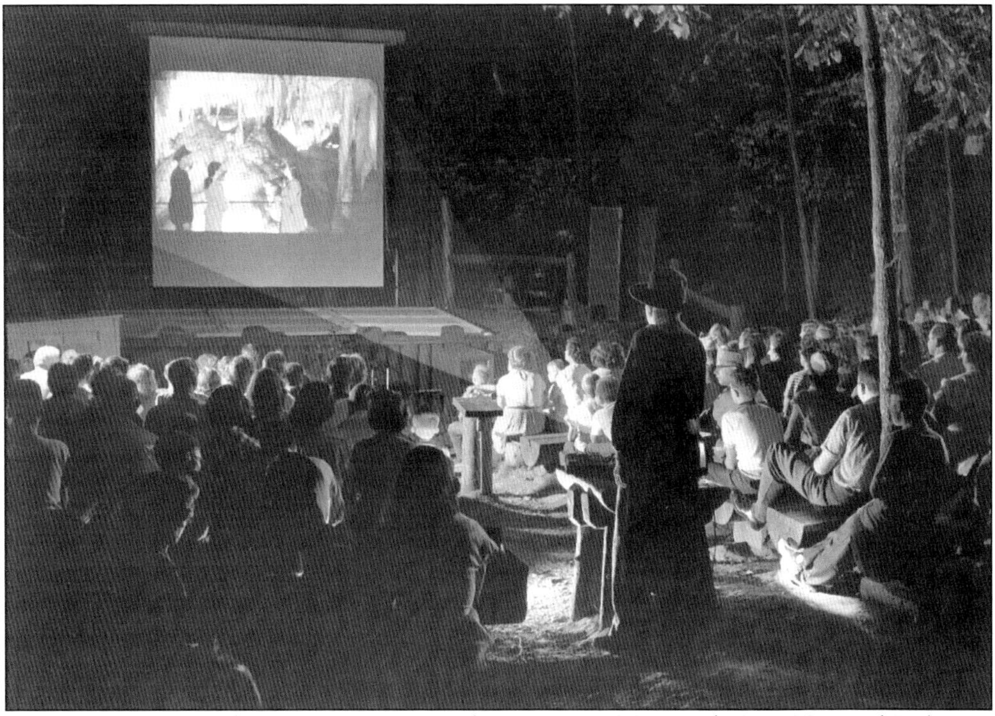

MOVIE TIME. During the warm summer months, visitors to Mammoth Cave National Park were treated to educational films about the cave and its environs. The outdoor setting proved to be a wonderful classroom. The cave was first photographed in 1866 and has been the subject of many filmed documentaries.

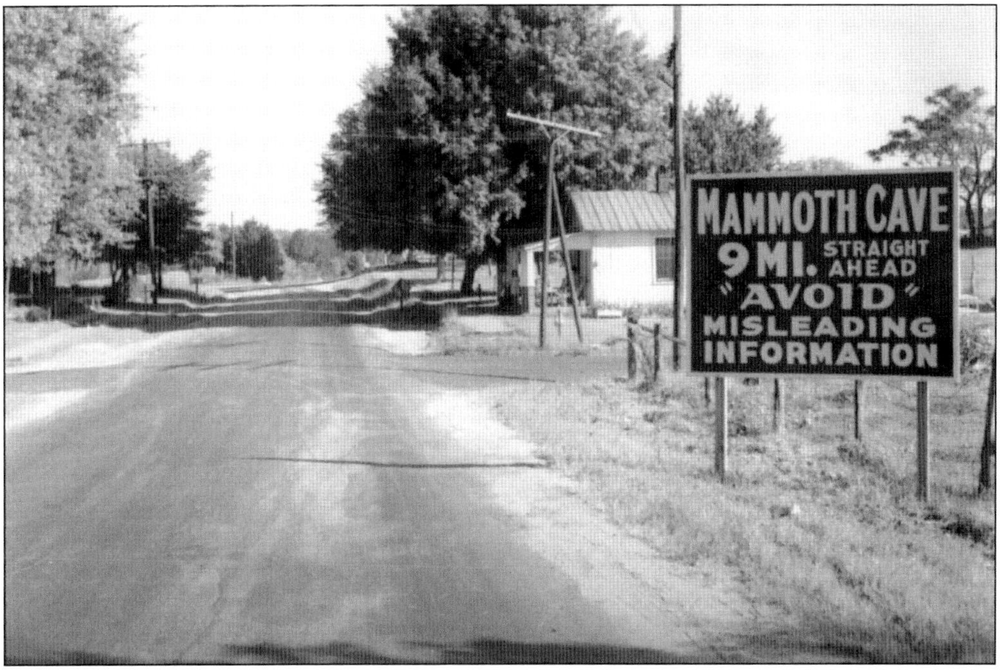

Finding Mammoth Cave. As tourism increased in the early 20th century, so did the fight for the visitors' dollars, as more than 17 caves were available for touring. Signs warn against the "cave wars," which were when unscrupulous people tried to waylay the unsuspecting visitors from their intended destination. (Courtesy of the National Park Service.)

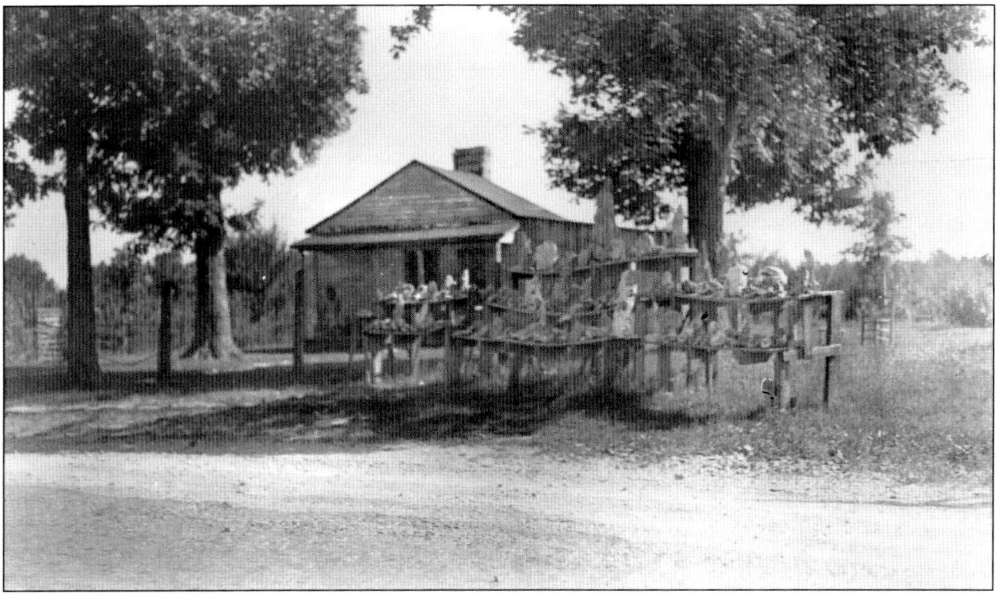

See Rock City. Everyone became an entrepreneur and wanted to cash in on the burgeoning tourist trade that the advent of the automobile produced. This type of makeshift stand sprouted all over the cave area. The stands sold rocks, stalactites, and the cone-shaped stalagmites that were taken from the caves in Barren and in the surrounding counties of Warren, Edmonson, and Hart. (Courtesy of the National Park Service.)

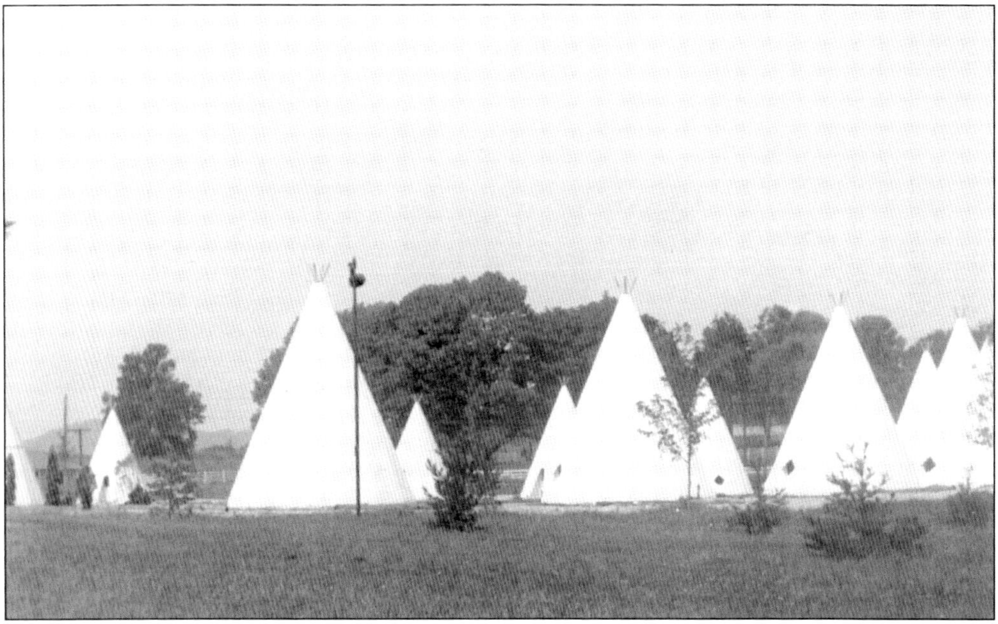

A NEAT PLACE TO SLEEP. Frank Redford loved the shape of ice cream cones and tepees, and so gained inspiration for his first Wigwam Village in Horse Cave in 1925. This 1940 photograph shows the second village in Cave City. Out of the original seven, three remain; the other ones are located in Holbrook, Arizona, and Rialto, California.

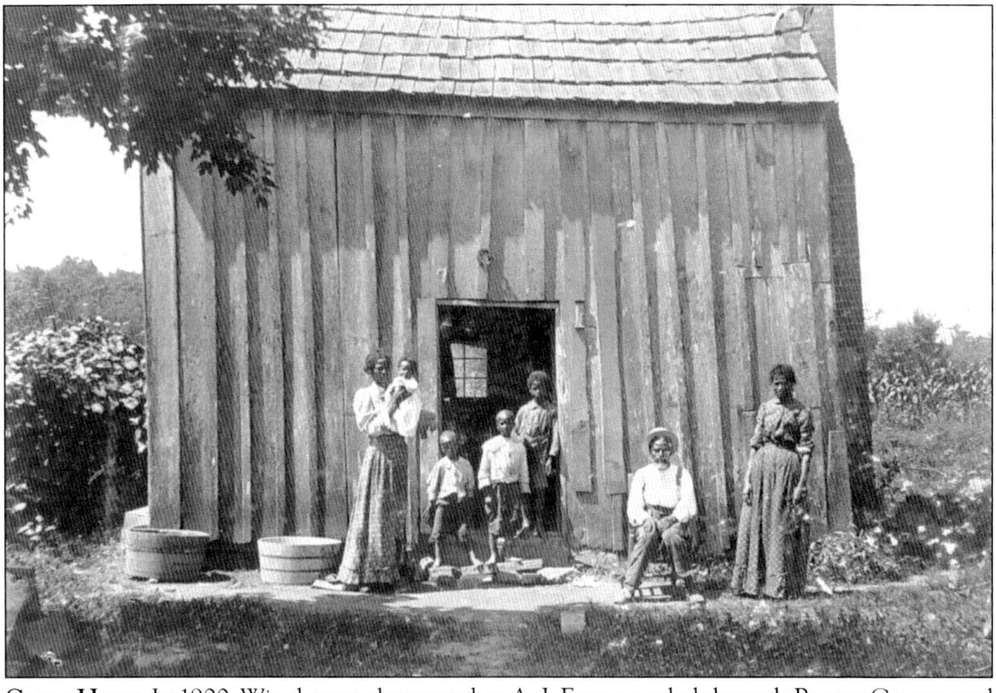

CABIN HOME. In 1900, Winchester photographer A. J. Earp traveled through Barren County and took this photograph of the dwelling of an African American family near Glasgow. The home has unpainted wooden boards and a tall brick chimney. A growing stand of corn can be seen behind the cabin. (Courtesy of Special Collections: Ekstrom Library, University of Louisville.)

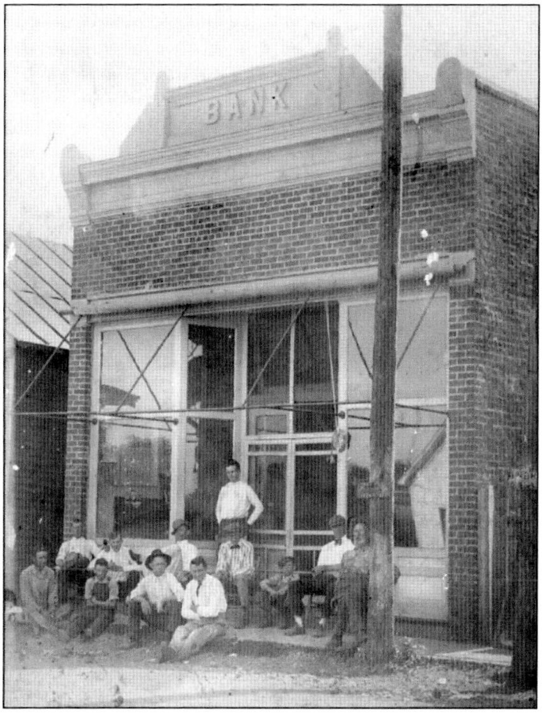

Hiseville Deposit Bank. Once known as Blue Spring Grove and Goosehorn, the small community of Hiseville was incorporated as a city in 1869, and its name was changed to honor Elijah Hise, a congressional representative. This 1905 photograph shows the Hiseville Bank with plenty of customers who seem to be waiting on the bank to open.

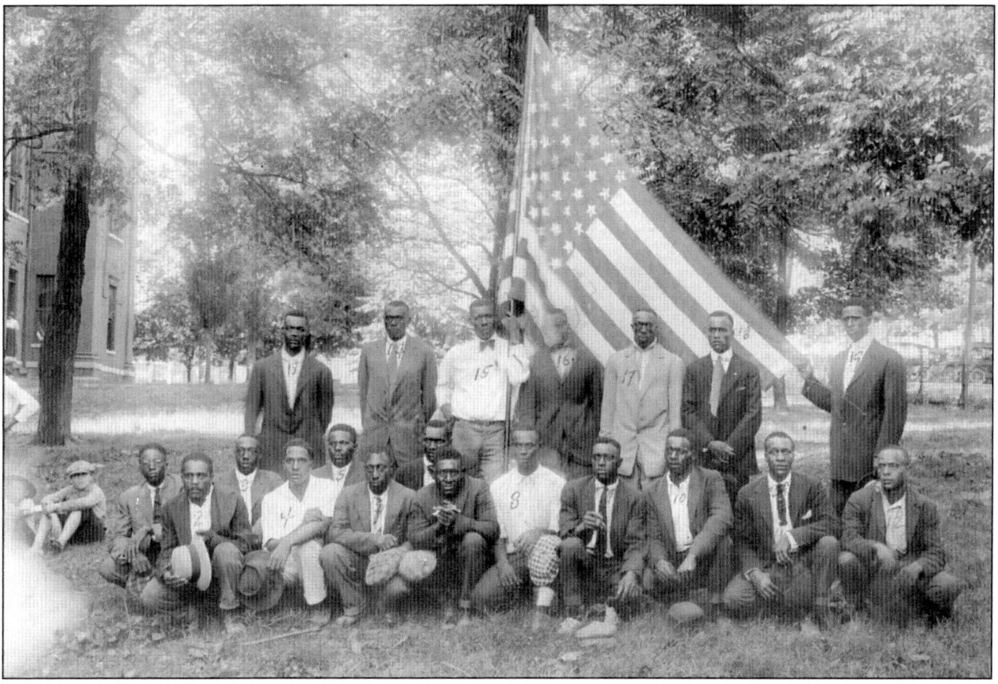

At the Ready! This representative group of Barren County's World War I African American soldiers pauses for a photograph on the courthouse grounds in August 1918. They were part of the 11th contingent and were on their way to Camp Taylor near Louisville, Kentucky. Camp Taylor was the largest artillery training camp in the United States. The camp was closed in 1920. (Courtesy of Perry Brantley.)

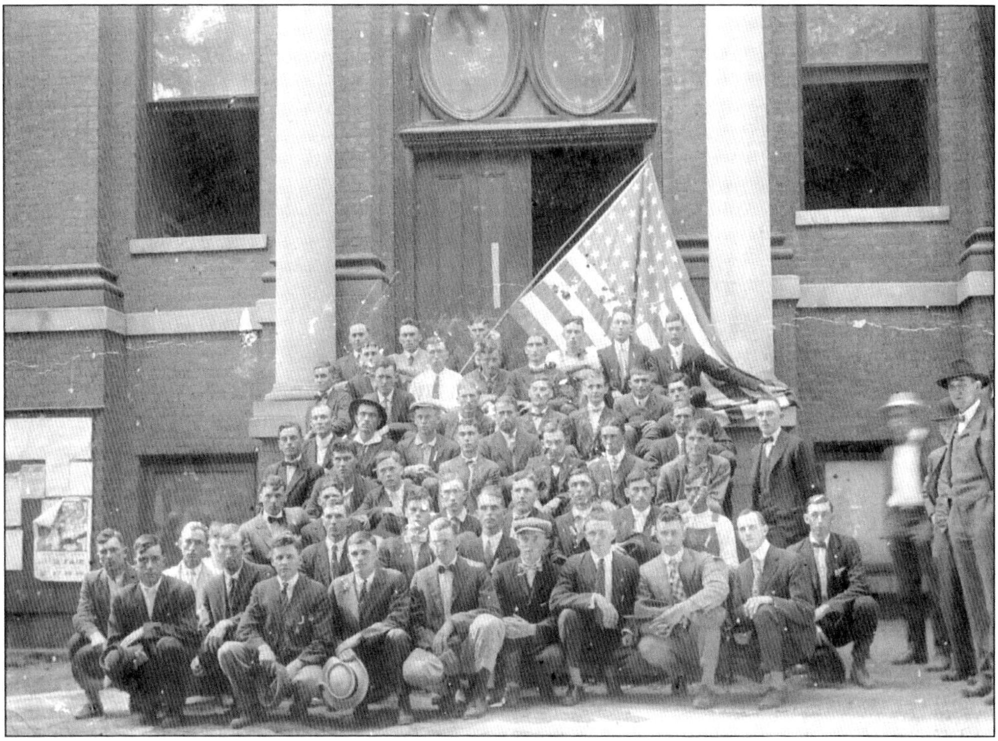

Together We Win. This group of 52 men, the county's second contingent, is also leaving for Camp Taylor in this photograph dated September 19, 1917. Barren County sent 900 men to the "War to End All Wars." The image also showcases the 48-star American flag and a close-up detail of the old courthouse. (Courtesy of Perry Brantley.)

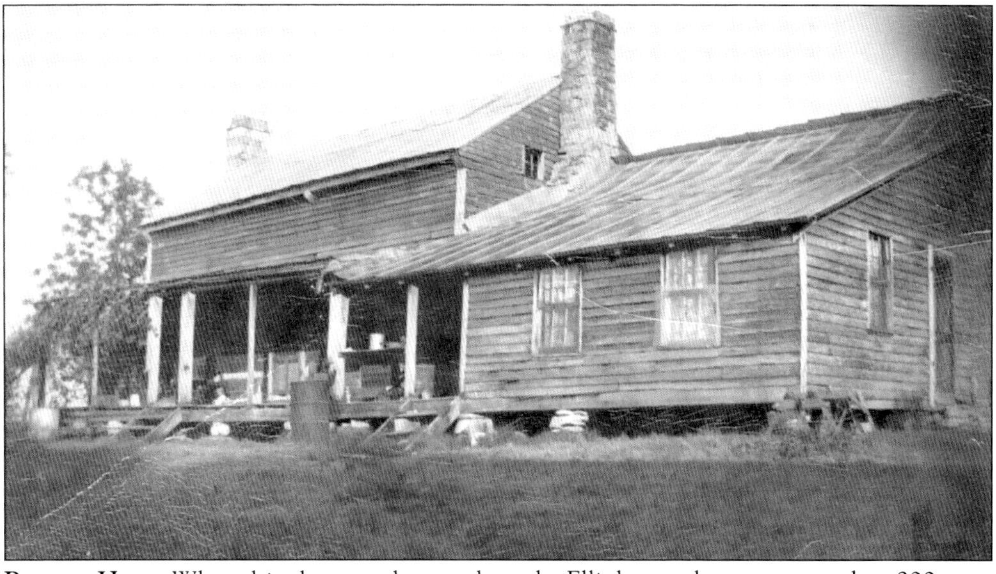

Pioneer Home. When this photograph was taken, the Ellis home place was more than 200 years old. The home was located in the Dry Fork community in the southern part of the county. After its demise, parts of the house were used to restore structures at U.S. president Andrew Jackson's home, the Hermitage in Nashville. (Courtesy of Mitchell Ellis.)

REMEMBERING WEDDING DAYS. Members of two of Barren County's most prominent families, these ladies had married the same day, May 17, 1870, and returned to the studio 28 years later to have their photograph remade in their wedding dresses. Eugenia Garnett (left) married one of Glasgow's more colorful politicians, John A. "Old Reb" Murray. Anne Rogers married E. Y. Kilgore, a druggist and publisher of the *Glasgow Times*. (Courtesy of Perry Brantley.)

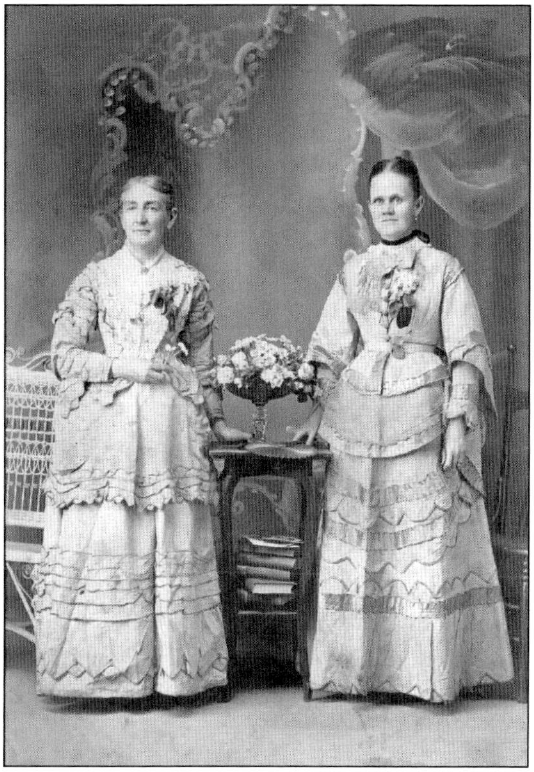

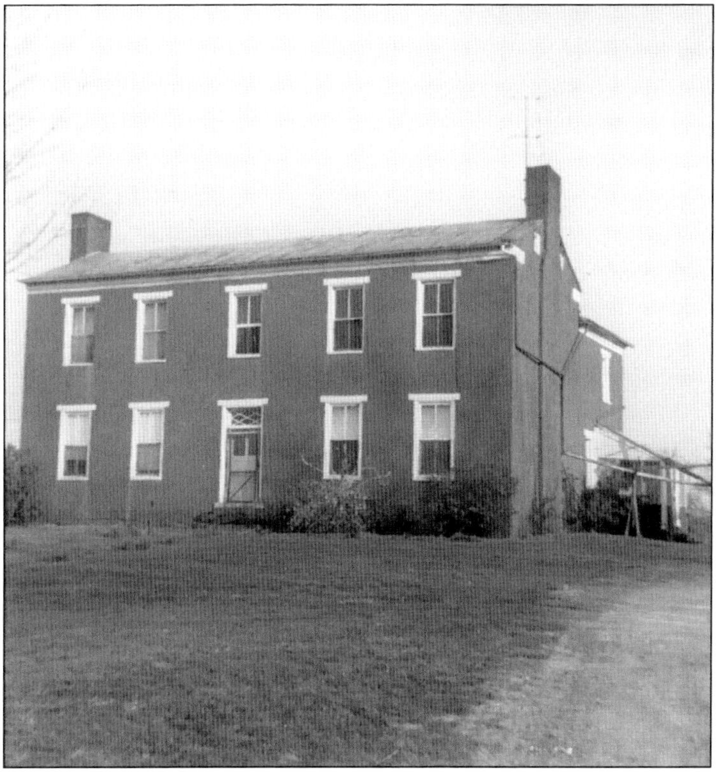

SURE SHOT. Felix Settle, the son of one of Barren County's earliest settlers, was the first gunsmith in the county and learned to make rifles from his father, William. The rifles, marked with the Settles name, can be seen today in the Kentucky Museum in Bowling Green. Built in 1842, the family's Federal and Greek Revival–style home is located in Rocky Hill and is listed on the National Register of Historic Places.

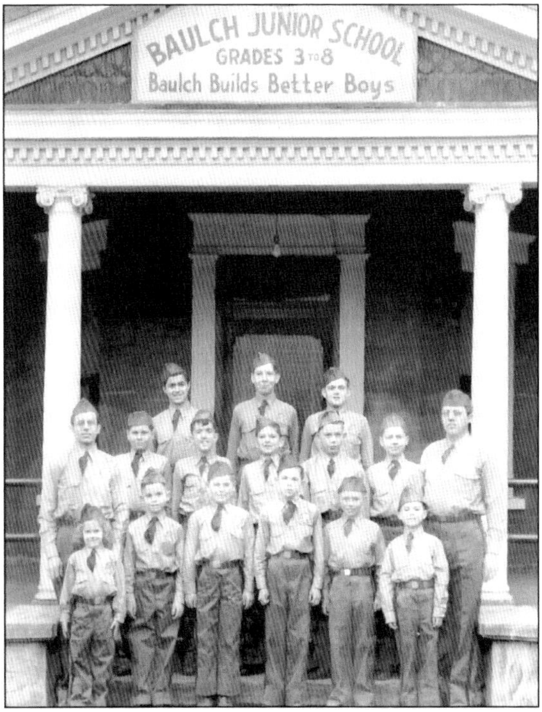

Building Better Boys. Ernest and James Baulch purchased the Mentz Hotel building in 1946 and opened the Baulch Junior School, a boarding school for boys in Park City. The photograph shows the boys ready for a trip to Mammoth Cave. The school's headmaster, Ernest Baulch, is the man on the far right, and assistant headmaster James Baulch is on the far left. The school was closed in 1952. (Courtesy of Howard Baulch.)

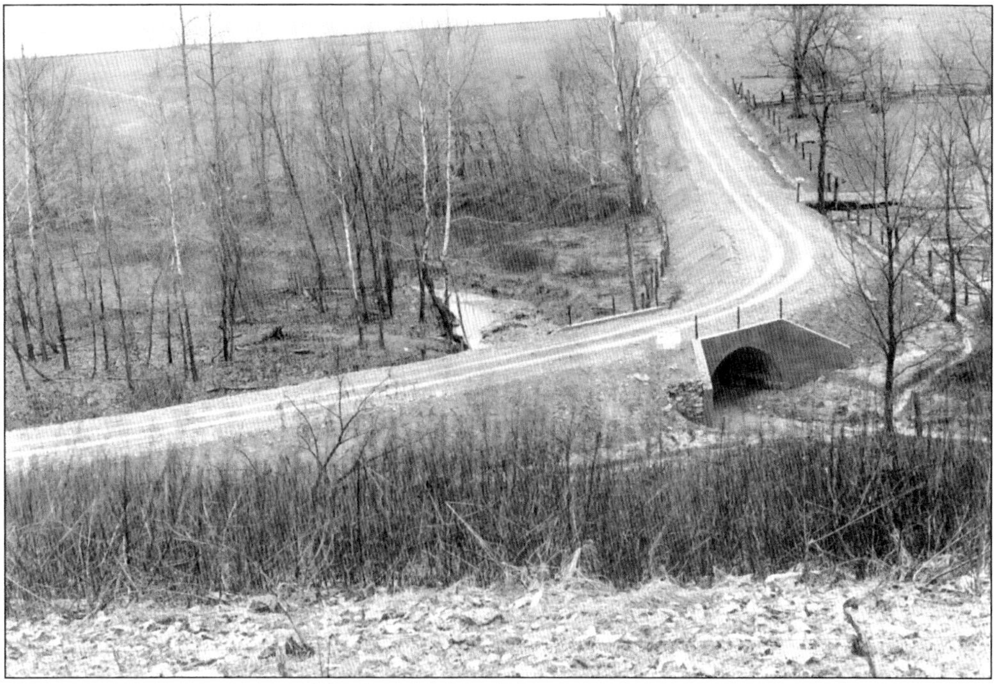

Around the Corner. One of the first thrusts of the WPA's road-building program in the county was to improve farm-to-market roads and to build new rural roads and bridges where they were needed. The Mount Herman–Etoile Road, shown in the 1930s, had drainage issues that were fixed as part of the Master Road Reconstruction Project. These rural and secondary roads were, for the most part, unpaved, and when it rained, many of them turned into swamps of mud.

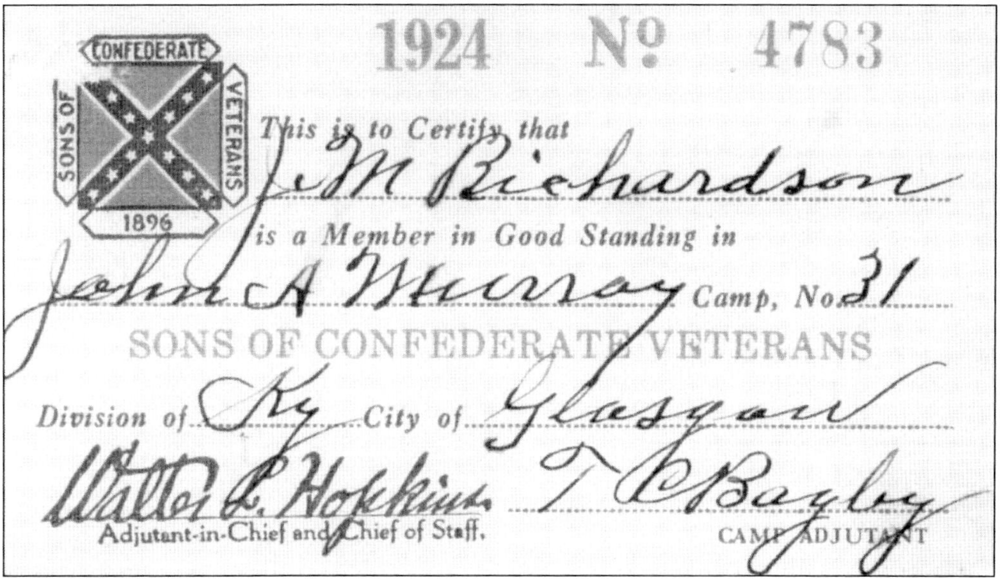
CONFEDERATE
SONS OF
VETERANS
1896
1924 Nº 4783
This is to Certify that J. M. Richardson
is a Member in Good Standing in
John A. Murray Camp, No. 31
SONS OF CONFEDERATE VETERANS
Division of Ky City of Glasgow
Walter L. Hopkins T. C. Bayley
Adjutant-in-Chief and Chief of Staff. CAMP ADJUTANT

Still Standing. In the aftermath of the war, a number of Civil War veterans' organizations came into being. The image above shows J. M. Richardson's Sons of Confederate Veterans membership card. The county, under John A. "Old Reb" Murray, had an active chapter. Murray was the driving force behind the erection of a monument to the Confederate dead in 1915, which still stands on the courthouse grounds, and in organizing the large reunions that took place each year. In the photograph below, Murray is the eighth person from the left. Frank Carter holds the flag honoring Col. Joseph H. Lewis, the last commander of the Orphan Brigade. (Both, courtesy of Perry Brantley.)

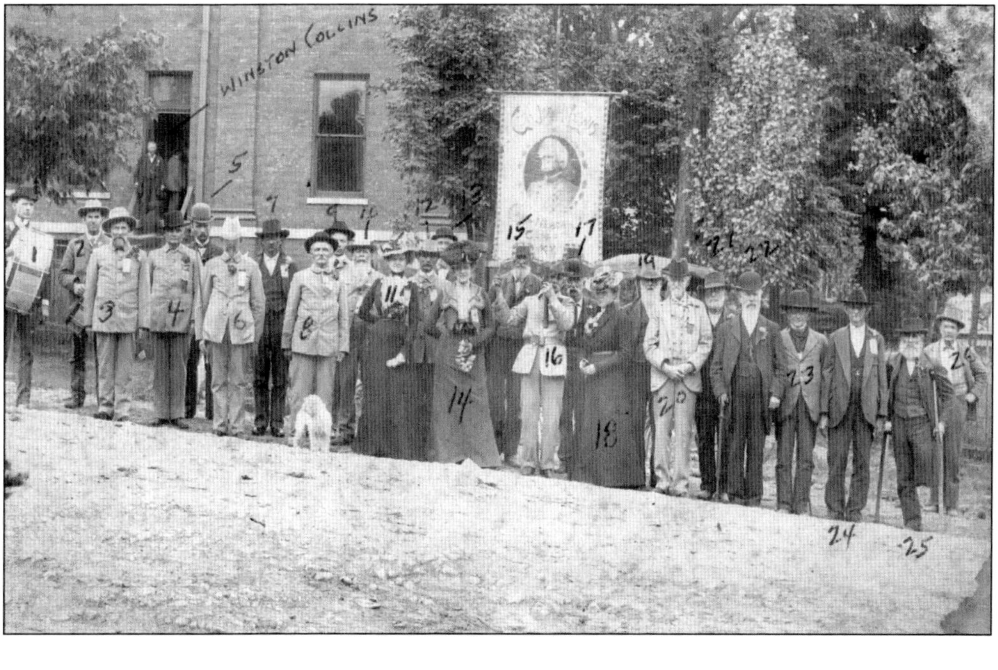

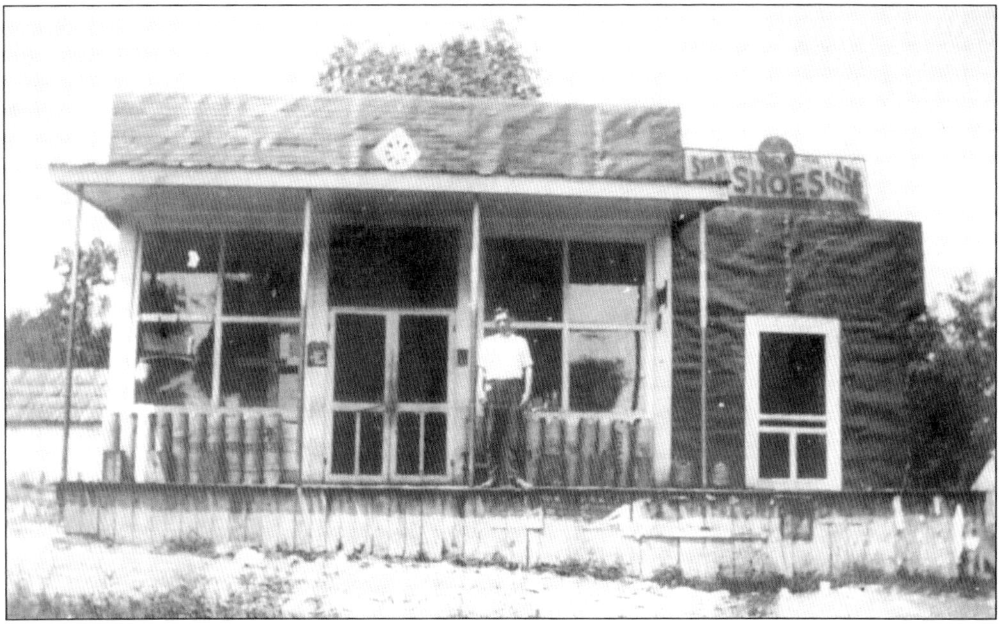

Store by the Side of the Road. The F. P. Bradshaw and Son store stood on the south bank of Peter's Creek in southern Barren County. Typical of stores in the early 1920s, the business served as the post office, community center, and the location of the horseshoe pits. It also offered everything from meal to medicine. One of the few female postal carriers, Verda Gosnell carried mail from this store to Austin on horseback. (Courtesy of Clifton Bradshaw.)

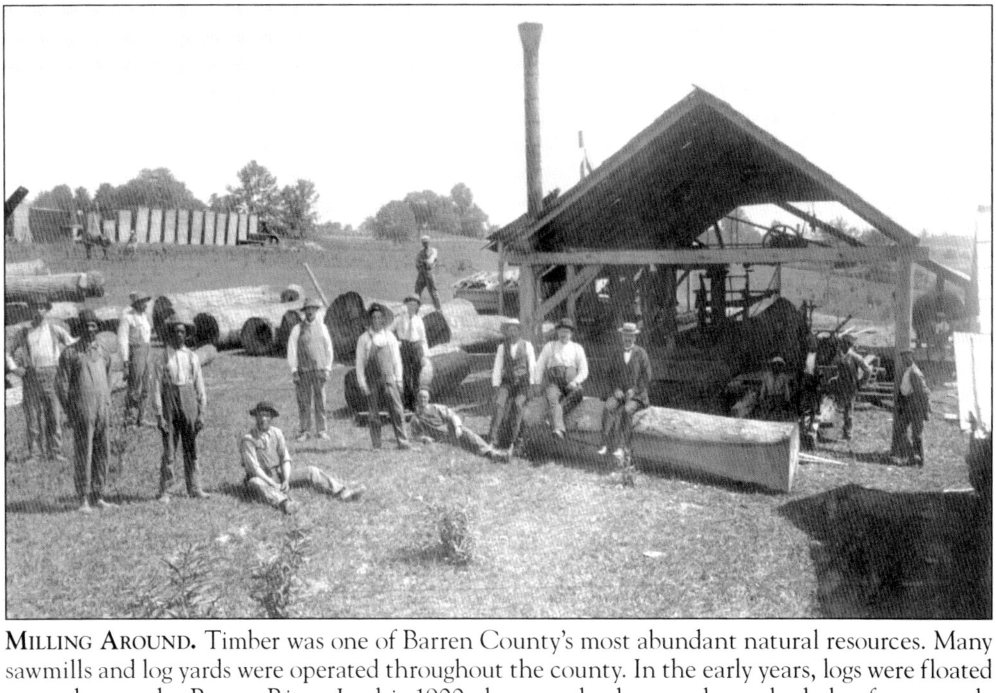

Milling Around. Timber was one of Barren County's most abundant natural resources. Many sawmills and log yards were operated throughout the county. In the early years, logs were floated to market on the Barren River. In this 1900 photograph, the men have the help of some early machinery for sawing the large logs. A horse and wagon wait nearby for the next load. (Courtesy of Special Collections: Ekstrom Library, University of Louisville.)

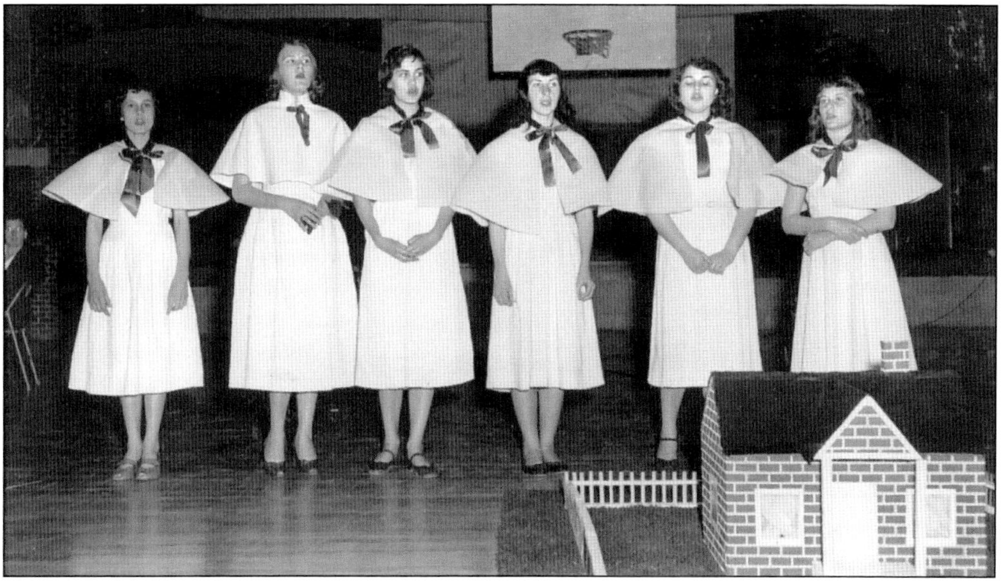

READY TO SOAR. These young ladies of the Austin Tracy Future Homemakers of America club have completed many projects and service hours, and are ready to be initiated into the organization. The new members were welcomed into the group by older members and sponsors. The girls are all proudly attired in their matching "winged" dresses and capes. (Courtesy of the Glasgow–Barren County Chamber of Commerce.)

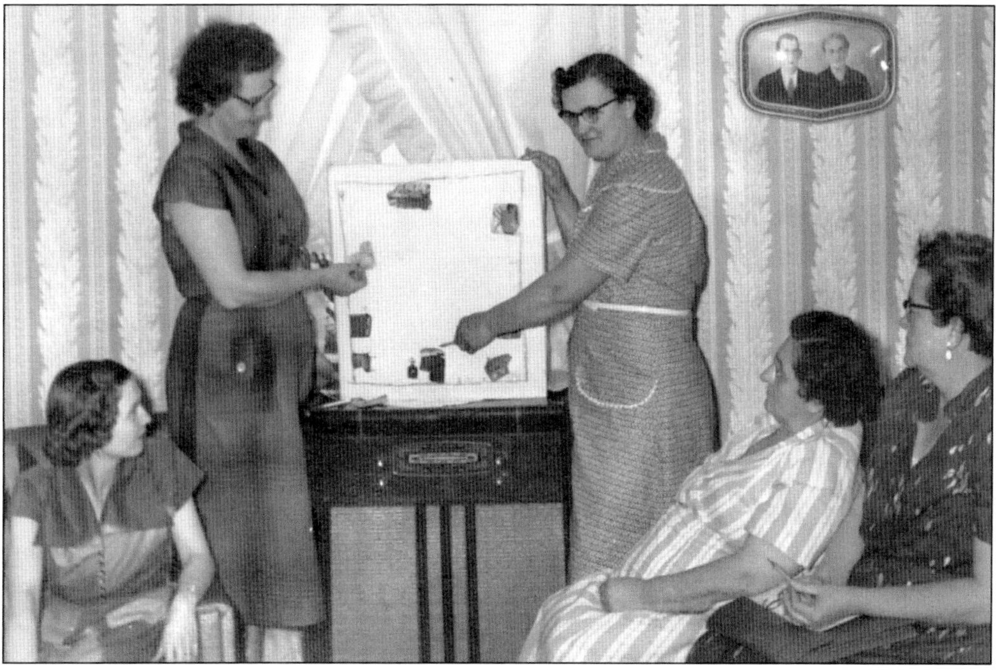

HAPPY HOMEMAKING. Barren County homemaker clubs have played an important part in the lives of the women of the county. A club's goals were to aid homemakers in increasing their skill level for everyday tasks and to learn new information about home, family, community, and country. This photograph shows the Bewleytown-Tracy Homemakers presenting a lesson on the best methods for furniture arrangement. (Courtesy of the Glasgow–Barren County Chamber of Commerce.)

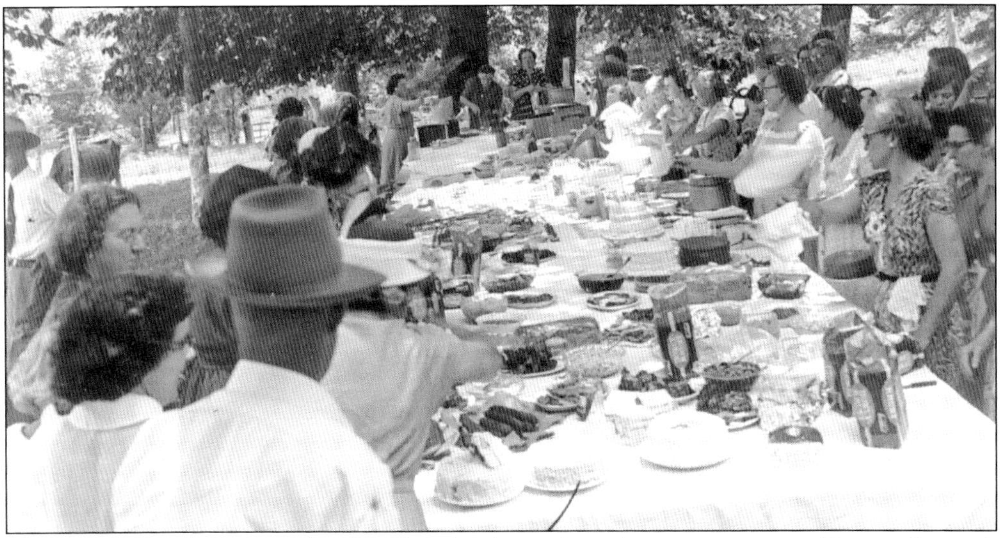

Dinner on the Grounds. Close-knit family relationships characterize many of Barren County's families, and every birthday and holiday was an opportunity to come home again. The Spillman family reunion was typical of the food, fun, and fellowship that one could enjoy. The only difficulty that usually arose was which dessert should be chosen.

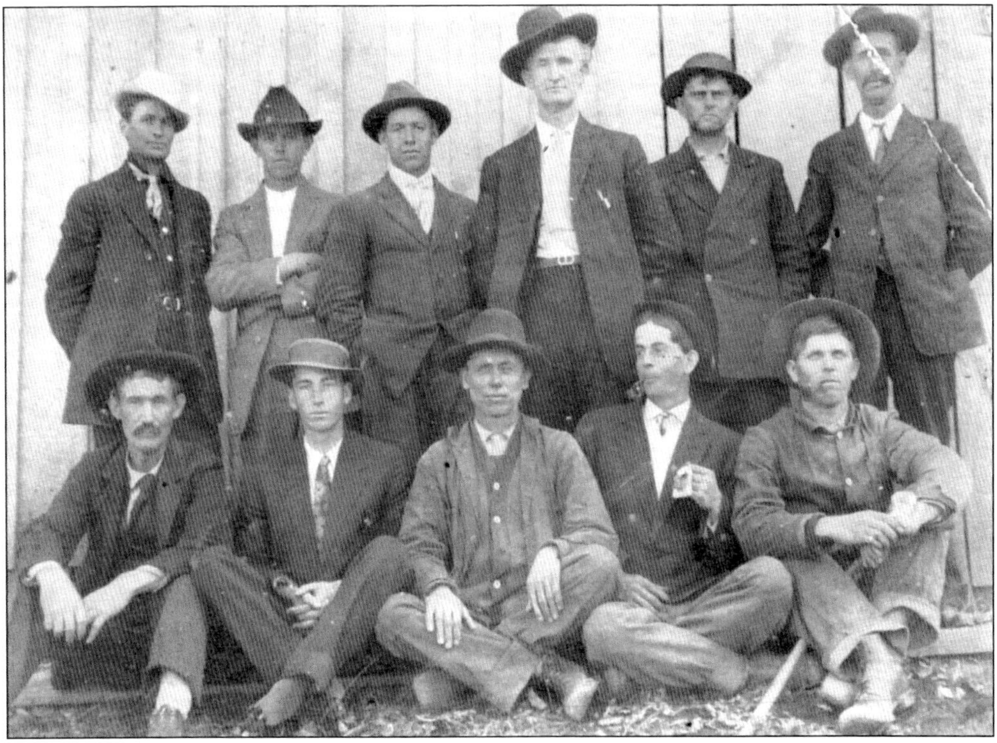

Hanging Around. These men of the Morrison Park area proudly pose with store owner Josh Barbour in 1909. The names listed are a "who's who" of Barren County families. From left to right are (seated) Hawk Barbour, Jim Bewley, William Mayo, William T. Bewley, and Arthur Bowles; (standing) John Bailey, Jimmy P. Bailey, Chris Rogers, Josh Barbour, Morgan Button, and Noon Barbour. Mayo was a well-known carpenter. (Courtesy of Gary Bewley.)

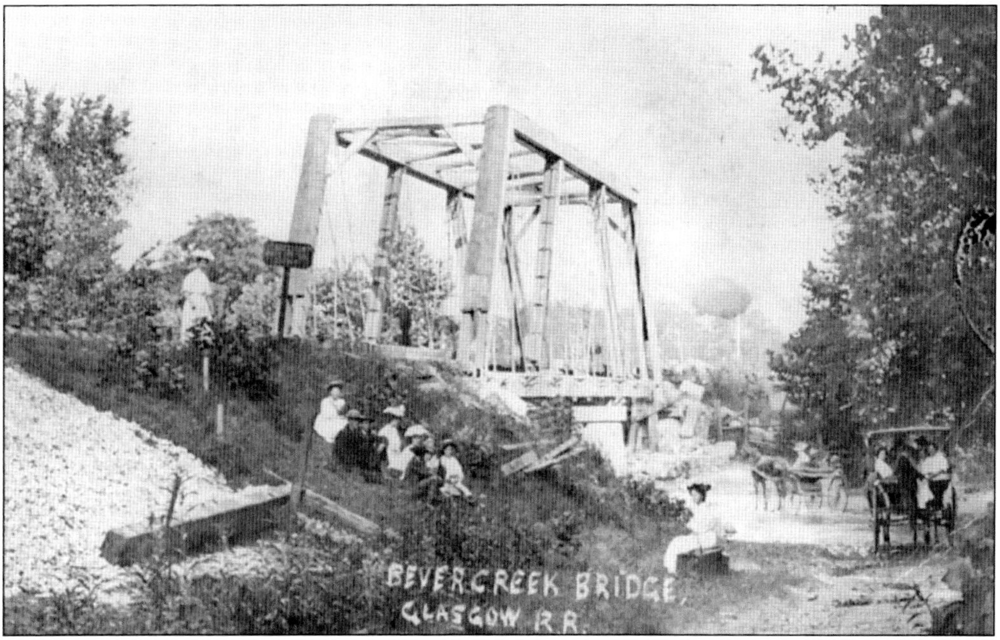

BRIDGE TO TOWN. The Beaver Creek Railroad Bridge area, shown above in September 1907, was the site of many happy outings and was located about 5 miles from Glasgow on Bowling Green Road. The creek is mentioned in many historical sources and as a marker in deeds, and it was one of the many waterways that defined the county. The photograph shows the trestle bridge of the Glasgow Branch Railroad. (Courtesy of Martha Harrison.)

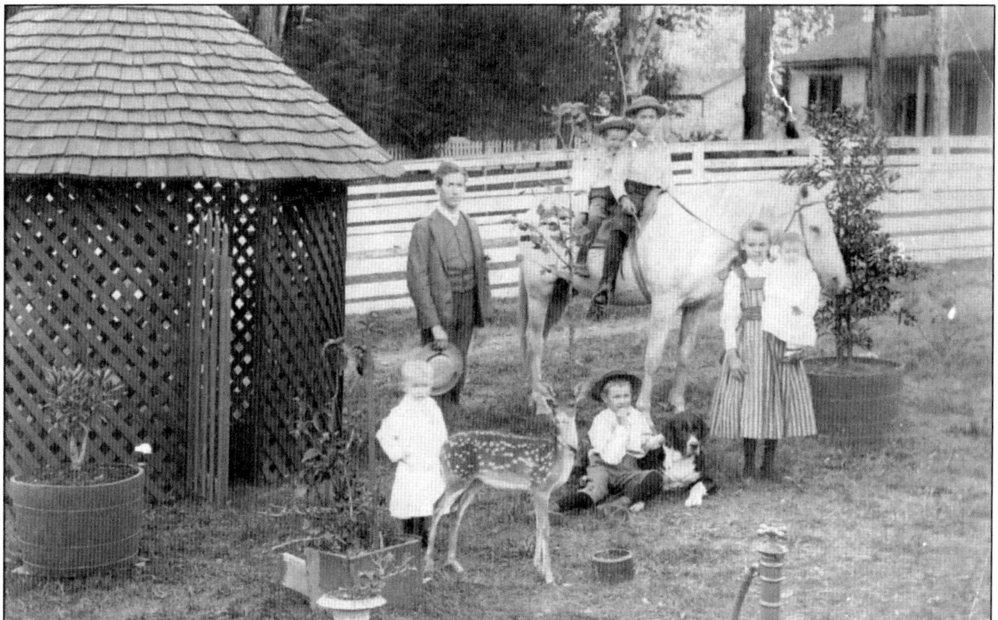

ALL PETS ON DECK. The children of the Edward Young Kilgore family certainly do not lack for pets. They have the usual faithful dog but also a horse and fawn. The garden atmosphere of the yard is accented by the gazebo, which actually served as a cage for the deer. (Courtesy of Perry Brantley.)

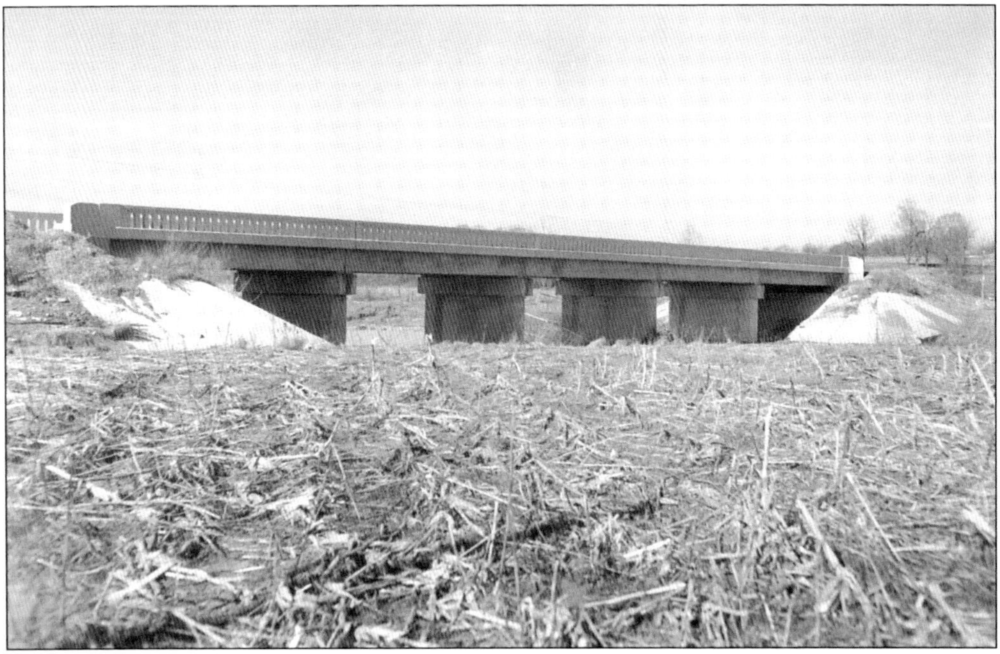

LONG AND WINDING ROAD. Highway 63, or Cordell Hull Highway, has a long history, which starts with its beginnings in 1805. The road had many dangerous hills and curves, and one of the most dangerous areas was removed in 1952 with the construction of this bridge. The entire highway is more than 50 miles long and is named in honor of Hull, who was known as the "Father of the United Nations."

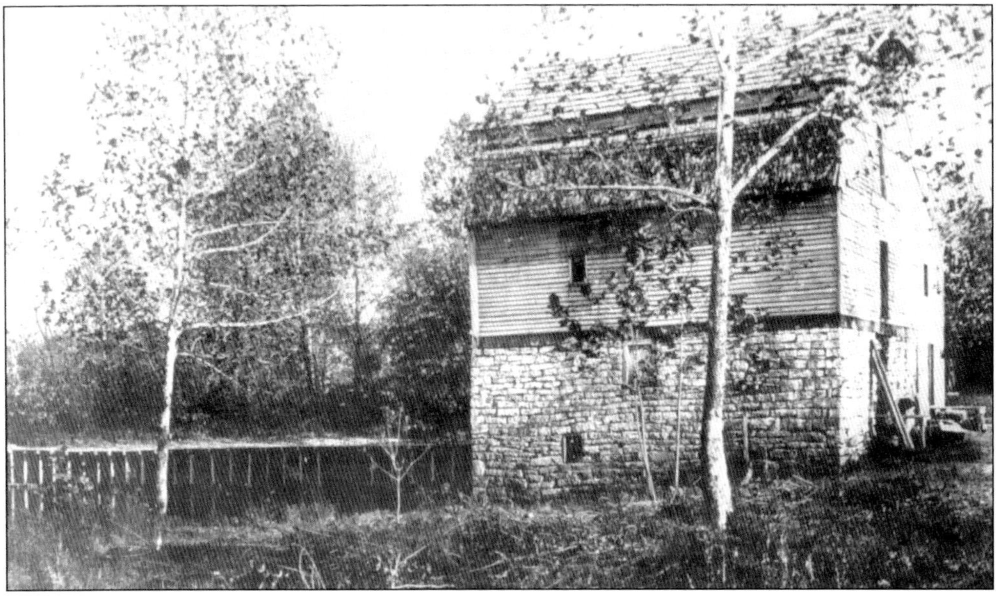

HISTORIC MILL. Barren County was still a part of Warren County when stonemason and landowner Killian Creek (Gullian Krieg) applied to the court for permission to build this mill in 1798. Over the years, it has passed ownership and has been known by the following names: Buford, Crenshaw, Staples, and Dentons. The mill's foundation walls were placed on the National Register of Historic Places in 1987 for its architecture and engineering details. (Courtesy of Martha Harrison.)

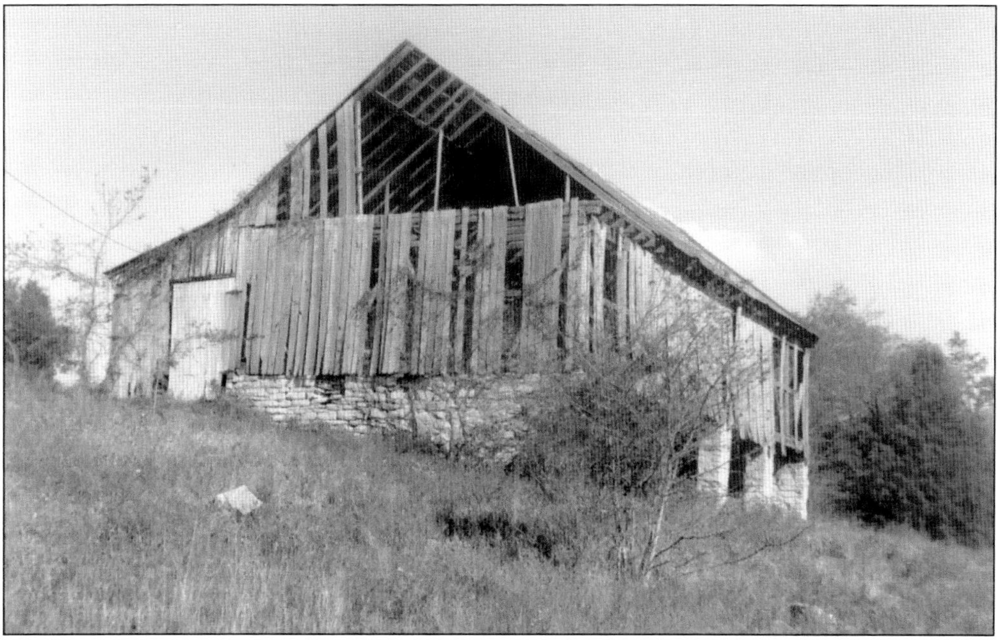

SIGHT UNSEEN. This barn is believed to have also been built by Gerig in the 1830s. It was the only one of its type known to exist west of the Appalachian Mountains. Its tilted, false-plate framing, the wood pegs, hand-hewn logs, hand-wrought hinges, and dry-laid stone foundation are building techniques that originated in England. Sadly, the barn is no longer standing.

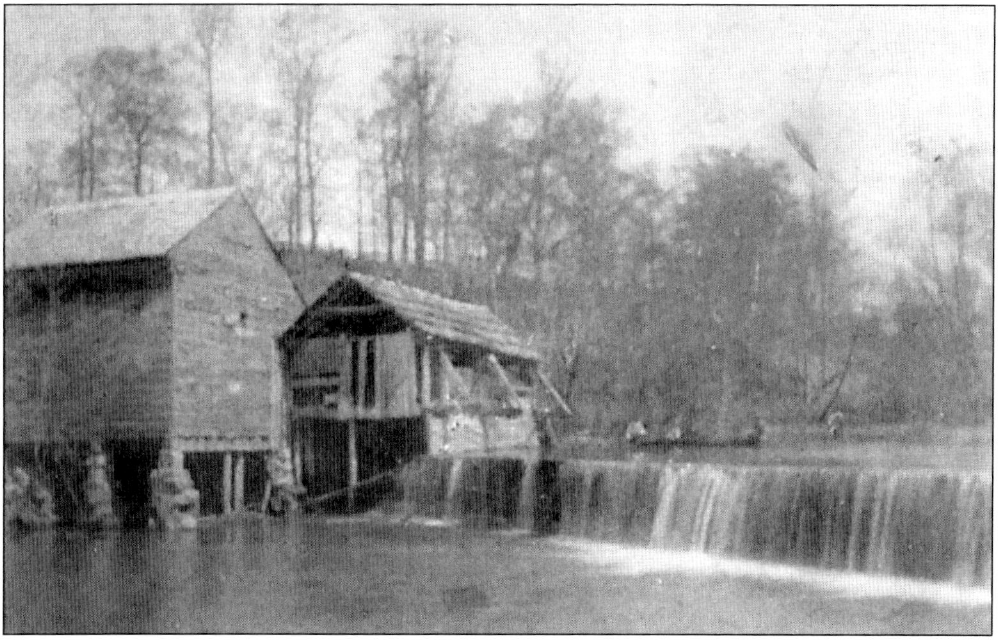

BARREN COUNTY MILL. Young's Mill, in the Dryfork community of Barren County, is shown in 1889. The mill was located on one of three forks of Dryfork Creek near the Tracy community, which is 10 miles south of Glasgow. The mill was water powered and well constructed, but as with other mills in the county, its decline and abandonment was caused by the steam mills being built across the state.

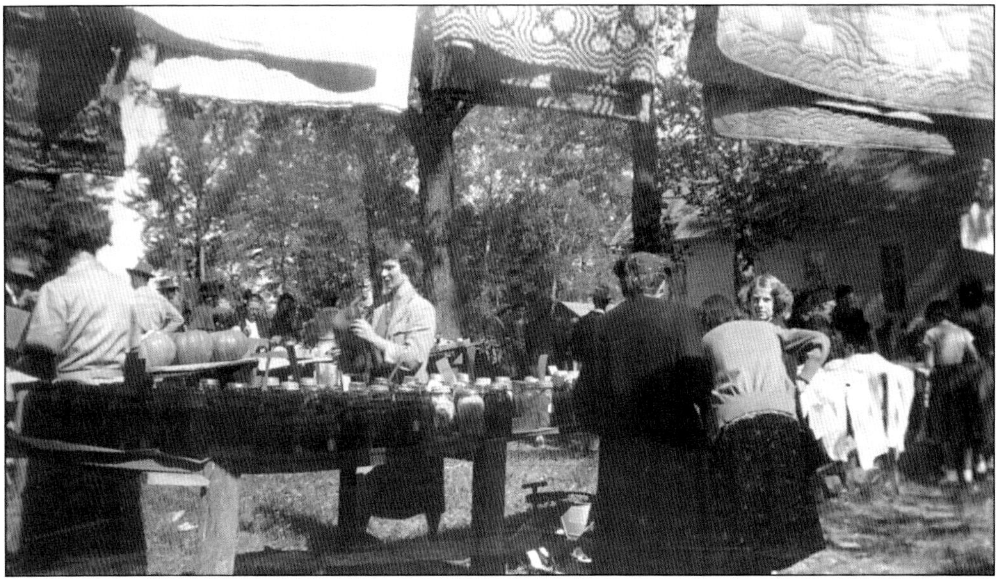

It's a Fair Day. The small community of Etoile annually sponsors one of the most popular fairs in Barren County. Now in its 69th year, the fair features the traditional baby and beauty pageants; tractor, horse, flower and quilt shows; a Tennessee Square marble tournament; and the ever-popular frog-jumping and rolling pin–throwing contests. The 4-H and homemakers clubs provide time-honored fair foods. (Courtesy of the Glasgow–Barren County Chamber of Commerce.)

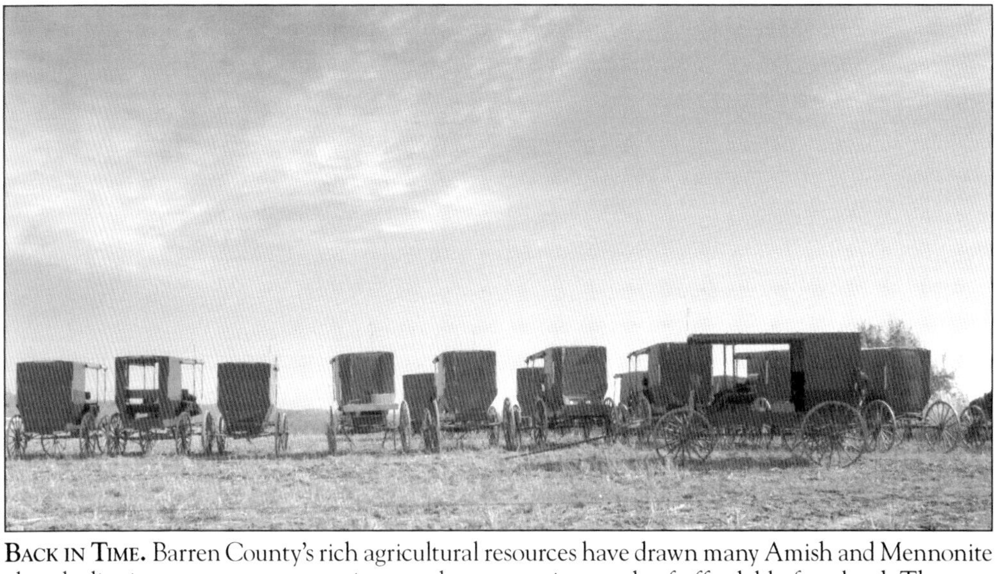

Back in Time. Barren County's rich agricultural resources have drawn many Amish and Mennonite church districts or compact groupings to the county in search of affordable farmland. They are known for their self-sufficiency, skill at handcrafts, hard work, and plain living. The photograph shows what seems to be an Amish parking lot but is actually the gathering of the families for Sunday worship services. (Courtesy of Tonya Archey.)

Four

Barren County Education

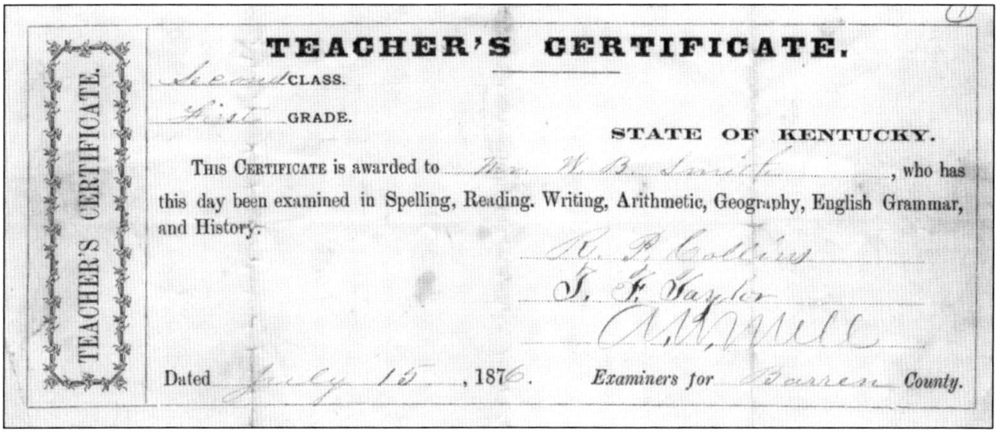

TEACHER'S CERTIFICATE.

Second CLASS.

First GRADE.

STATE OF KENTUCKY.

THIS CERTIFICATE is awarded to Mr. W. B. Smith, who has this day been examined in Spelling, Reading, Writing, Arithmetic, Geography, English Grammar, and History.

R. P. Collins

T. F. Taylor

Dated July 15, 1876. Examiners for Barren County.

TEACHER'S CERTIFICATE.

Teachers Certificate. W. B. Smith worked hard and passed the examination to earn his teacher's certificate from Glasgow Normal School. Many students began teaching right after high school. The normal school concept had a shortened course of study and quicker graduation times. Everything, including costs, was geared toward quickly producing qualified teachers. The Glasgow Normal School was founded in Glasgow in 1874, and Smith was among the first to receive his certification.

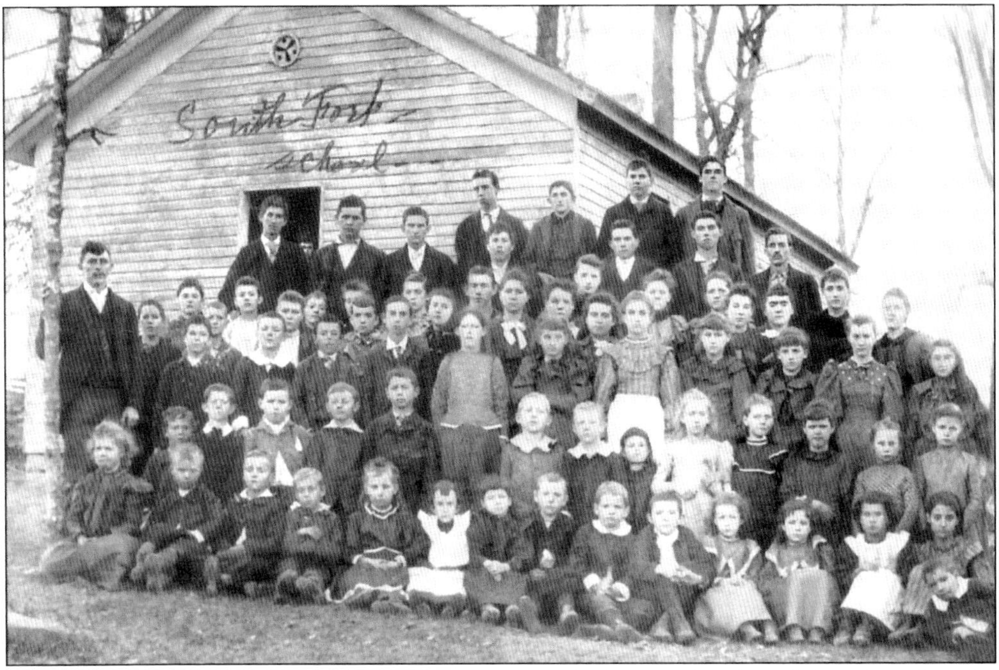

LONG GONE. South Fork School students are shown with their teacher, J. A. White (standing, far left), in 1870. The school was located in the Haywood-Bruce community of central Barren County. New and modern for its time, with its whitewashed clapboard siding, the school stands in stark contrast to its wooded surroundings. The students, dressed in their finest, pose for the camera and are, along with the school, the pride of the community. (Courtesy of Martha Harrison.)

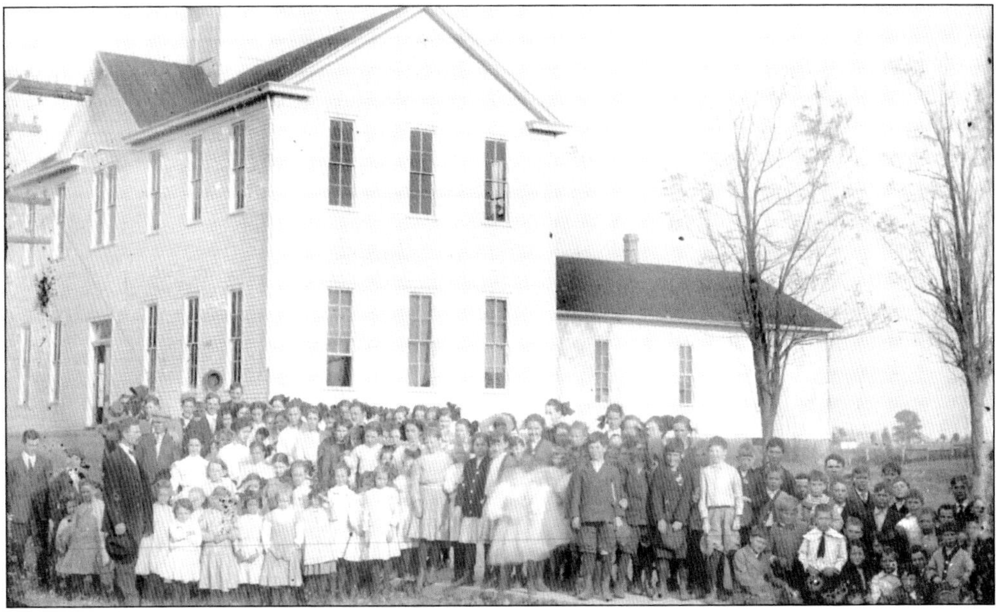

CAVE CITY SCHOOL. One of more than 7,000 schools in operation in Kentucky at the beginning of the 20th century, the Cave City School is shown at the intersection of KY 70 and U.S. 31-W. The principal was Lucian N. Richards, and the teachers were Mrs. J. R. Branson, Nellie Richard, and Beulah Ferguson. The Cave City School was torn down in 1923. (Courtesy of Linda Hunt.)

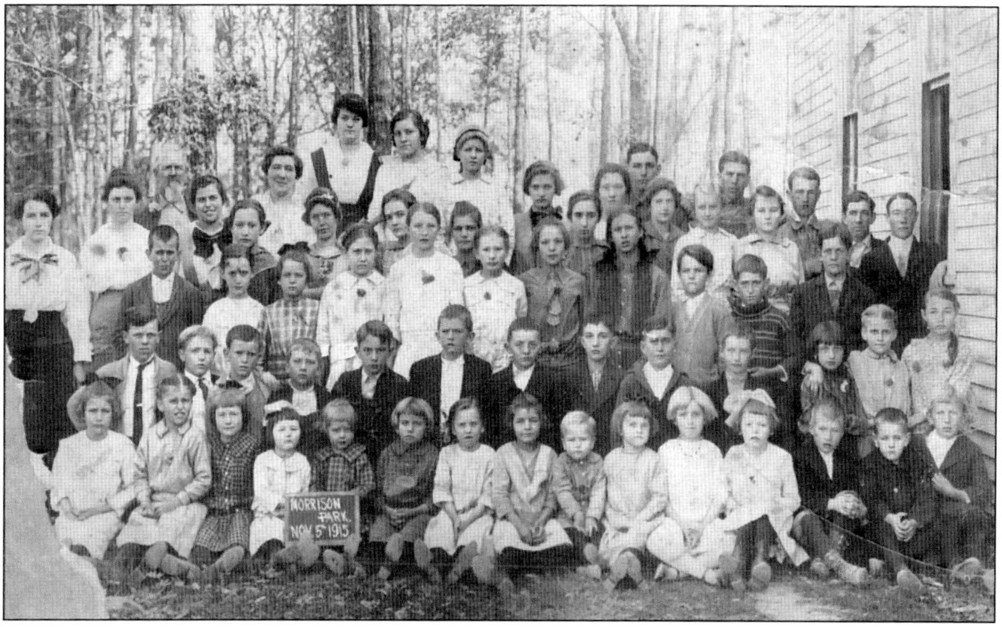

SCHOOL DAYS. Morrison Park School students are captured in the above photograph from 1915. The students were being taught by Mayme Eaton Myers. Some parents and neighbors came by to have their picture taken also. The school district was located in the southeastern part of the county on land purchased by John O. Morrison. It was noted that the land had an everlasting stream. It was from this spring that the students obtained their drinking water. It was a special treat to be picked to fill the water bucket. Some of the surnames of the students shown in the photograph above are Fisher, Eatman, Matthews, Williams, Button, Nuckols, Quick, Smith, Bailey, Mayo, Barbour, and Boles (Bowles). The Bald Knob and Morrison Park Schools were both located on Bristletown Road off of Highway 63. The Bald Knob students are pictured below in 1899. (Both, courtesy of Gary Bewley.)

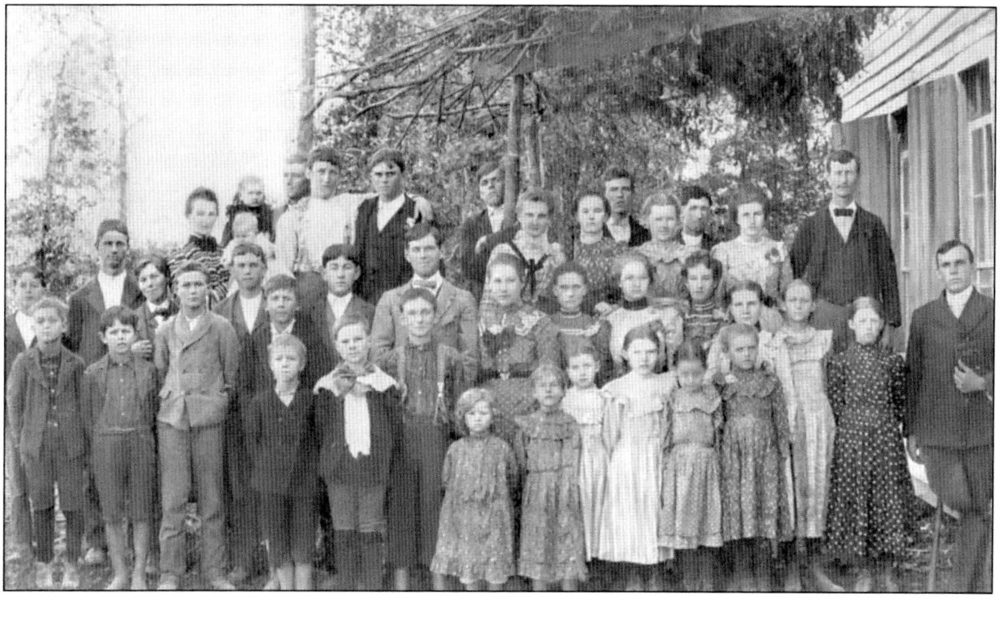

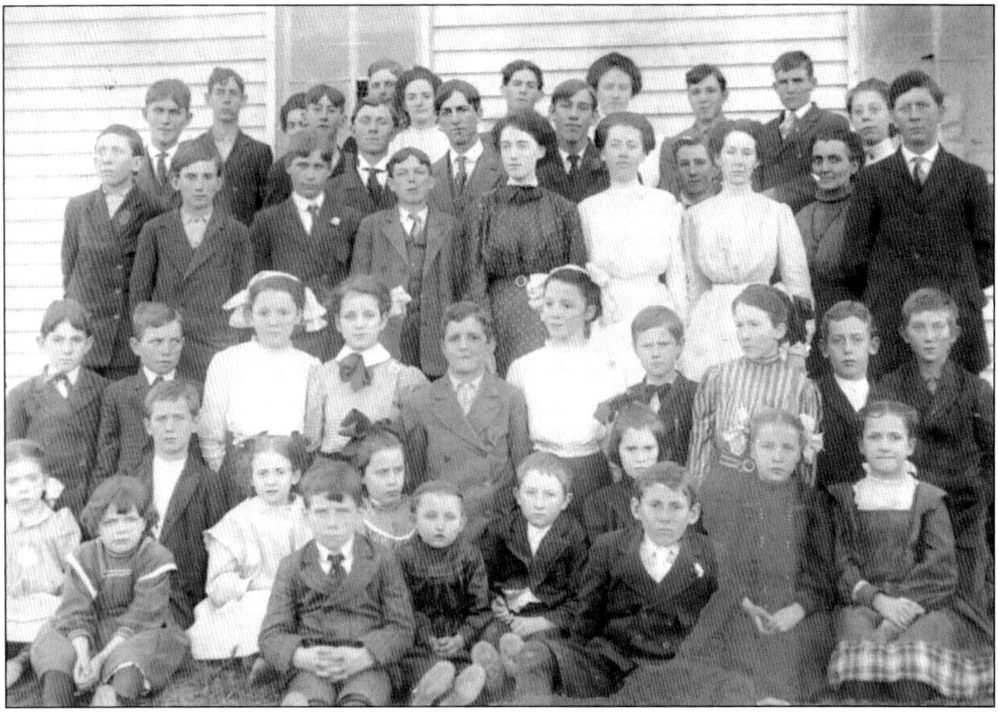

Beech Grove School. Beech Grove School was one of the earliest schools organized. This photograph is from 1909. The teacher is listed as a Mrs. Kidd. In many one-room school photographs, distinguishing the teacher from the pupils can be a difficult task, as they were often only a few years older than their charges. Barren County's first school, and one of Kentucky's, was the Vineyard School, which was organized in 1850. (Courtesy of Martha Harrison.)

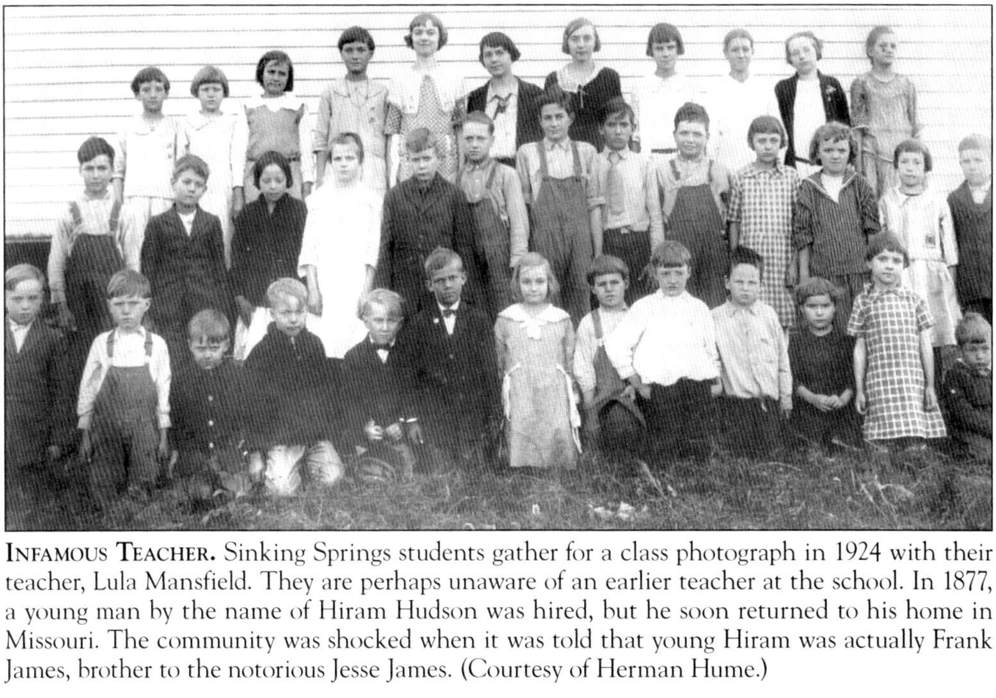

Infamous Teacher. Sinking Springs students gather for a class photograph in 1924 with their teacher, Lula Mansfield. They are perhaps unaware of an earlier teacher at the school. In 1877, a young man by the name of Hiram Hudson was hired, but he soon returned to his home in Missouri. The community was shocked when it was told that young Hiram was actually Frank James, brother to the notorious Jesse James. (Courtesy of Herman Hume.)

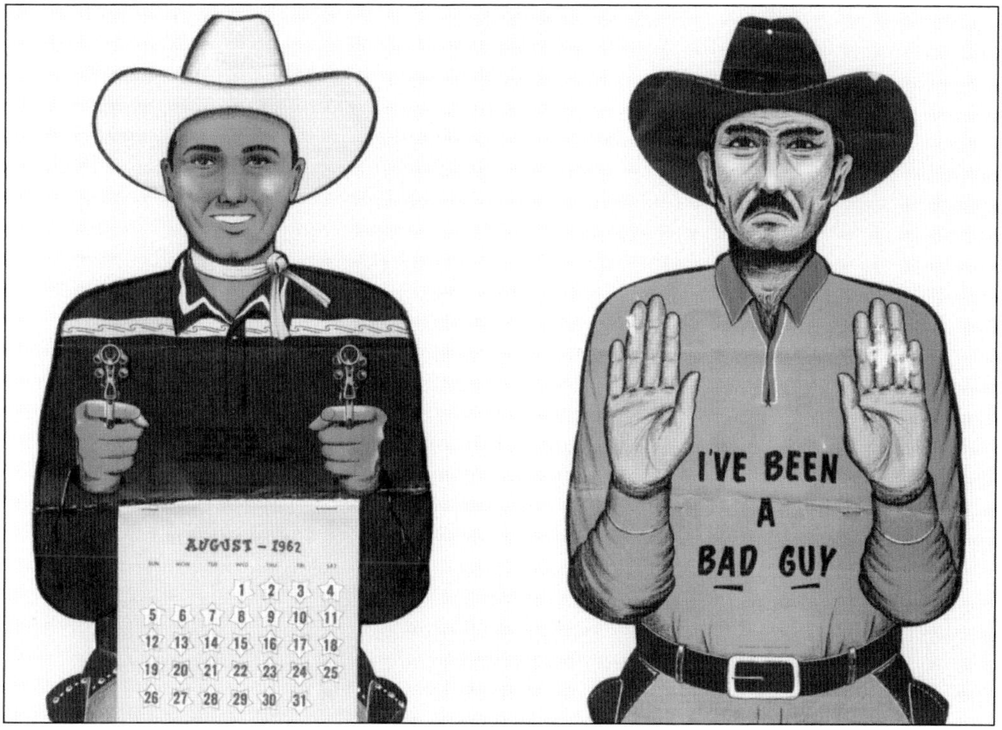

STICK 'EM UP. This advertisement poster from Ely Drugs might have been helpful for teachers and parents in disciplining their students and children. Everyone wanted the shiny gold star of the good guy and not the sad blue face of the bad bandit, which was depicted on the flip side.

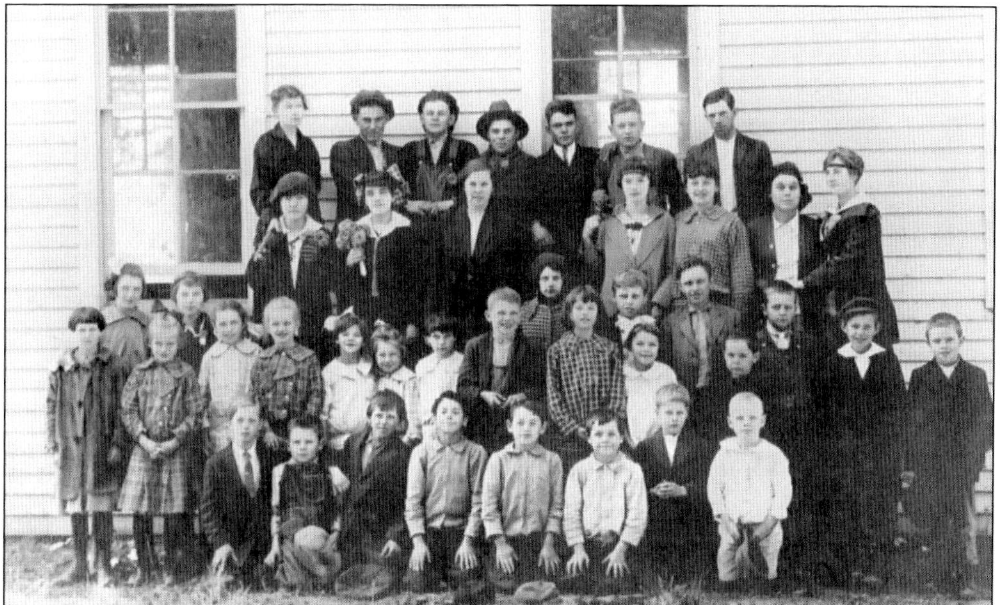

ALL TOGETHER. This group constitutes the students of Union Hill in 1915. Everyone is wearing his or her best, and the photographer must have told everyone to smile. The teacher is Jessie Powell Commings, at left, near the window. (Courtesy of Martha Harrison.)

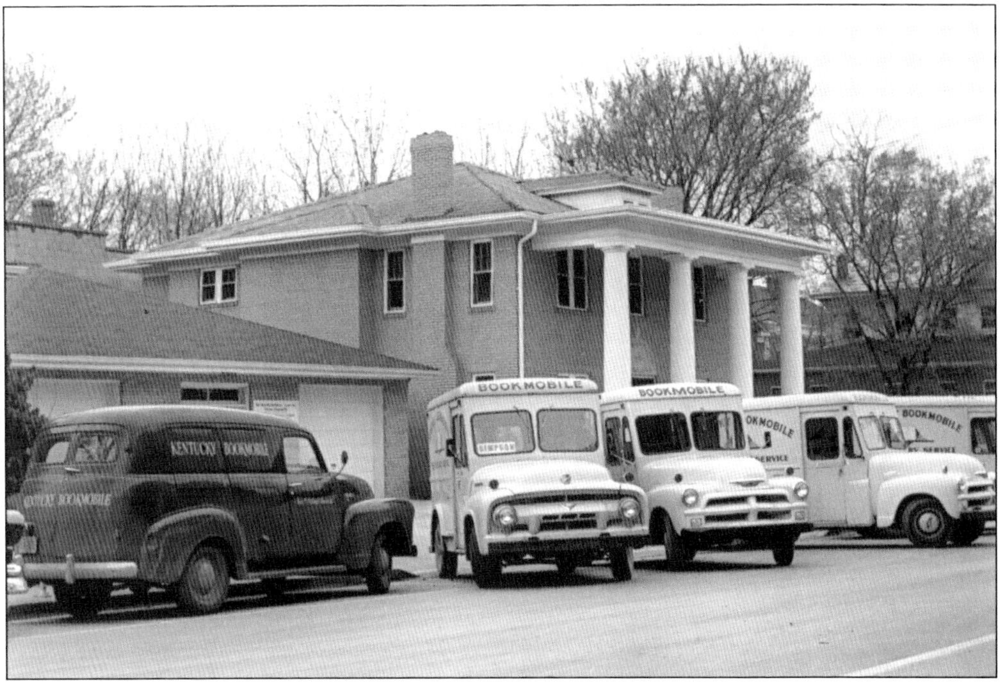

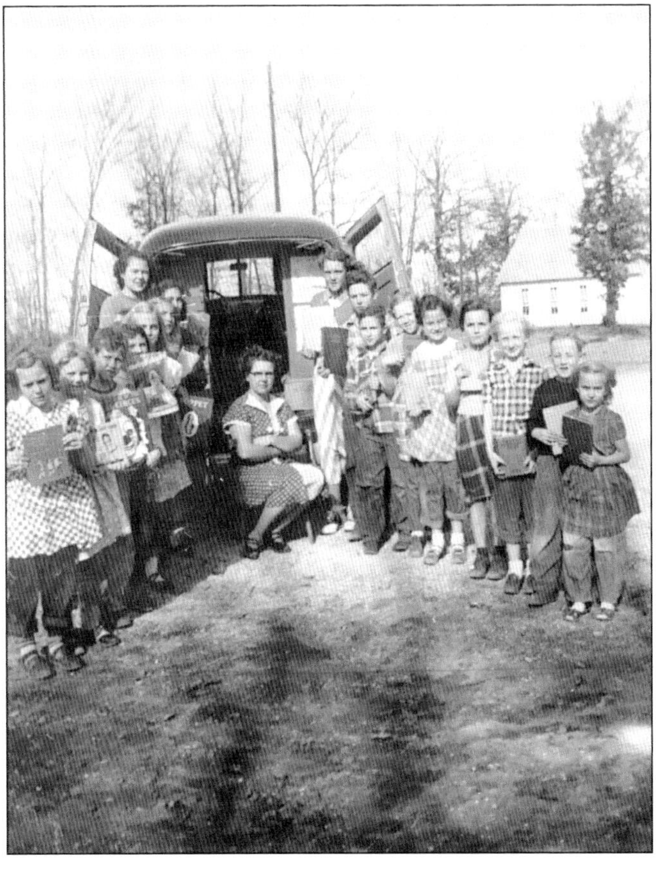

Around the Bend. Coles Bend School students are happy to see the traveling Barren County Bookmobile. The bookmobile would visit all the one-room schools and also made stops at country stores. The bookmobile was part of the service provided by the Mary Wood Weldon Memorial Library and made access possible to books that the students might not have had otherwise. Circulation statistics for a six-month period in the early 1950s show the students checked out almost 10,000 books. Verne Martin was the first bookmobile librarian. Dr. William Adair Weldon deeded an apartment building on College Street that was home to the library for more than 65 years. The library moved in 2009 to a larger facility. (Both, courtesy of the Glasgow–Barren County Chamber of Commerce.)

Book Lovers. The students of the one-room Hiseville School, shown at right in 1952, are pleased to see the bookmobile making its rounds. It was noted with pride that one student at the school was such a voracious reader that she read 85 books during one six-month period. The bookmobile librarian could hardly keep up with her. The enthusiastic students of the Allen School are also shown below, each holding tight to their treasured selections. All states still offer traveling branch library services, but Kentucky is No. 1, with its 98 bookmobiles. The customized step vans have changed throughout the years but remain a welcome sight. (Both, courtesy of the Glasgow–Barren County Chamber of Commerce.)

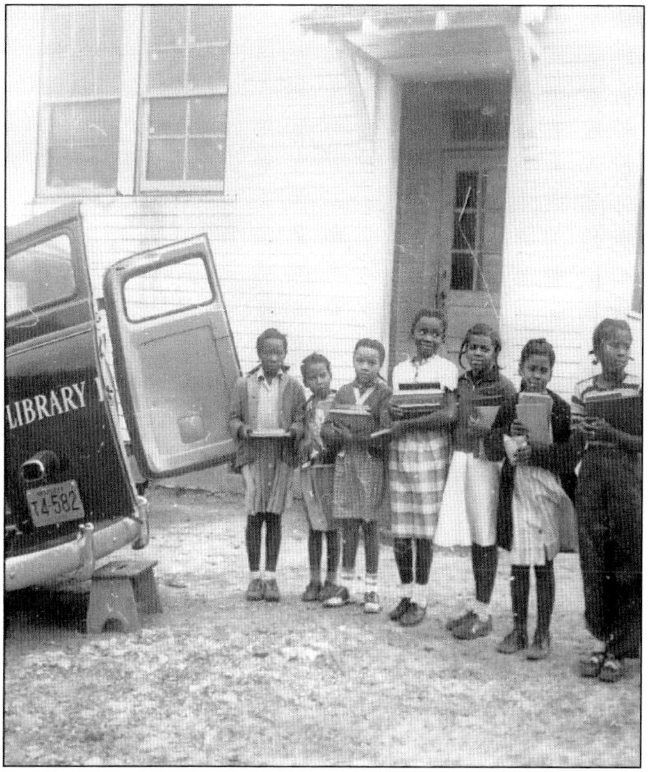

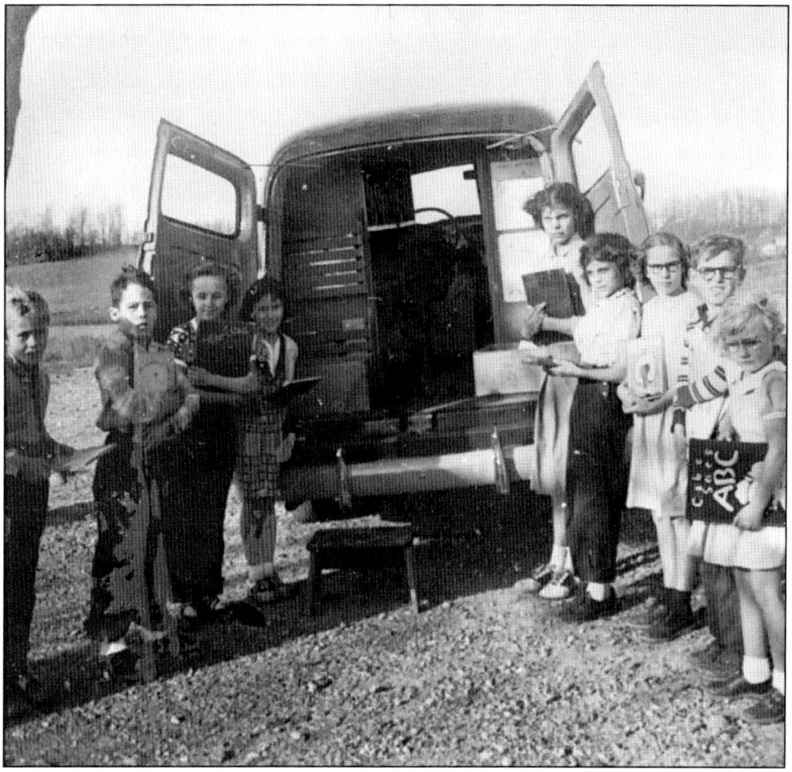

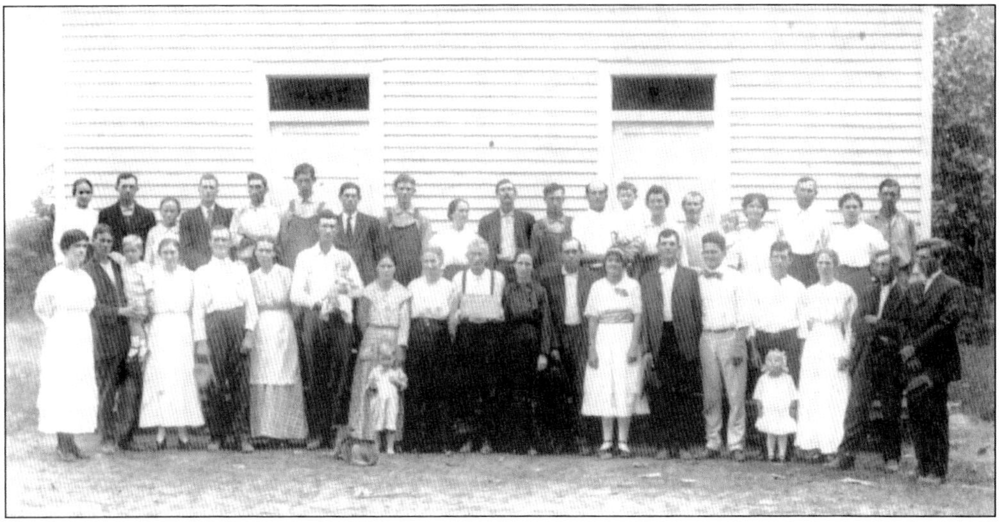

MOONLIGHTING. Kentuckian Cora Wilson Stewart was a pioneer in adult education and started the concept of "Moonlight" schools in 1911. The idea spread throughout the state as teachers volunteered their time on moonlit nights to teach anyone who found their way to the schoolhouse. This photograph from 1917 shows one of the first in the county at the Capitol Hill schoolhouse. The teacher is Ethel Arterburn. Throughout the county that year, through the efforts of such volunteer teachers, 265 adults were taught to read and write. (Courtesy of Scott Fife.)

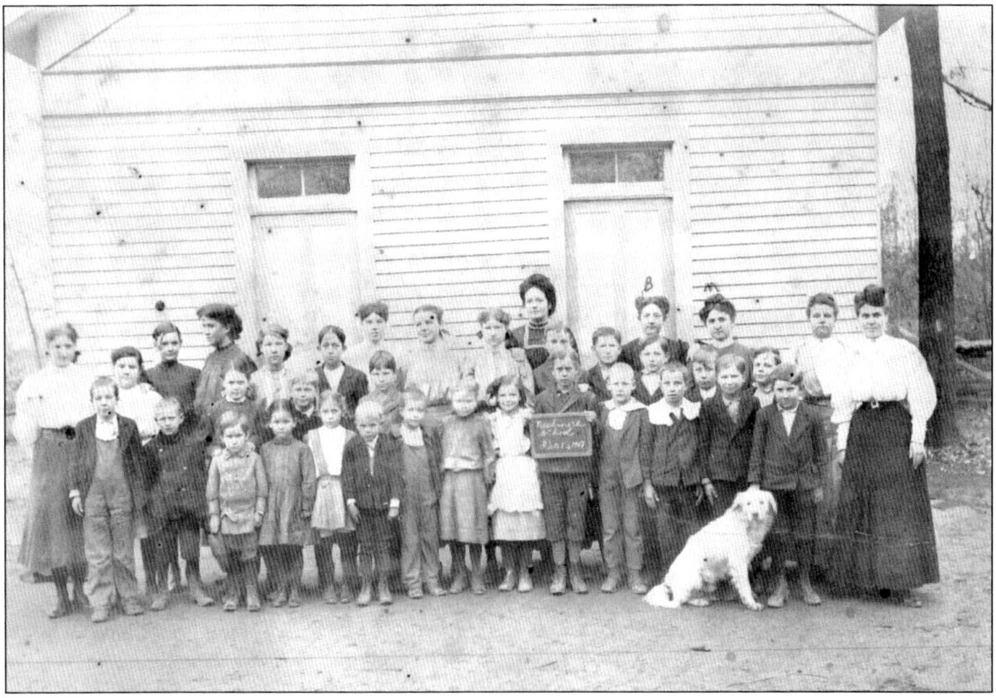

DOG DAYS. Needmore School was located southwest of the Haywood community. In this photograph from 1907, identified students are Willard Carver, with his hand on the dog, and Bertha and Myrtie Carver, in front of the right-side door. Teachers in schools such as Needmore were paid $35 a month if they had a teaching certificate, and they could board with one of their students for $2 or $3 dollars per month. (Courtesy of Runell Houchen.)

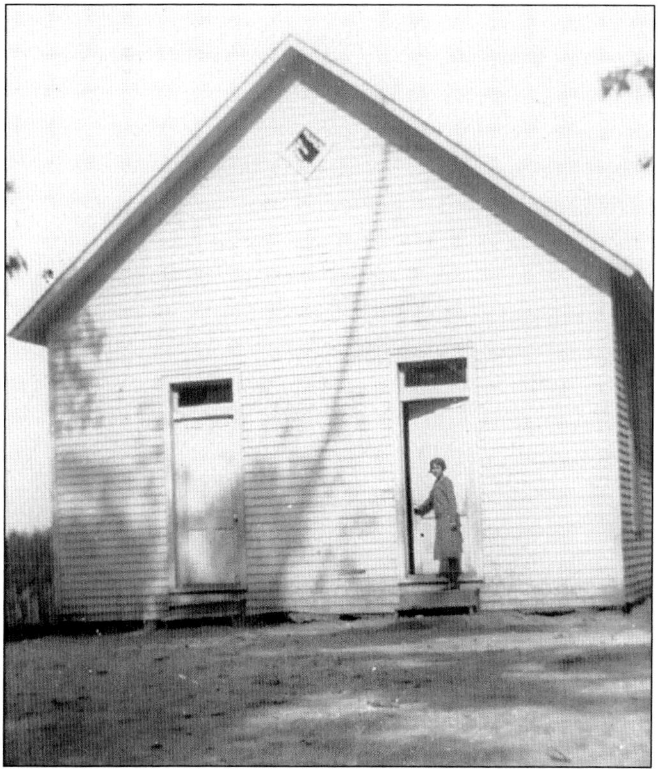

WELCOME! Shown in 1926, the one-room Tracy School was typical of the rural schools at the beginning of the 20th century. The schools had been locally controlled at the county level since 1908, when Kentucky school law left administration to the "sound discretion of the county boards." Other one-room schools in the area were Capitol Hill, Lucas, Devasher, Needmore, Winn, Union Hill, Moore, and Walnut Grove or "Seed Tick." (Courtesy of Martha Harrison.)

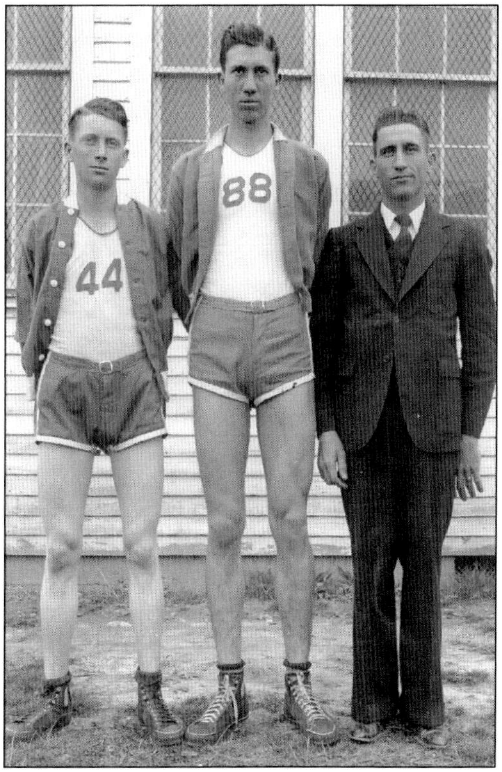

THE LONG AND SHORT OF IT. From left to right, Leo Bewley, Grover Wyatt, and principal George R. Helm pose in front of the newly consolidated Austin Tracy High School. The high school students of Lucas, Finney, Austin, and Tracy were first able to attend this new consolidated high school in 1933. A total of 15 students enrolled the year it opened. Though the school had its talented basketball teams, it did not have a gym until 1949. (Courtesy of Danny and Carolyn Wyatt.)

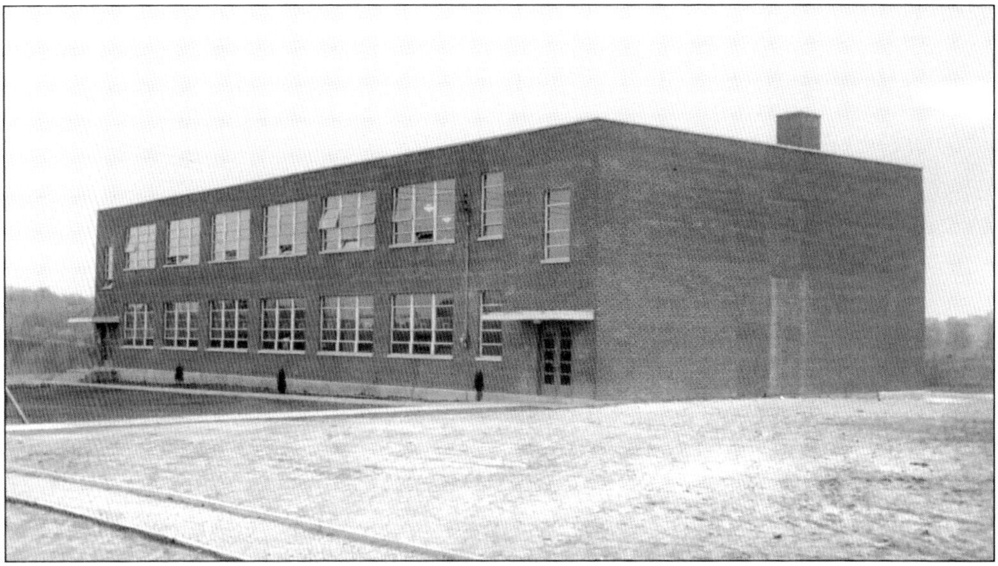

School Pride. Ralph Bunche School is built on land donated by one of Barren County's African American philanthropists, Stephen Landrum. Originally, the school was a wooden four-room building and one of the 27 public schools that the county had for African Americans at the beginning of the 20th century. The school was also known as the Glasgow Training School, and the above photograph shows the newly constructed and renamed Ralph Bunche School. The building housed all 12 grades and was the first state-accredited 12-year program for African Americans in the county. The school also had a librarian with a master's degree in library science, Carrie Robinson Morrison. The building is still standing but is owned today by the Liberty District Association, a group of African American Churches. Students are shown below in the library. (Both, courtesy of the Glasgow–Barren County Chamber of Commerce.)

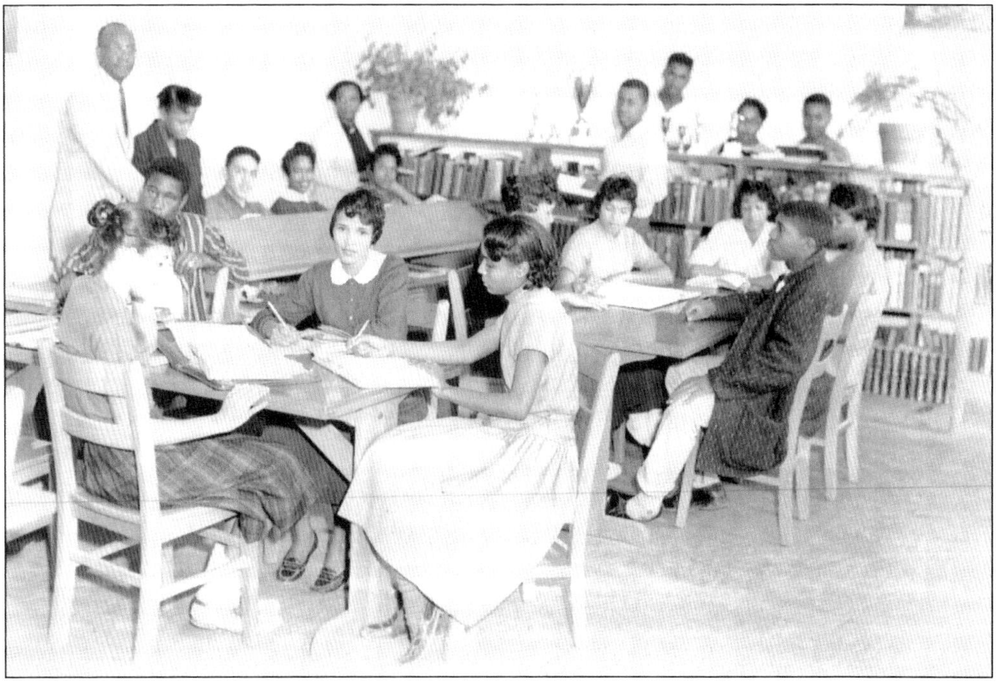

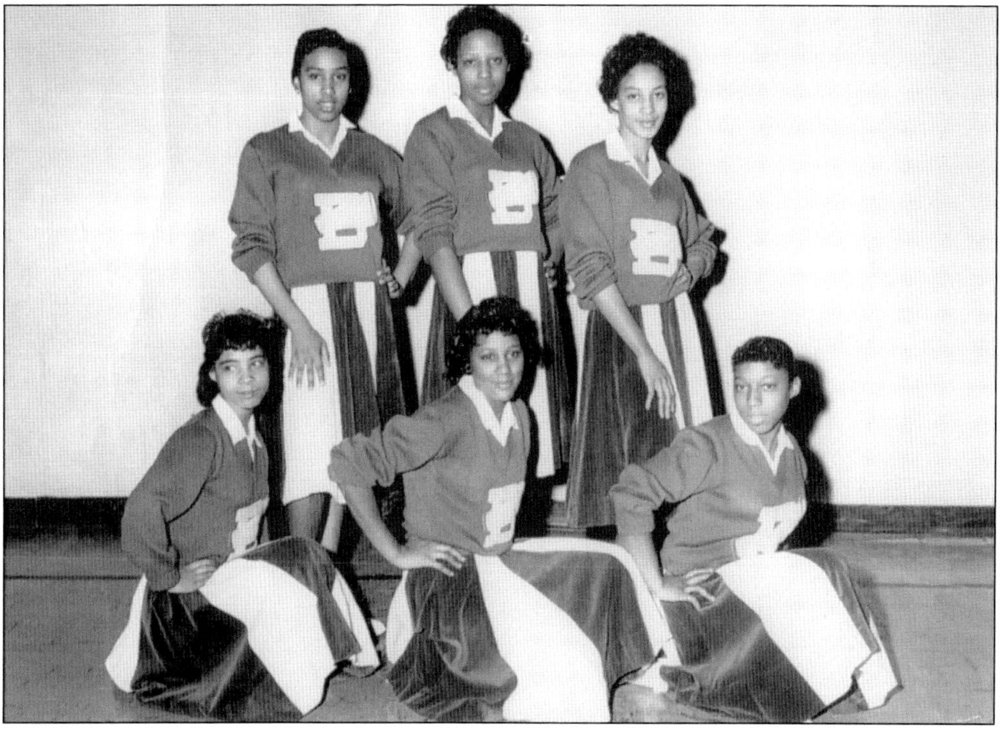

Something to Cheer About. These young women are proud to be on the cheering squad for the Ralph Bunche School in Glasgow. From left to right are (kneeling) Juanita Curd, Esther Webb, and Shirley May Mansfield; (standing) Billie Anne Bridges, Gerri Lewis, and Clara Glover. Opened in 1951, the school was named in honor of Nobel Prize winner and American diplomat Ralph Bunche. A gym and an industrial arts shop were added in 1955. The school remained the African American school for the area until 1964. In the photograph below, the Bunche Blue Hawks marching band are decked out in school colors as they march in the Glasgow Christmas Parade. (Both, courtesy of Alma Glover.)

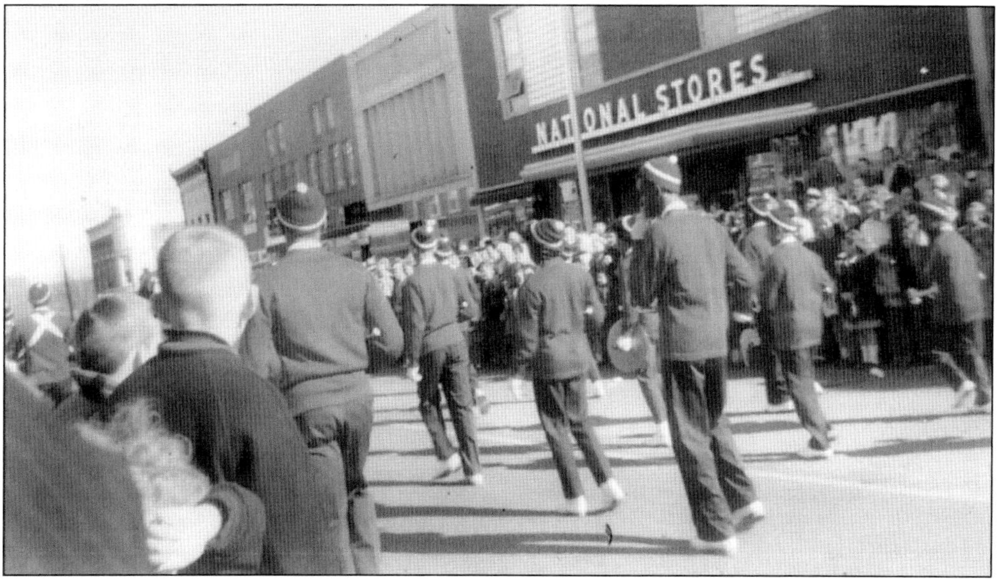

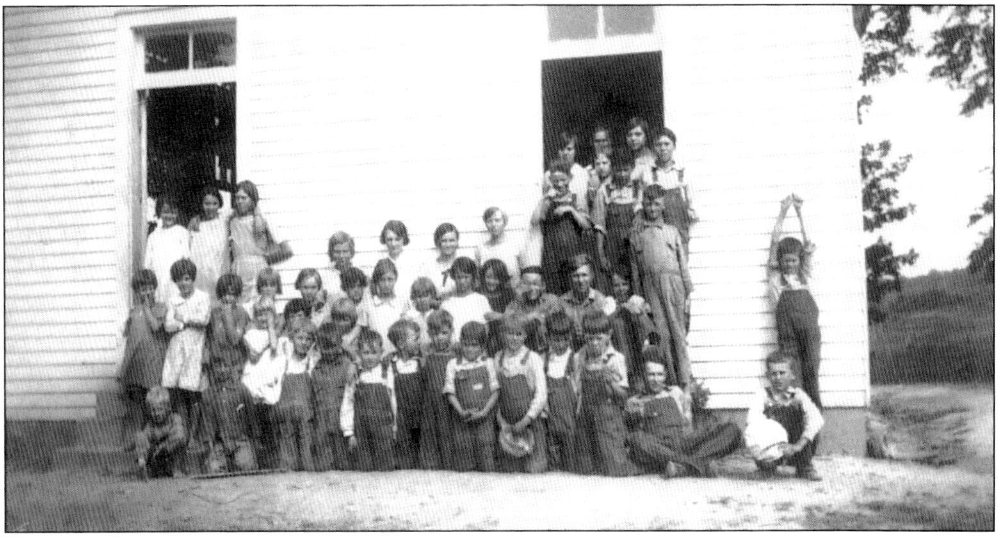

Not So Far Away. Many fondly remember the Lyons School, as shown in this 1930 photograph. The teacher at this time was Thelma Young, but the school's most beloved teacher was Hannah Kinslow Greer. She taught for many years and influenced the lives of all the students. Many did not mind the 4 or 5 mile walk to school just to be with "Miss Hannah." (Courtesy of James and Olene Richey.)

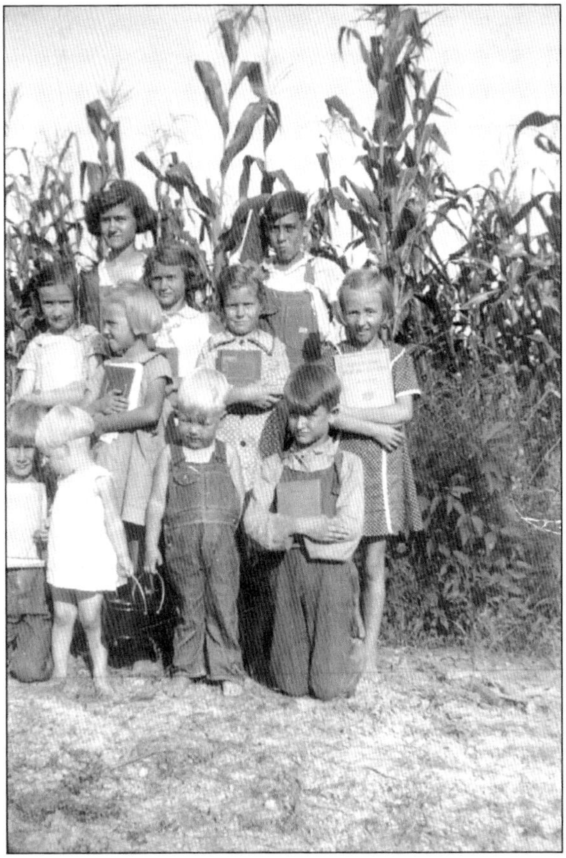

Lyons School Days. In 1937, James Henry Richey and Virginia Richey Bowman are too young to attend classes but have come along for the picture and to help carry the lunch pails. With them are Richard and Julian Ritter. Shown, from left to right, are (second row) unidentified, Helen Frances, Elizabeth "Snooks" Button, and Jean Frances; (third row) Mary Ellen Ritter, Frankie Mae Ritter, and Wilbur Oliver. (Courtesy of Virginia and Garnett Bowman.)

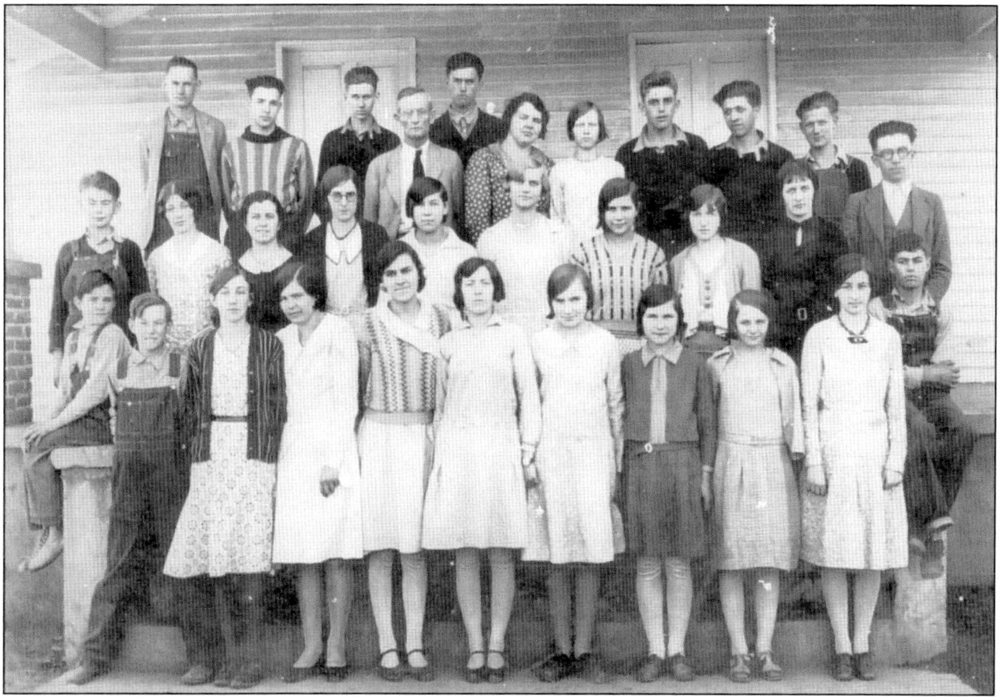

All Together Now. These students of the 1930–1931 school year stand on the porch of the old Temple Hill High School in the photograph above. The teacher for that year was Hazel Johnson, and J. E. Bryant was principal. The high school started out in the elementary school building, constructed in 1888, and occupied the second floor. All students had to use outdoor bathroom and water facilities. The first class in 1925 had 14 students. The students always did well and scored some of the highest grades in the county on their eighth-grade exams. Shown below in 1934, the new brick building, a WPA project, had been constructed, and it became a four-year program for its graduates. It has been stated by many that "the school turned out numerous noted people and good citizens." (Above, courtesy of Herman Hume; below, courtesy of Linda Dickson.)

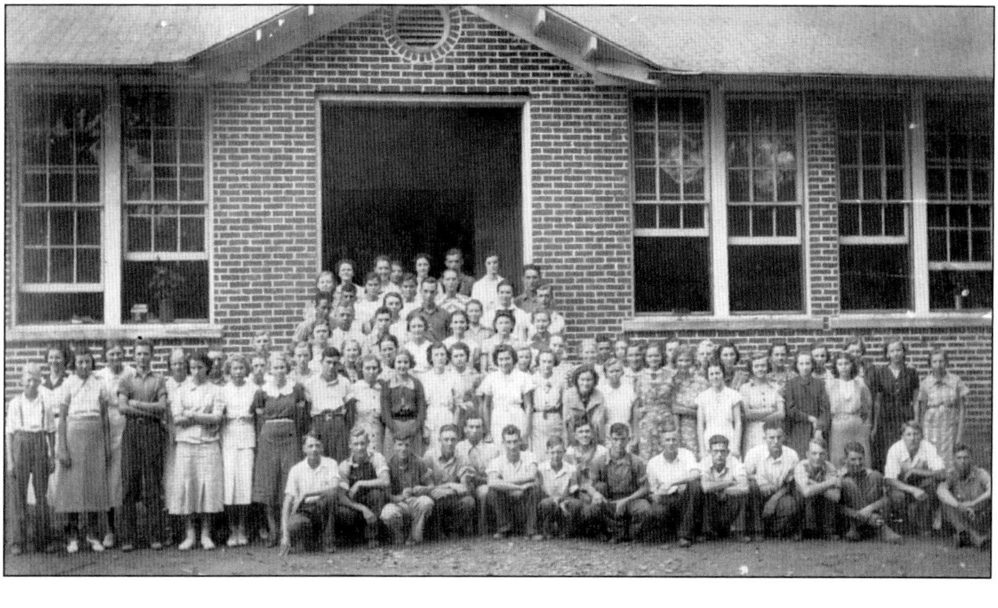

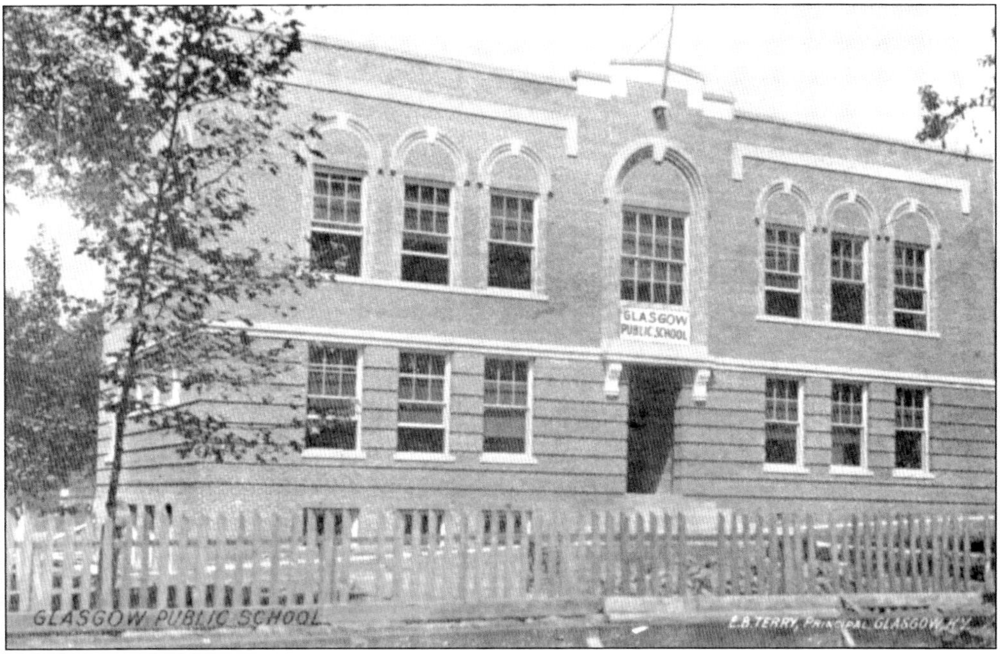

GLASGOW PUBLIC SCHOOL. This postcard shows the Glasgow Public School when E. B. Terry was its principal. Terry would later become superintendent of the school system. The *Handbook of Kentucky* from 1907 exults that the school was one of two commodious and modern schoolhouses in the city, having had extensive renovations at a named cost of $15,000.

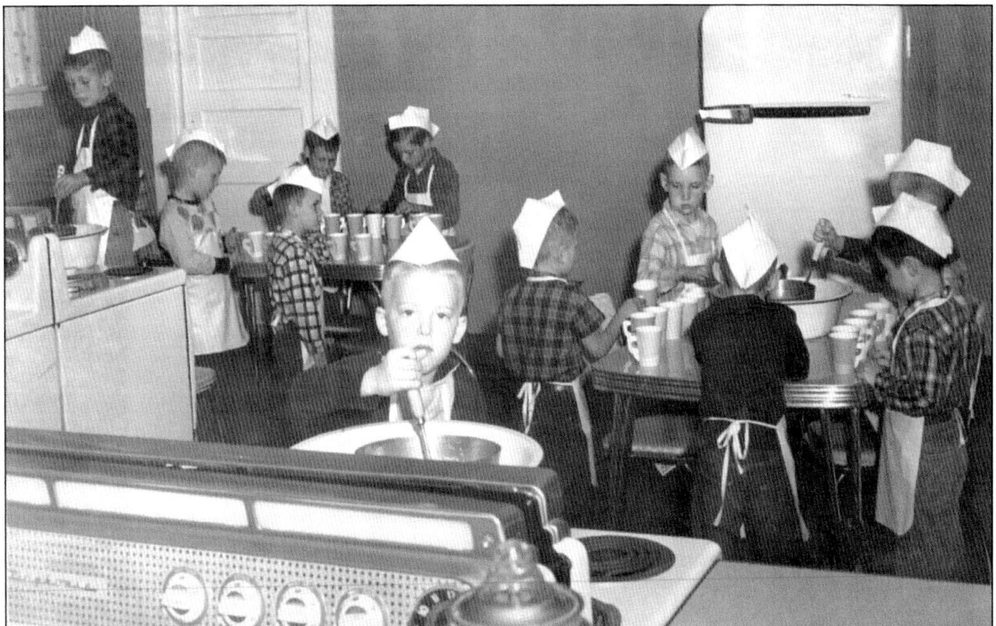

TOO MANY COOKS SPOIL THE BROTH! It is never too early to begin learning self-sufficiency skills, safety, and simple food preparation. This wonderful photograph shows what happens when a first-grade class takes over a home economics department in the early 1950s. The image features young boys as the "cooks." (Courtesy of the Glasgow–Barren County Chamber of Commerce.)

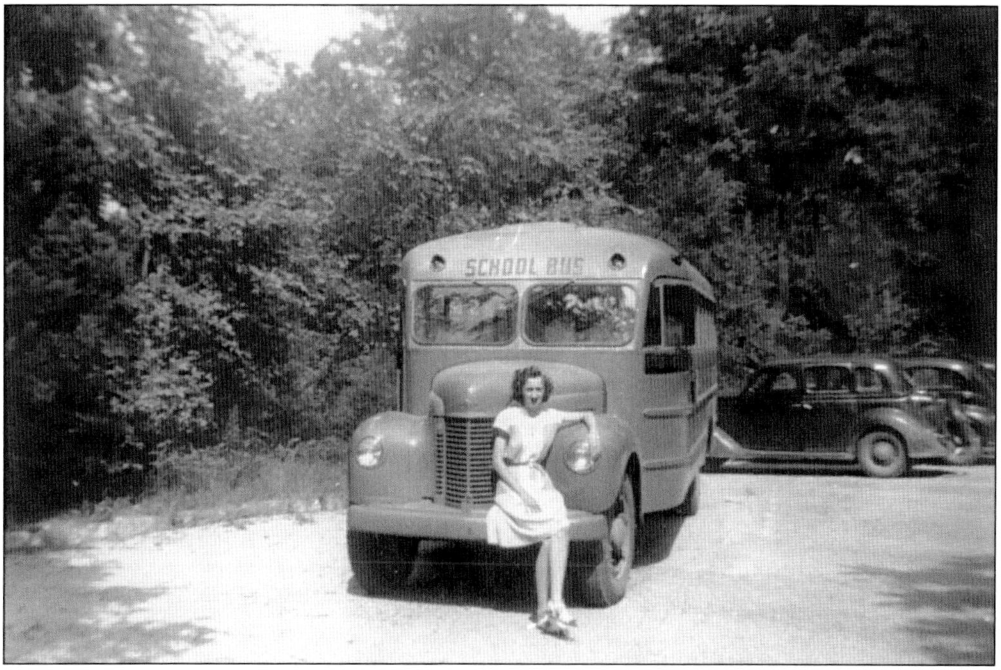

BEAUTY AND THE BUS. Rebecca Miller sits in front of one of the county's early school buses in a photograph from 1944. The need for reliable transportation came with school consolidation in the 1930s. Many in the county would have had to walk long distances to get back and forth to their schools. The buses at first were really "school trucks" that were improvised to accommodate students. (Courtesy of John Robert Miller.)

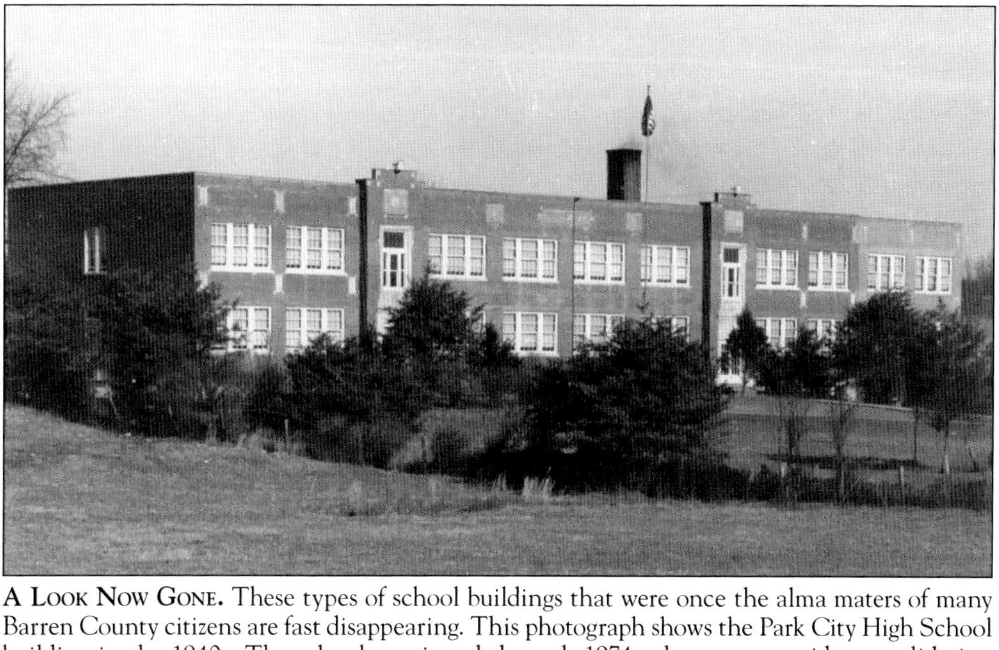

A LOOK NOW GONE. These types of school buildings that were once the alma maters of many Barren County citizens are fast disappearing. This photograph shows the Park City High School building in the 1940s. The school continued through 1974, when county-wide consolidation melded the individual schools into the newly built Barren County High School. (Courtesy of the Glasgow–Barren County Chamber of Commerce.)

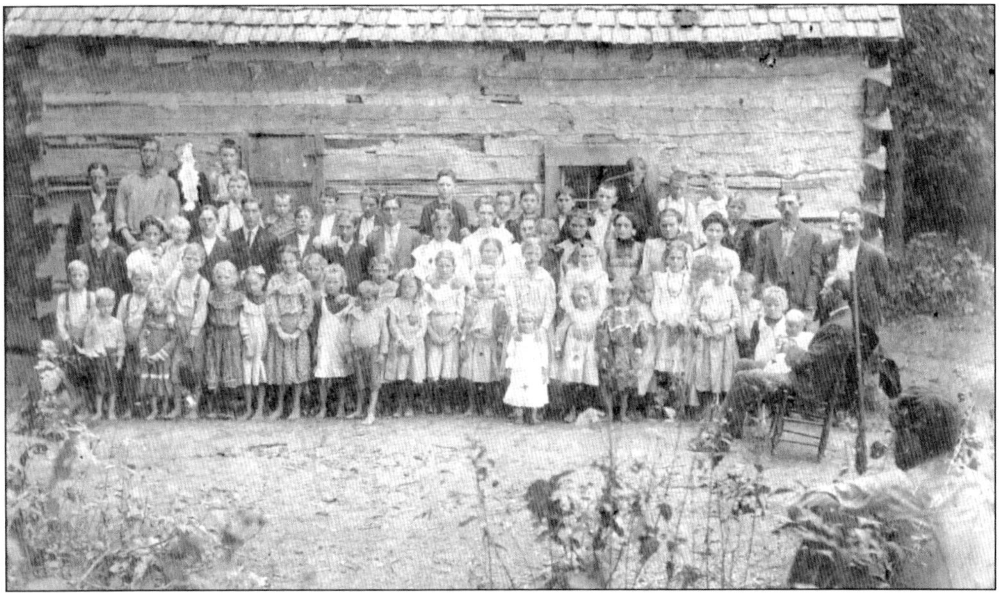

In the Woods. The location and name of this school is not known, but the image is striking. The youngest children in the first row are all barefooted but dressed in their Sunday bests. A suited man sits in the only chair, while the man in the far right of the photograph holds a gun. His presence accentuates the rural nature of the photograph, as there may have been wild animals still running about.

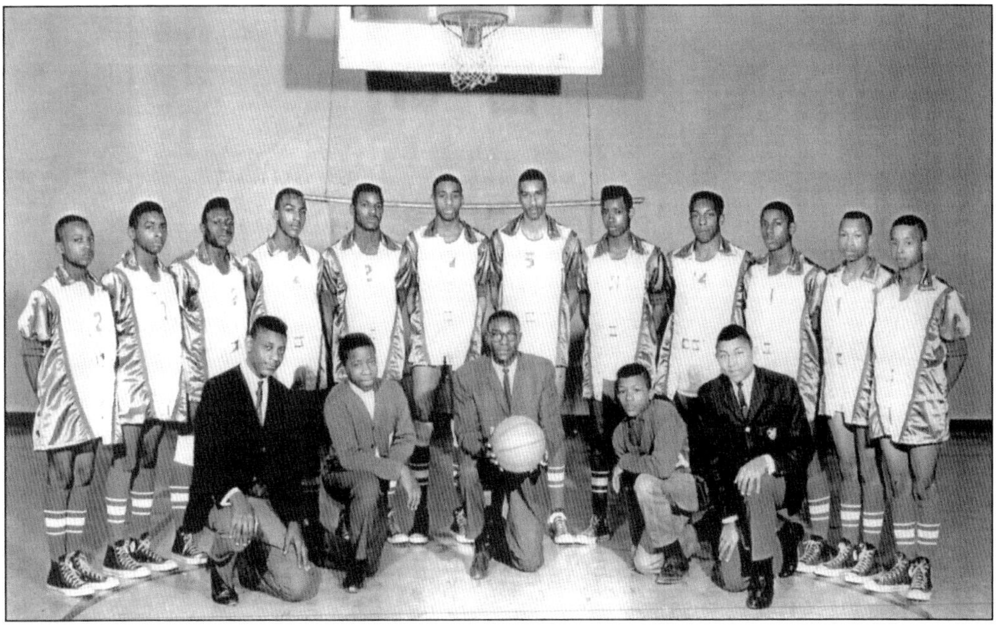

Glasgow's Champs. The Ralph Bunche "Bluehawks" team won the 15th district championship in the 1963–1964 school seasons. Members of the team shown standing are, from left to right, James Stockton, Jerry Stockton, Alonzo Tinker, Clifton Tobin, Joe Webb, Lawrence Curd, Floyd Bridges, Paul Breeding, Jerry Childress, Alonzo Webb, William Bailey, and Walter Rhodes. The coaching staff and ball boys are, from left to right, Joe Rhodes, Harry Francis, Johnny Herron, Rex Bailey, and Donnie Bransford. (Courtesy of Alonzo Webb.)

Five

Working, Playing, and Praying in Barren County

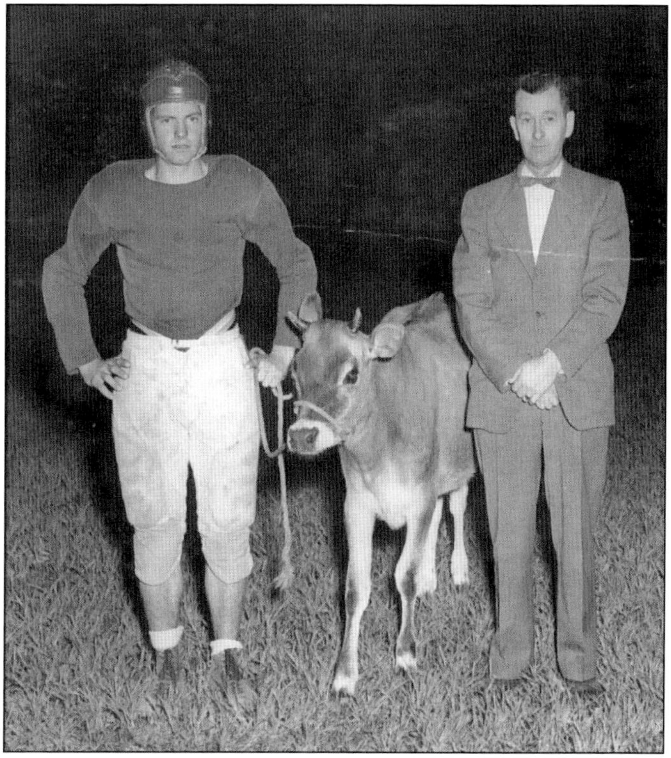

Work and Fun. This unusual photograph highlights two of Barren County's reasons for pride. Local sports are followed with great interest, and the county and city teams enjoy friendly rivalries. The county has large numbers of Hereford, Angus, and other registered cattle breeders and dairy producers. Barren County is the No. 1 producer of milk, hay, and cattle for the state of Kentucky. (Courtesy of the Glasgow–Barren County Chamber of Commerce.)

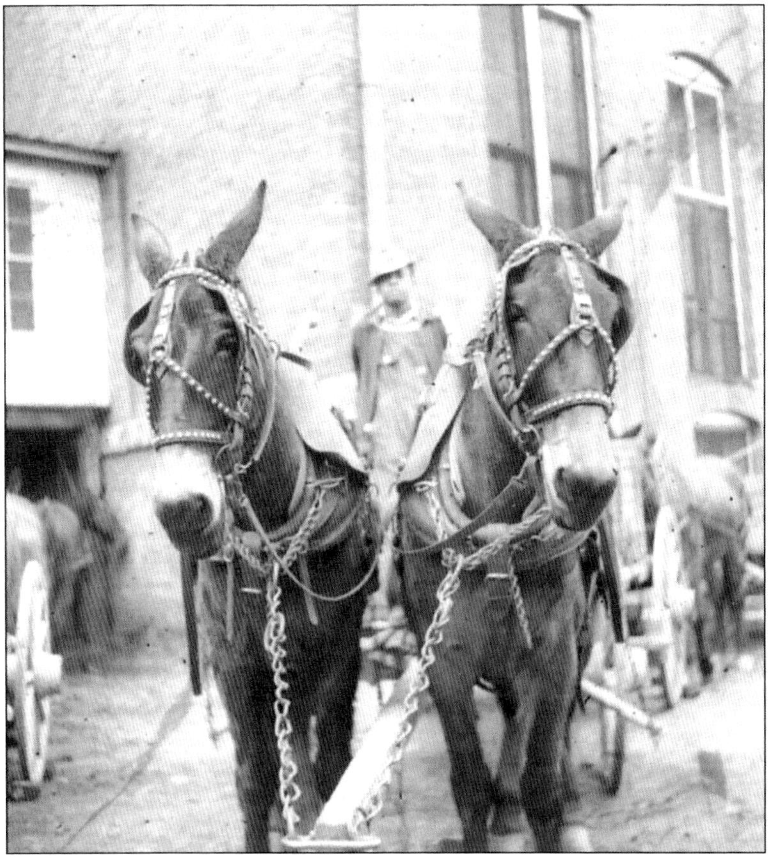

MULEING AROUND. This team, equipped and loaded down for the long trip home, waits patiently behind the buildings off the square for their owners to return. The curious intelligent strong-willed mule was valuable property and was used for riding, pulling, plowing, and packing. At the time of this early-20th-century photograph, the State Bureau of Agriculture reported that there were 5,895 mules in the county.

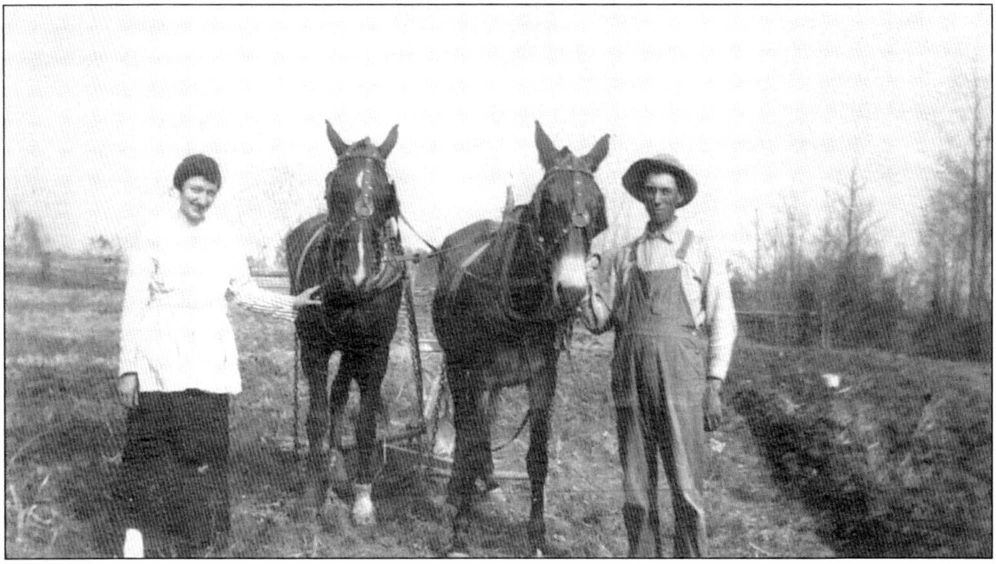

PROUD TEAM. Martha and Henry Miller pose with a pair of fine mules as they ready their farmland for spring planting in 1917. The mules were an essential part of farming and industry. On county court days, everyone gathered on the third Monday of each month and traded mules, horses, wagons, and tools. Glasgow was known as a mule-trading center. (Courtesy of John Robert Miller.)

Kentucky Proud. The rolling countryside and wide-open spaces of the county's farms were perfect for raising quality horses and cattle. Barren County still has more cattle than any other county east of the Mississippi River, and there are a number of horse-related businesses in the county, including boarding, breeding, and training. (Courtesy of the Glasgow–Barren County Chamber of Commerce.)

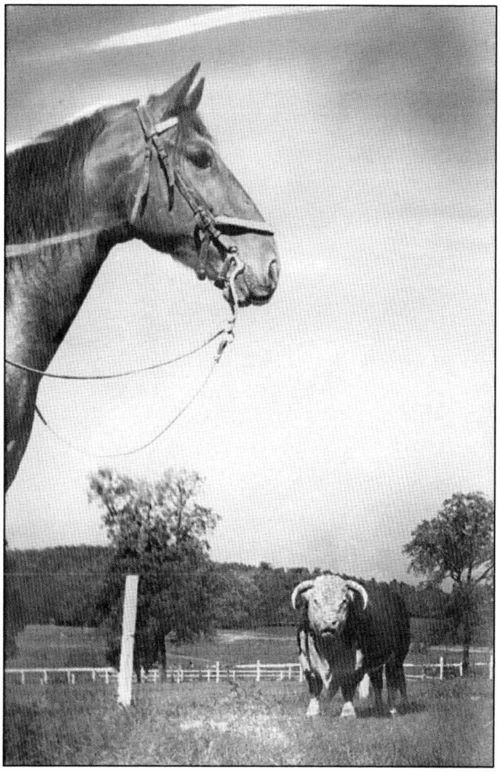

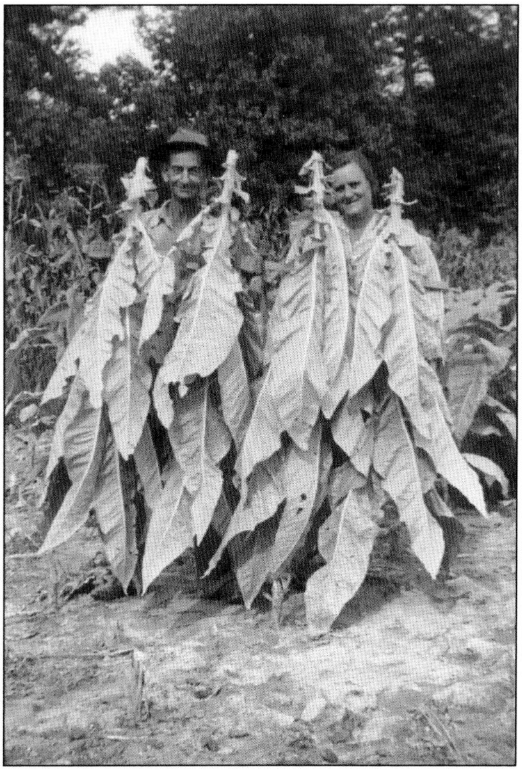

Barren's Bounty. The county's leadership in the production of tobacco is recognized as starting in the 1820s. In 1920, only about 12 percent of farms had tractors available, so the arduous process of cultivating the crop began by tilling the ground with a turning plow and mules. Care and harvesting of the plants took the effort of everyone. Will and May Bewley show off some of the effort of their labor. (Courtesy of Gary Bewley.)

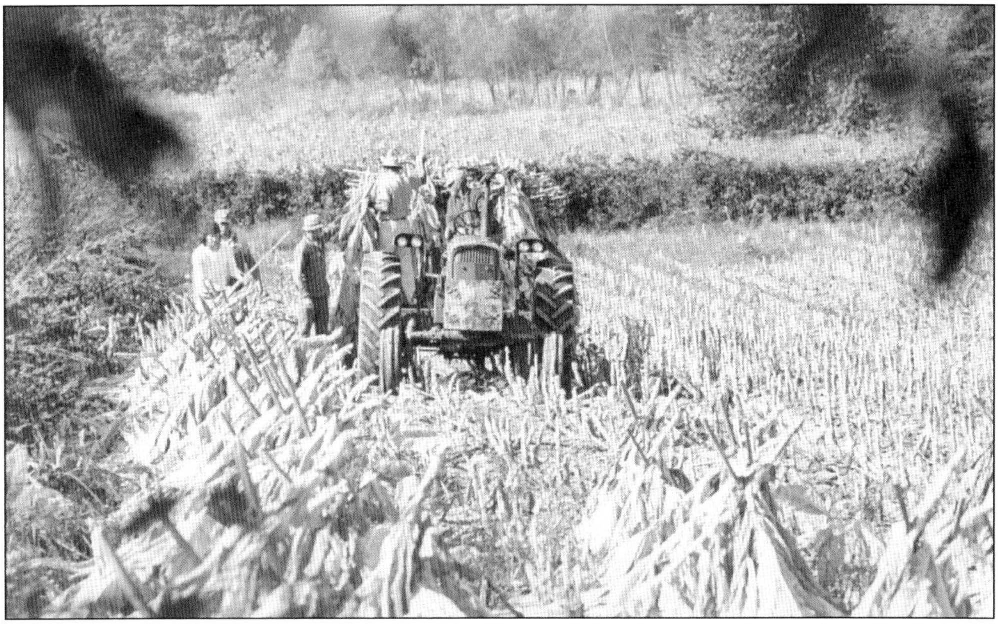

CASH CROP. Barren County consistently topped Kentucky's tobacco production lists. But because of health concerns, production has declined in importance in Barren and other Kentucky counties as farmers are looking to grow more varied and diversified crops. From 1997 to 2007, the number of Kentucky tobacco farms dropped from 93,530 to 16,234. The photograph above shows burley tobacco being loaded on a wagon to be taken to barns for drying. (Courtesy of Jimmy Lowe.)

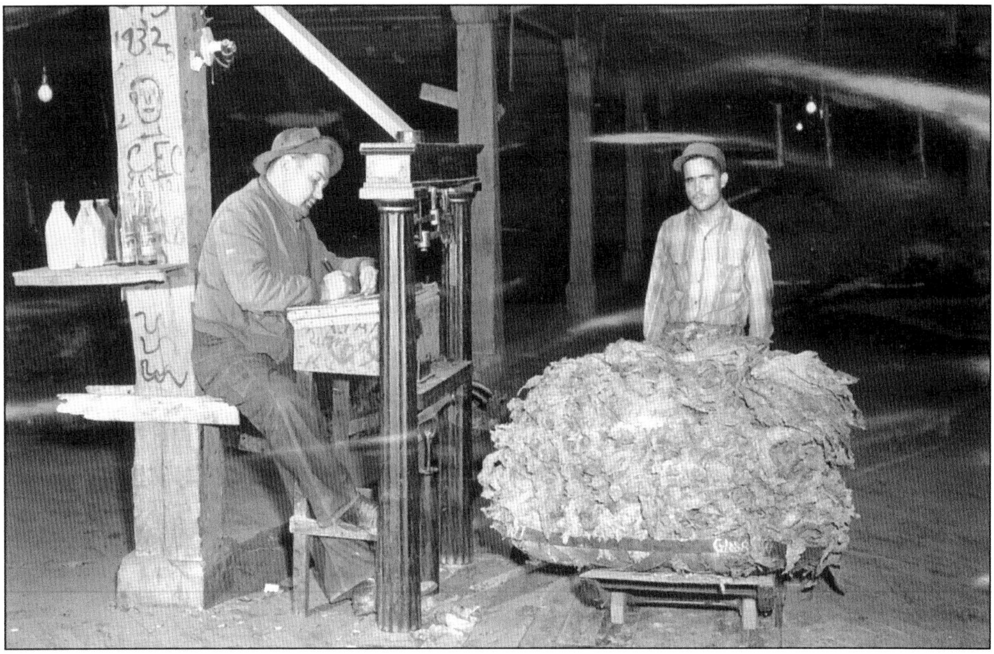

WEIGHING IN. All the hard work for the farmer is about to pay off as he presents his tobacco to be weighed. The leaves have been sorted into matching grades and positioned on the warehouse floors, ready for inspection, auction, and selling. The weigh master seems ready for work, with his milk and soft drink bottles at hand. (Courtesy of the Glasgow–Barren County Chamber of Commerce.)

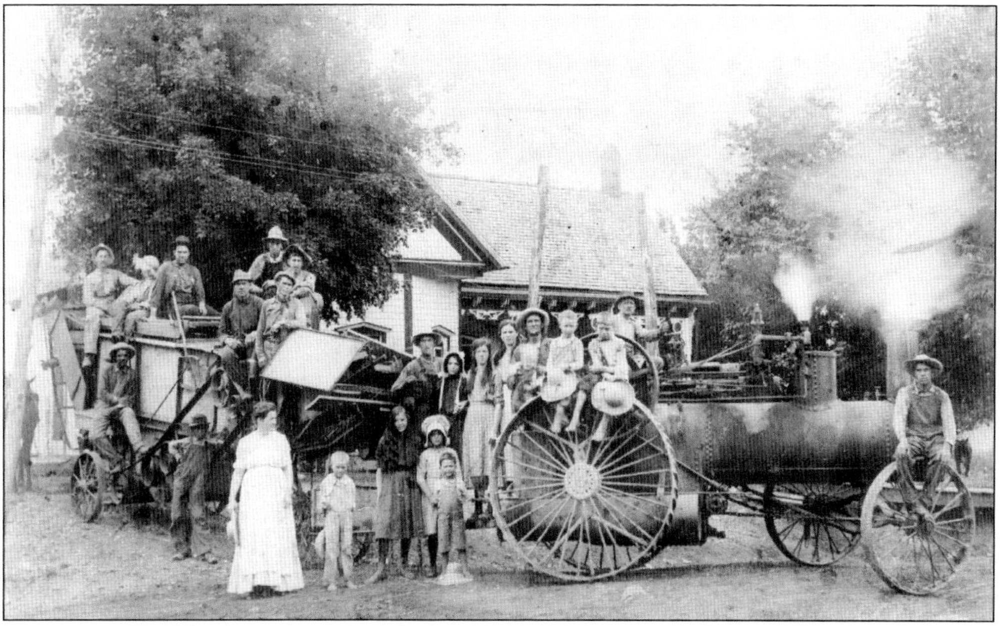

COME AND SEE. Charlie Simmons made the rounds, going from farm to farm with his marvelous steam thresher. The machine was beneficial in reducing the manual labor that was needed for harvesting the crops, and it eased the reliance on horses. However, the machines were cumbersome, and only the larger farmers relied on these machines. They were exciting to see, as everyone has come to take a look at the new marvel. (Courtesy of Scott Fife.)

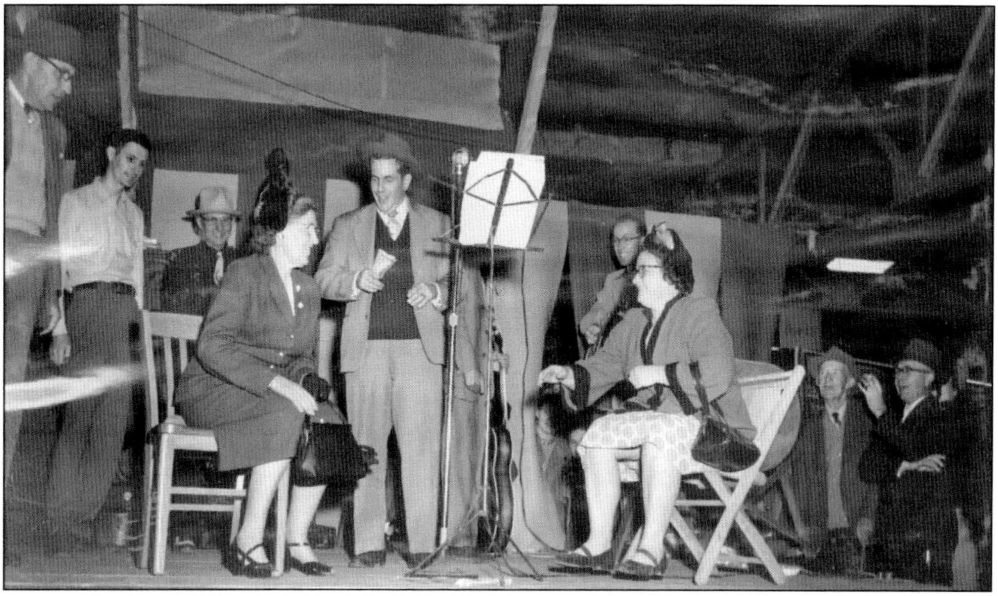

TOBACCO FUN. Preceded by tobacco fairs and enlarged by tobacco company support, these festivals offered a chance for the entire community to come together for many exciting events. The homemaker clubs served delicious food, and there were many contests offering prize monies. Popular contests were square dancing and the "balloon bursting" contest. It was one of the most requested contests and produced some of the festival's funniest moments. (Courtesy of the Glasgow–Barren County Chamber of Commerce.)

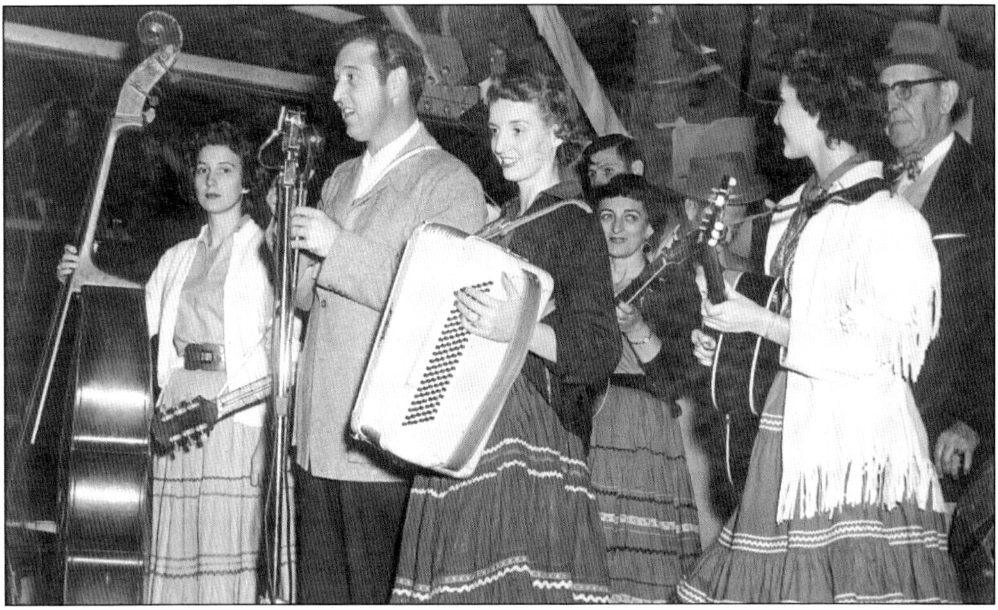

FUN FESTIVAL. The Tobacco Festival celebrated and promoted the importance of tobacco to the economy of Barren County and had a joint sponsorship by the chamber of commerce and the Glasgow Tobacco Board of Trade. The festival was usually scheduled for November and was held in the cavernous tobacco warehouses that used to make up part of the city's landscape. The festival featured music and other stage performances, both amateur and professional. The photograph above shows, from left to right, Anita Carter, Floyd "Lightnin" Chance (at the microphone), Helen Carter, "Mother" Maybelle Carter, and unidentified. As shown in the photograph below, attendance and support from the community was outstanding and was marked one year as record breaking, with more than 8,000 people. (Both, courtesy of the Glasgow–Barren County Chamber of Commerce.)

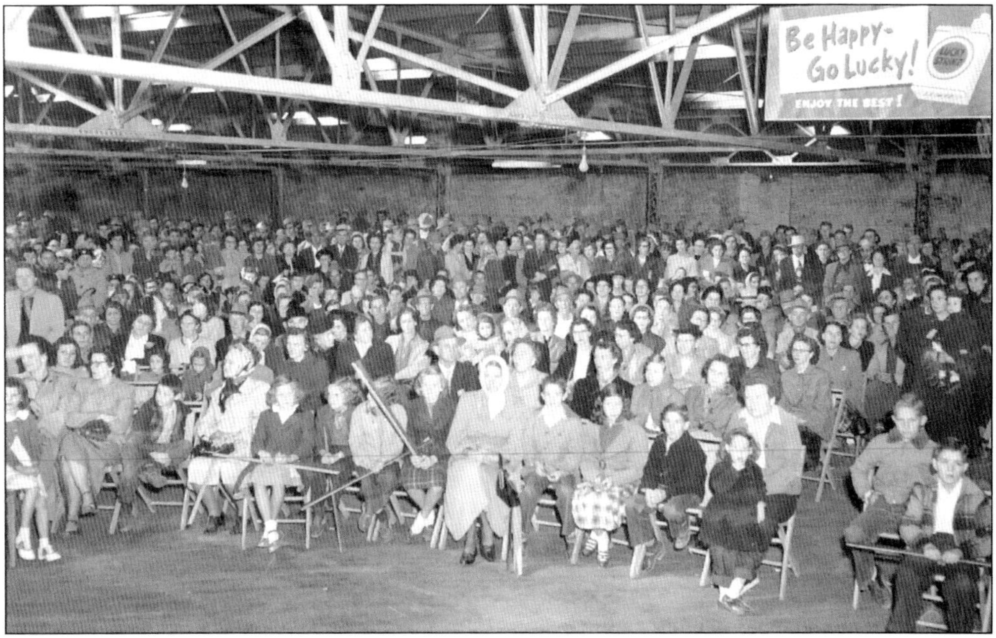

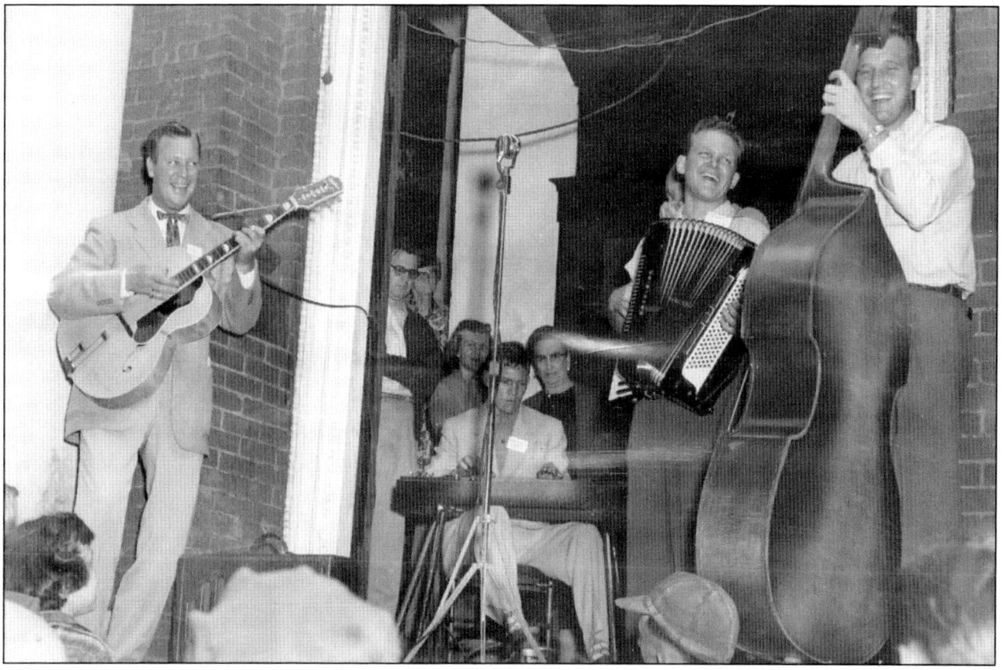

Let Me Entertain You. Nashville entertainers stop by the Glasgow Courthouse during a goodwill tour sponsored by the Nashville Chamber of Commerce. The tours featured Nashville artists as they promoted reciprocity and friendship between cities. "Smiling Eddie" Hill is on the guitar, Bud Isaac is playing the steel guitar, Floyd "Lightnin" Chance is on bass, and Tony Ceneola adds the sounds of the accordion. (Courtesy of the Glasgow–Barren County Chamber of Commerce.)

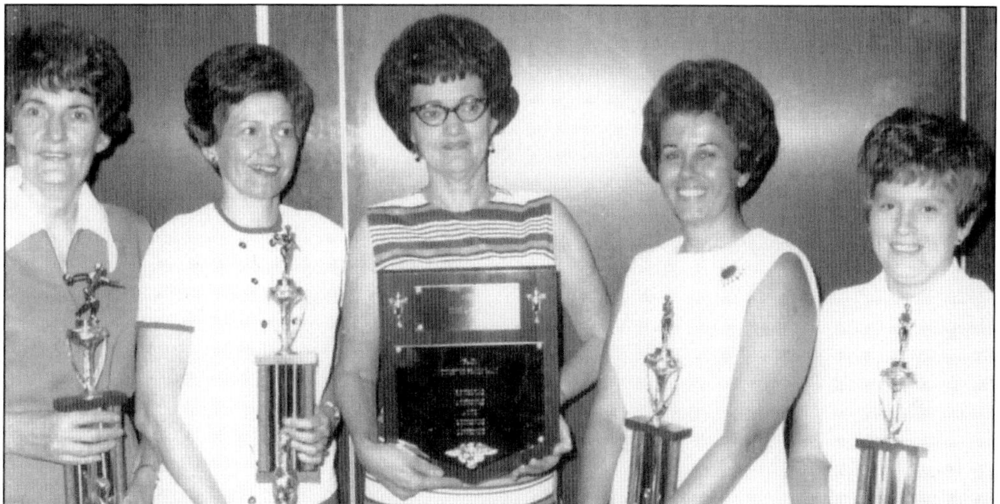

Winner's Circle. This group of women is justly proud of their trophies and is representative of the group leagues that were popular in Barren County in the 1950s. Bowling's popularity grew with the first broadcast of "Championship Bowling," and the game quickly became the great American pastime. The women shown here were representing Underwood's Beauty Shop. From left to right are Zelma Underwood, Betty Underwood, Lucille Underwood, Maxine Underwood, and Shirley Estes. (Courtesy of Maxine Underwood.)

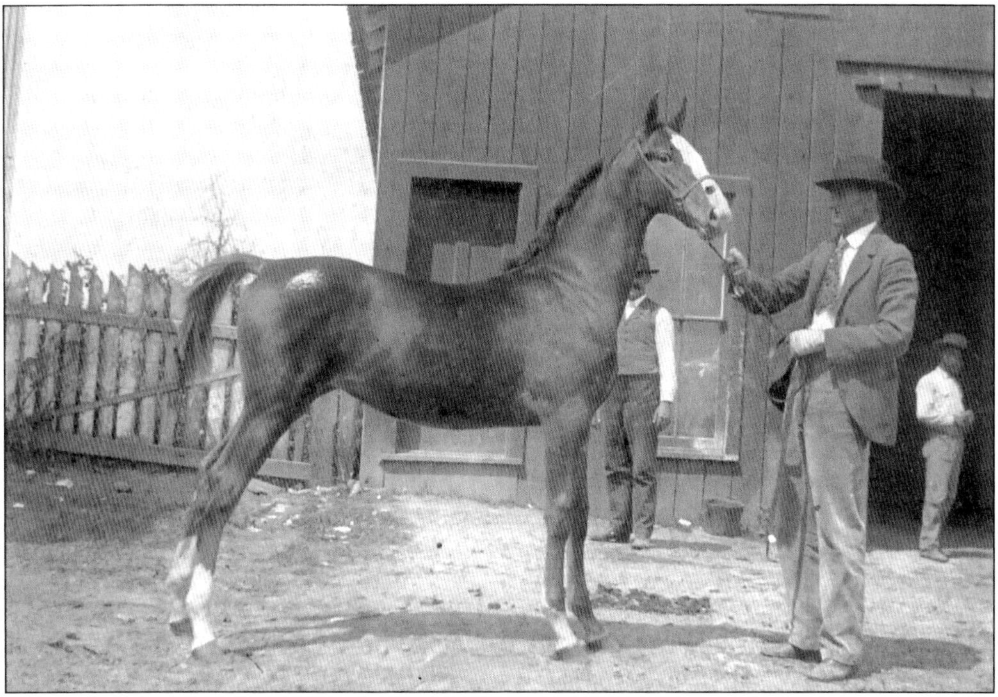

Ready for a Show. Though Barren County is not known as a horse-breeding region, many people did breed and raise high-quality stock. Raised on a Barren County farm in 1900, this colt is ready to be shown at the state fair. Both horses and mules were highly prized, and their sale could produce a year's income for the family. (Courtesy of Runell and Terry Houchen.)

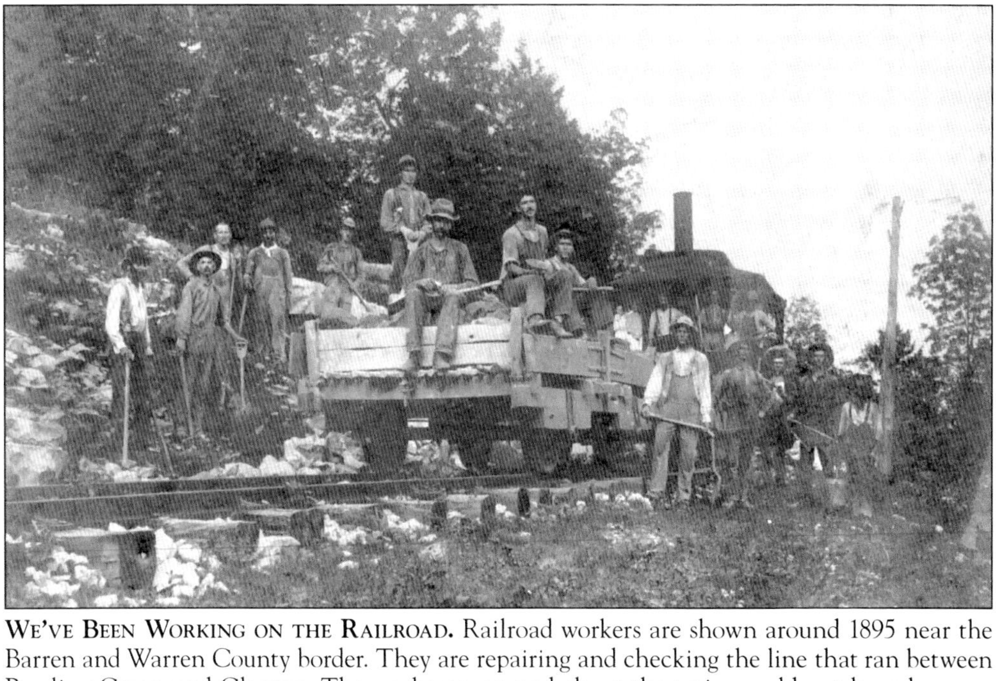

We've Been Working on the Railroad. Railroad workers are shown around 1895 near the Barren and Warren County border. They are repairing and checking the line that ran between Bowling Green and Glasgow. The workmen on and about the train would not have been an unusual sight, but one must wonder about the woman and child in the engine car.

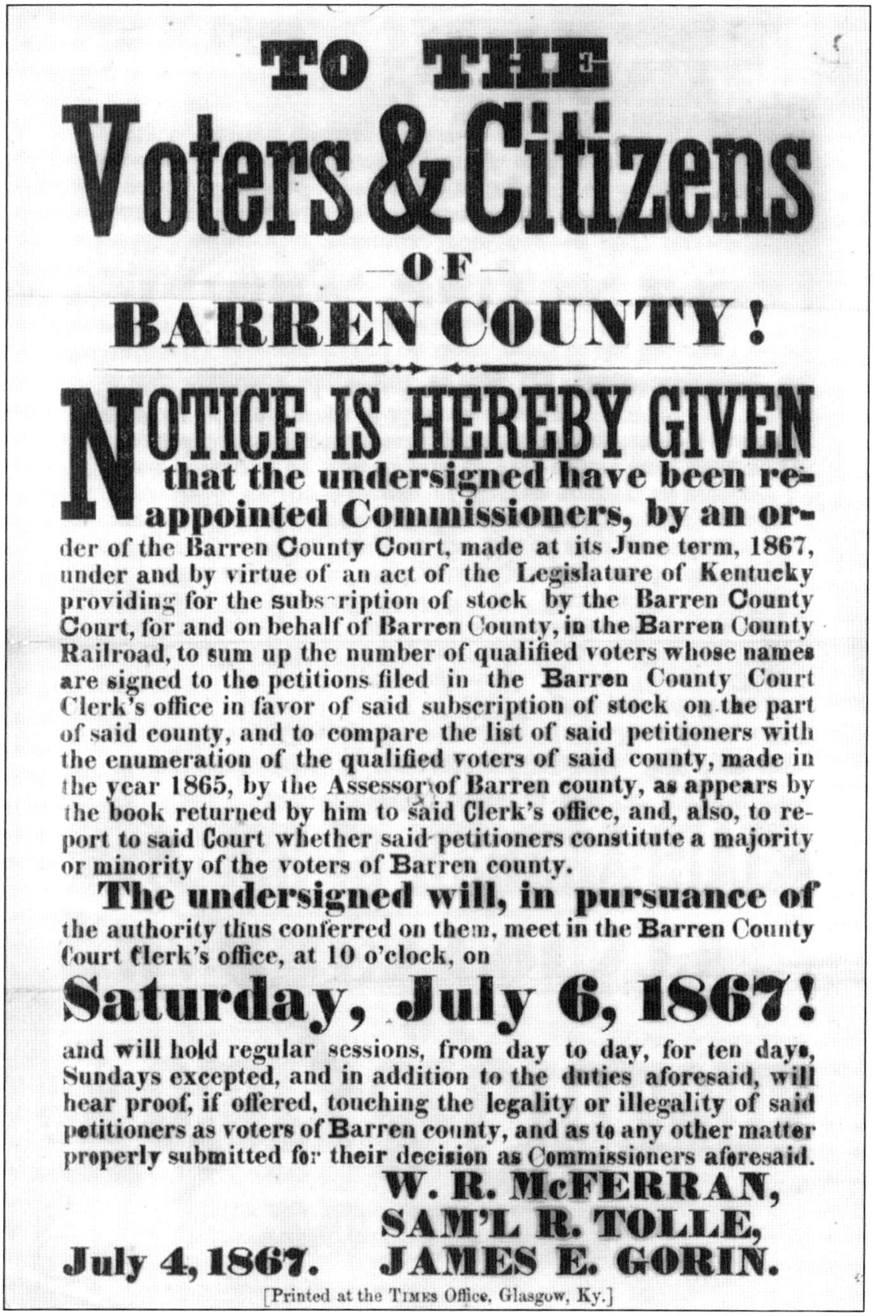

TO THE

Voters & Citizens

—OF—

BARREN COUNTY!

NOTICE IS HEREBY GIVEN that the undersigned have been re-appointed Commissioners, by an order of the Barren County Court, made at its June term, 1867, under and by virtue of an act of the Legislature of Kentucky providing for the subscription of stock by the Barren County Court, for and on behalf of Barren County, in the Barren County Railroad, to sum up the number of qualified voters whose names are signed to the petitions filed in the Barren County Court Clerk's office in favor of said subscription of stock on the part of said county, and to compare the list of said petitioners with the enumeration of the qualified voters of said county, made in the year 1865, by the Assessor of Barren county, as appears by the book returned by him to said Clerk's office, and, also, to report to said Court whether said petitioners constitute a majority or minority of the voters of Barren county.

The undersigned will, in pursuance of the authority thus conferred on them, meet in the Barren County Court Clerk's office, at 10 o'clock, on

Saturday, July 6, 1867!

and will hold regular sessions, from day to day, for ten days, Sundays excepted, and in addition to the duties aforesaid, will hear proof, if offered, touching the legality or illegality of said petitioners as voters of Barren county, and as to any other matter properly submitted for their decision as Commissioners aforesaid.

W. R. McFERRAN,
SAM'L R. TOLLE,
July 4, 1867. JAMES E. GORIN.

[Printed at the TIMES Office, Glasgow, Ky.]

TRAIN'S A COMING. In 1859, Barren County was bypassed by the main north and south line of the Louisville and Nashville Railroad. Citizens quickly recognized the need for a connection to this main line and issued this notice for subscribers to a Barren County railroad spur line. The line was built in 1870 and was connected with the Louisville and Nashville line at Glasgow Junction (Park City). Subscription stocks played an active role in early railroad development in the United States, but litigation followed quickly on the heels of such developments, as property owners fought and disagreed with the location of the tracks. Joe Creason of the *Courier Journal* stated it well when he said, "probably no other town in Kentucky owes so much to so little railroad."

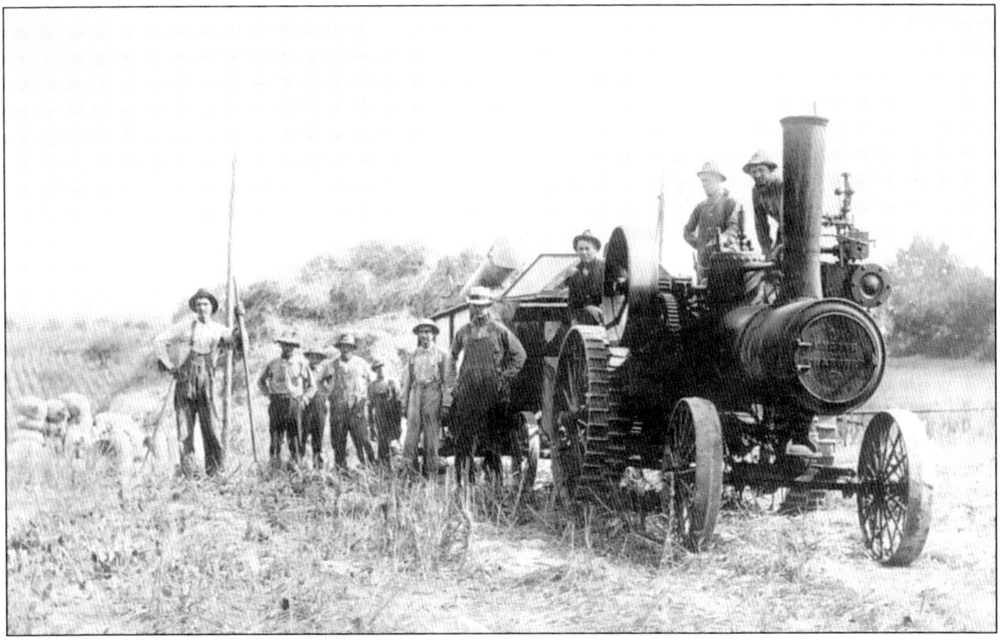

Harvest Time. The old saying, "make hay while the sun is shining" applied to the group effort it took to gather the crops. The threshing machine made quicker work of the process of harvesting, but as the photograph shows, it still took many hands to complete the job. The owner of the machinery would charge a set fee per acre or ask for a percentage of the crop in exchange. (Courtesy of Martha Harrison.)

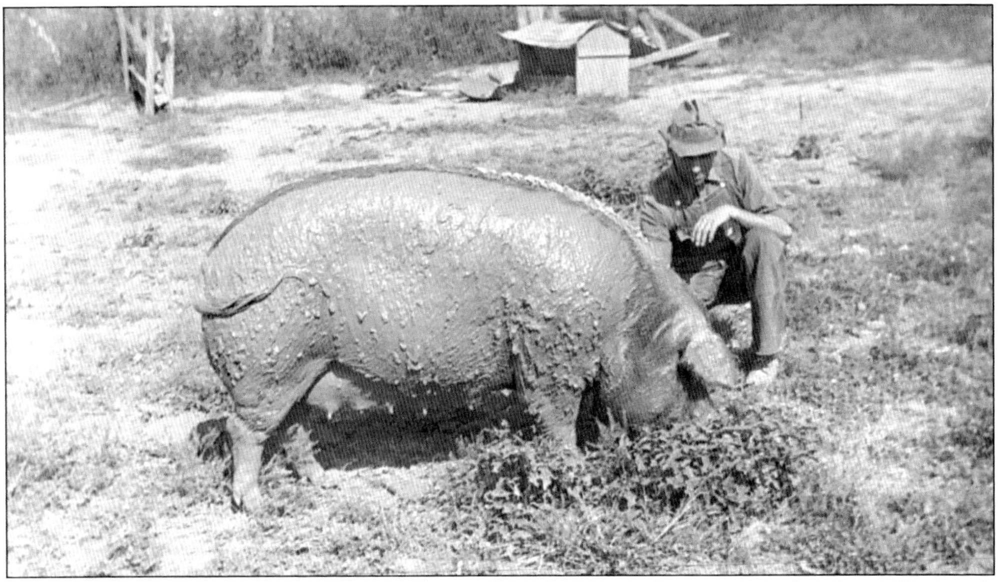

What a Ham. Barren County's agricultural preeminence is well known. Sample values of livestock from the 1950s show that the county held fifth place in the state for hogs on farms. This large hog would feed the Miller family through the coming winter, providing months of food. Hog killing time was also a tradition in the late fall and involved all the family and community, as it was labor intensive. Henry Miller is shown in 1920 with one of his prized animals. (Courtesy of John Robert Miller.)

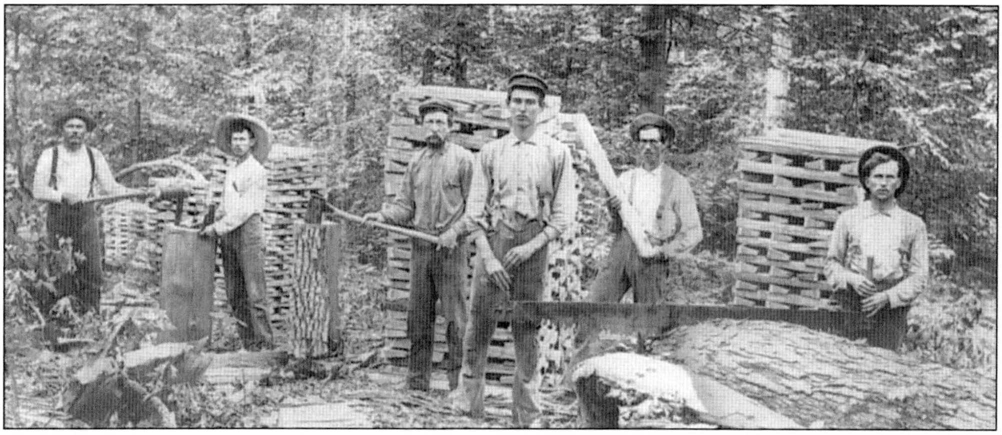

From Start to Finish. Making axe handles is an old craft that was an important and valued skill. The county's wooded areas provided all types of wood for making axe handles and other products. Of the different types of woods, hickory became the best material for axe handles. Granville Wheat Bunch (with suspenders) is shown in this early photograph, with other laborers, sawing and preparing logs to make axe handles and other items. (Courtesy of Gary Bewley.)

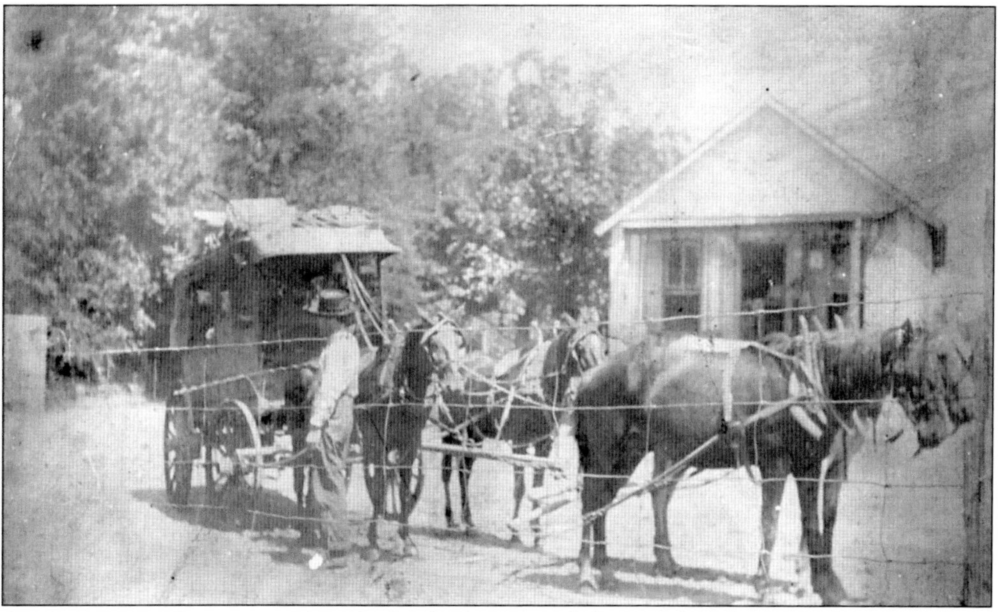

On Our Way. The stage, with its high wheels, covered the rutted roads regularly to Burkesville and other locations. The trips could take 24 hours and several changes of horses, depending on the distance. The fare was 10¢ per mile or $4 for a one-way trip. Riding a stagecoach was a high adventure, and the newspaper carried many flamboyant reminisces of the travelers. (Courtesy of Perry Brantley.)

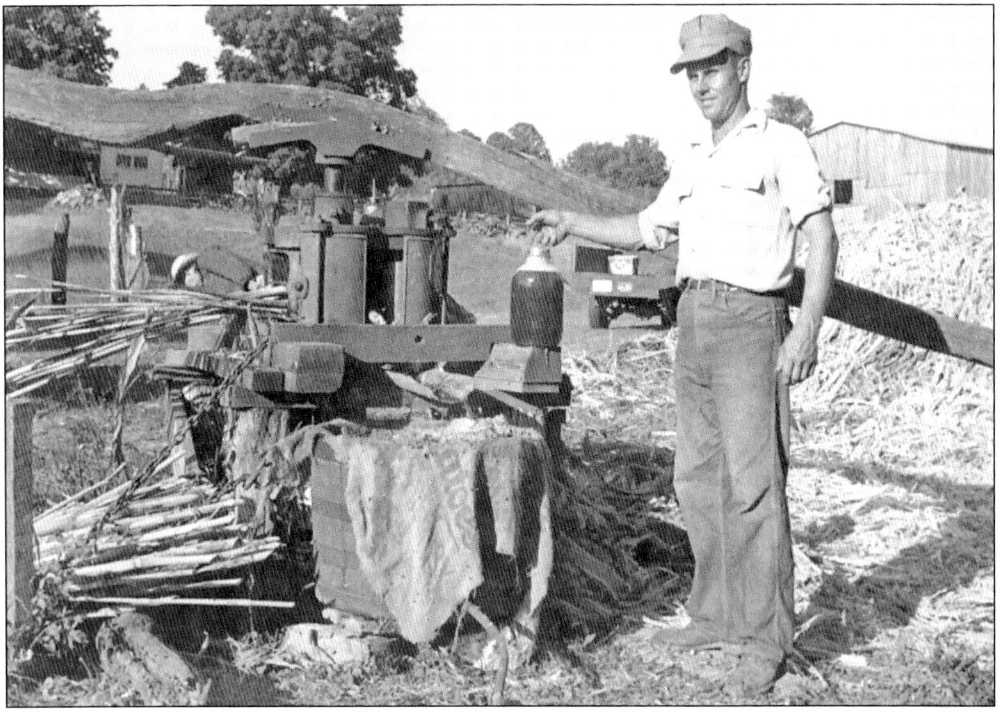

Sweet Makings. The production of molasses was a fall tradition on many farms that has disappeared. The process involved using mule or horsepower to squeeze the juice from cane, and then cooking the juice down until it was the consistency desired. Many remember the excitement of the time and waiting in anticipation of the first taste of the new molasses. Elton Lee is shown with some of the sweet product. (Courtesy of Winston Nunn.)

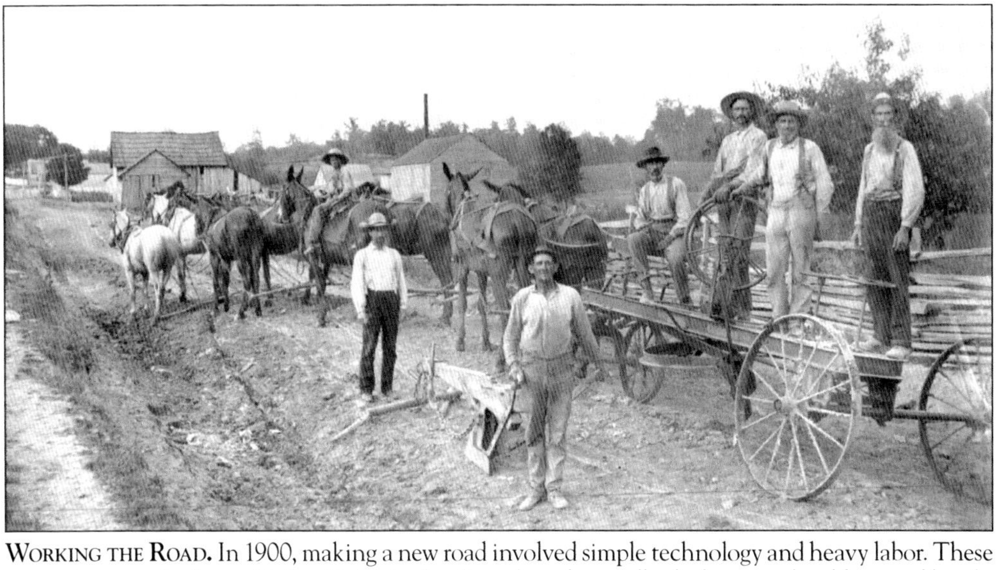

Working the Road. In 1900, making a new road involved simple technology and heavy labor. These men, photographed near Eighty-Eight, had to first clear the roadbed of stumps, boulders, and brush. Usually this was done entirely by hand or with the help of horses and mules. After the debris was cleared, leveling began using handheld rakes, hoes, or scrapers to create a surface amenable to wagon and stage travel. (Courtesy of Special Collections: Ekstrom Library, University of Louisville.)

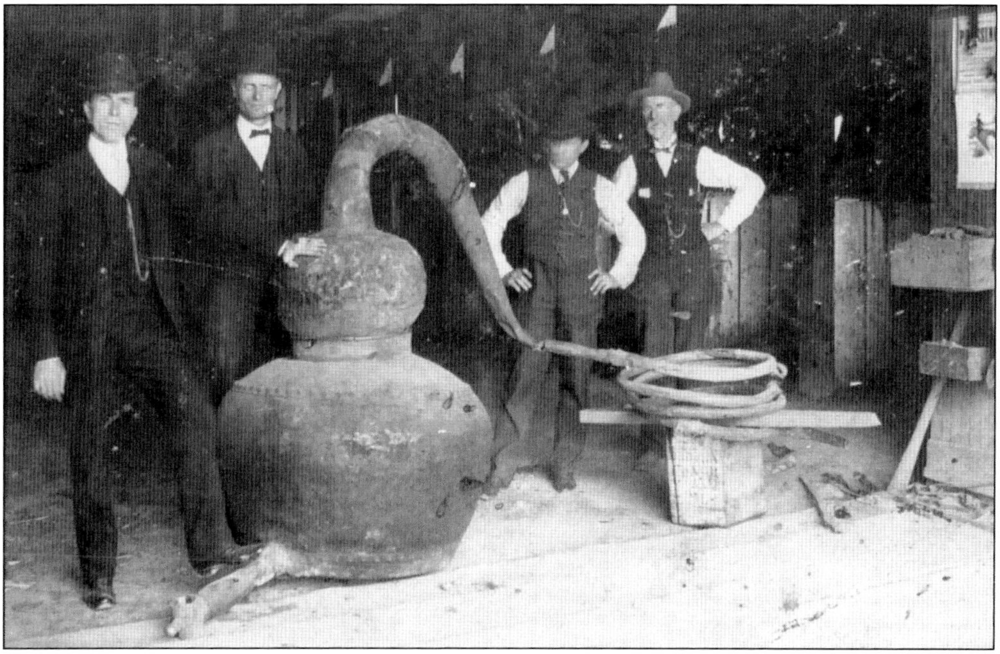

WHAT IS IT? This typical Kentucky moonshine still, found near Glasgow in the 1920s, was impounded and destroyed by law enforcement officials. The men are unidentified. The hilly and hidden terrain and rurality combined made the state an ideal location for the production of illegal spirits. During the years of Prohibition (1920–1933), there was an average of more than 600 stills that were annually seized. Additionally, there were more than 2,800 related arrests, and 21,681 gallons of distilled spirits confiscated yearly.

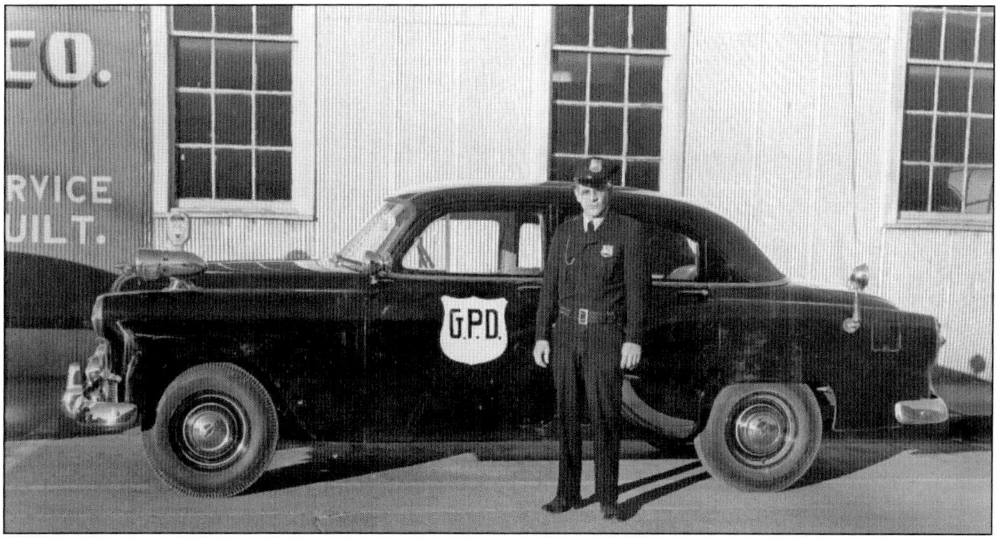

GLASGOW POLICE DEPARTMENT. Police cars, like police work, have changed considerably over the years. One of the Glasgow Police Department's officers, Herbert Brooks stands next to a new squad car that the department purchased in the 1950s. This one has some of the pieces of specialized equipment that were available. It would not be until after World War II that major auto companies would begin offering "police packages." (Courtesy of the Glasgow–Barren County Chamber of Commerce.)

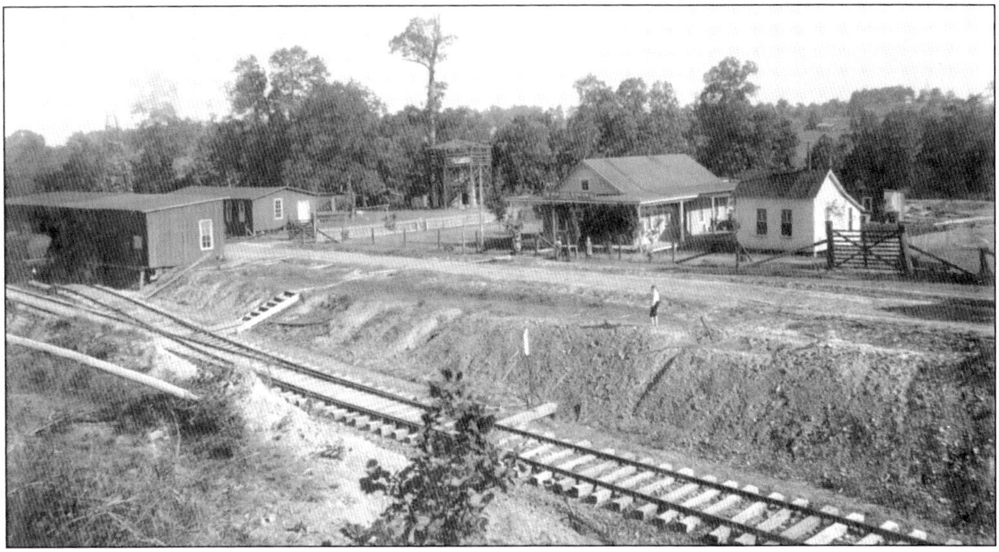

Discovering Oil. In 1865, an oil deposit was discovered along Boyds Creek, and the well was listed as the first well in the county. Oil fever developed as petroleum and mining companies promised that other pools of oil and riches were to be found in the county. Taken in 1900, this photograph shows "Oil City," which is near Glasgow, with an oil derrick and an office building that says "The Inter-State Petroleum Company." (Courtesy of Special Collections: Ekstrom Library, University of Louisville.)

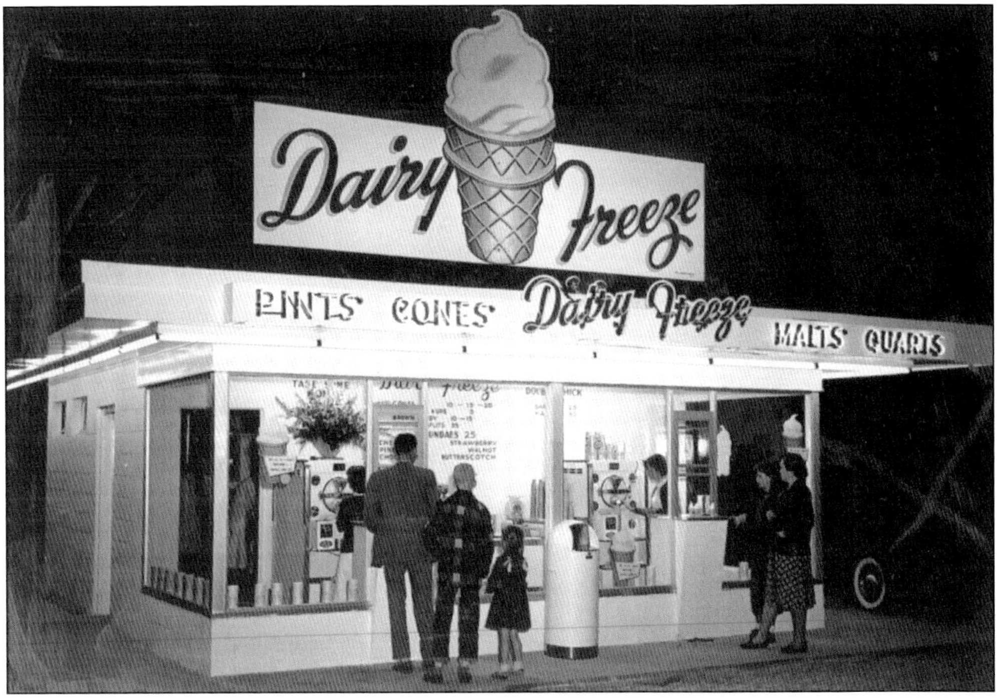

Taste of the Past. A place of tasty treats and happy memories, the Dairy Freeze was located near the Happy Valley Shopping Center. Soft-serve ice cream was the main attraction. Restaurants of this type were beginning to become part of the fun of eating out and were also the hubs of the mobile youth culture. (Courtesy of the Glasgow–Barren County Chamber of Commerce.)

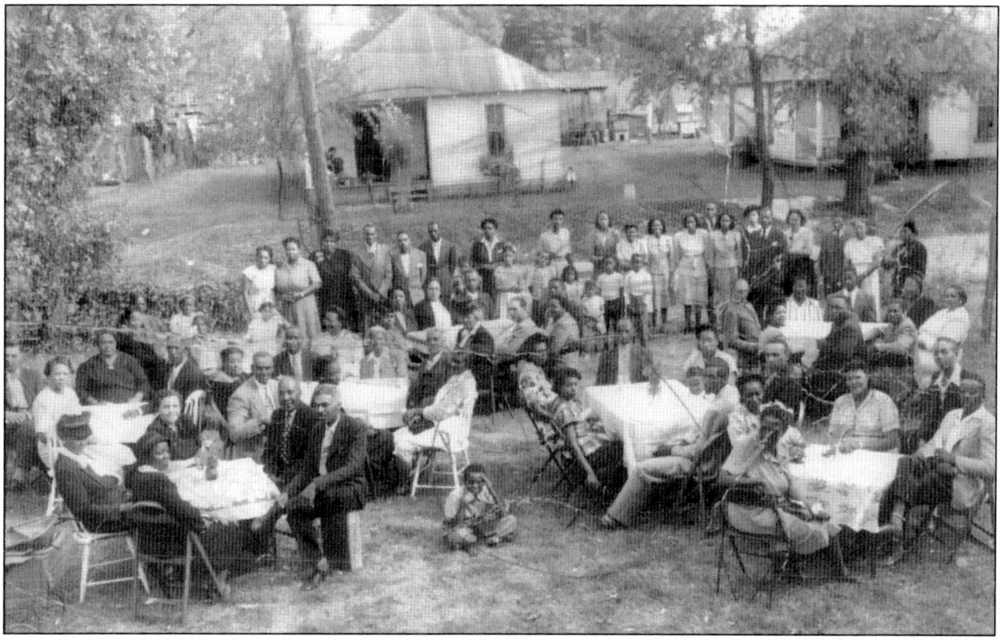

A Happy Get-Together. First Baptist Church members gather for an informal time of food, fellowship, and fun. This event took place in the late 1940s on Morgan Street. The tables are set and ready for the feasting to begin. One man has improvised a chair out of a Coca-Cola container. The children will have to make do with sitting on the ground picnic style. (Courtesy of Alonzo Webb.)

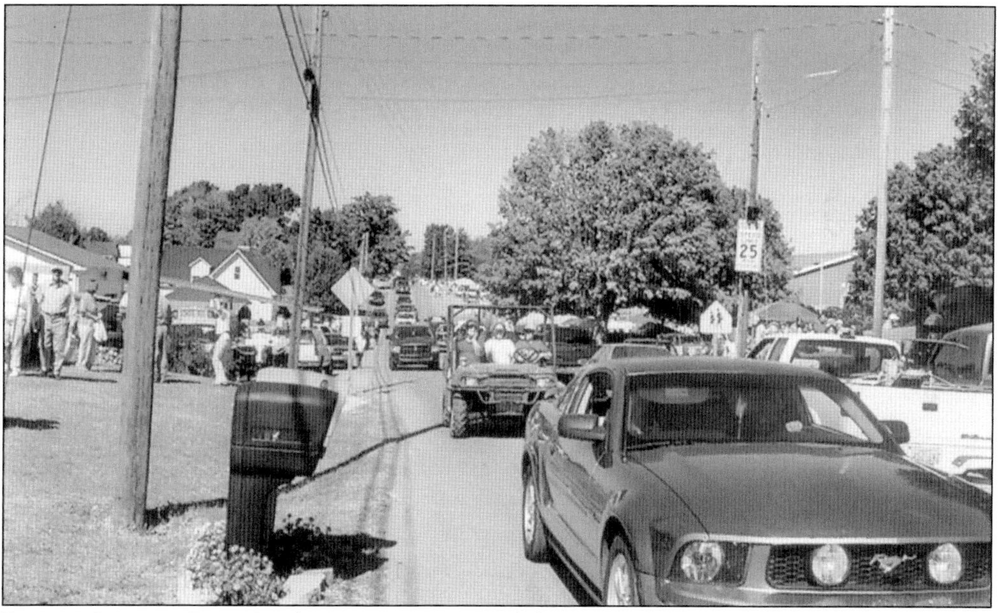

Roller Coaster Fair. Sarah Ann Bower started the 150-mile-long yard sale in 1986. The fair follows the winding and twisting Cordell Hull Highway. Attendance at the three-day-long event, which takes place the first weekend of October, has been counted at more than 140,000. The photograph shows downtown Temple Hill with its own traffic jam. In 2010, the yard sale celebrated its 25th anniversary. (Courtesy of James Richey.)

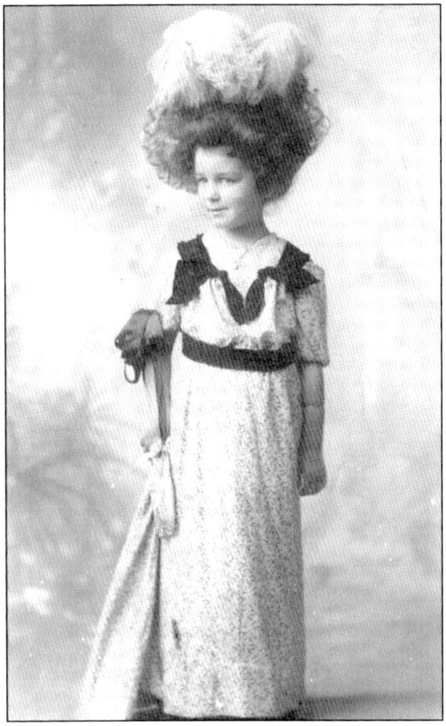

Tea Time. Beautiful Helen Frances Rogers is shown dressed as "Anabella White" for her part in her kindergarten play, *The Tea Party*. The image was printed on a postcard to share with all her relatives. She was the daughter of Edmund Rogers and Attelia Fowler. Her Revolutionary War ancestor, Edmund Rogers had settled in Barren County in 1800 and laid out the town of Edmonton. (Courtesy of Perry Brantley.)

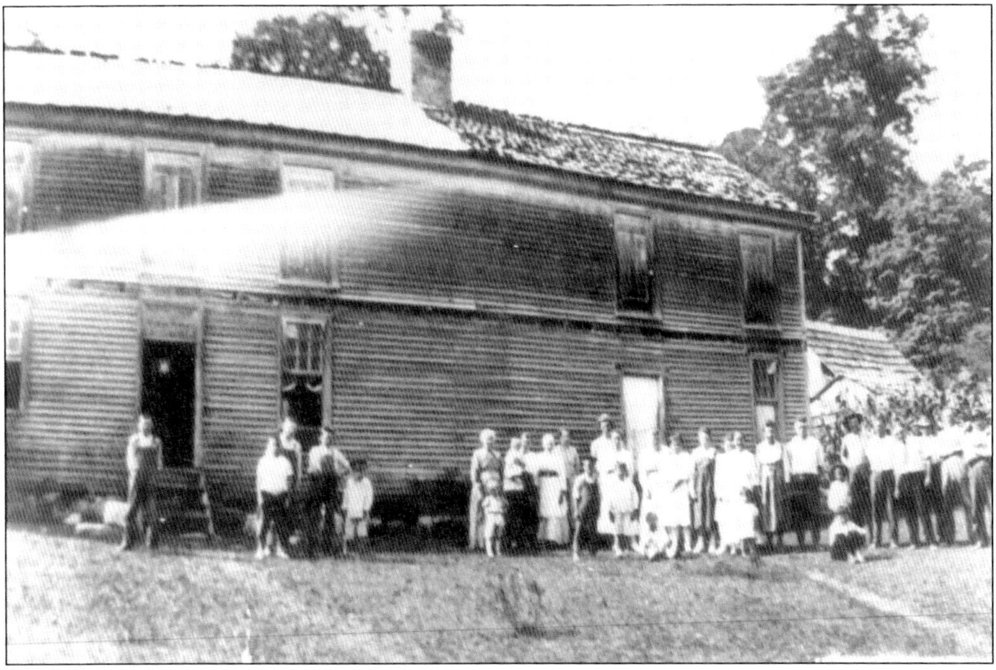

Jackson's Hotel. This image, taken in 1920, shows the Holman Hotel that was located on Buck Creek. The hotelkeeper was Joseph Holman. Legend tells that this was the hotel that U.S. president Andrew Jackson stayed at on his way back from Washington, D.C., to his home in Nashville. Ports near here could handle small steamboats as they made their way down the Green River to the Barren River. (Courtesy of Martha Harrison.)

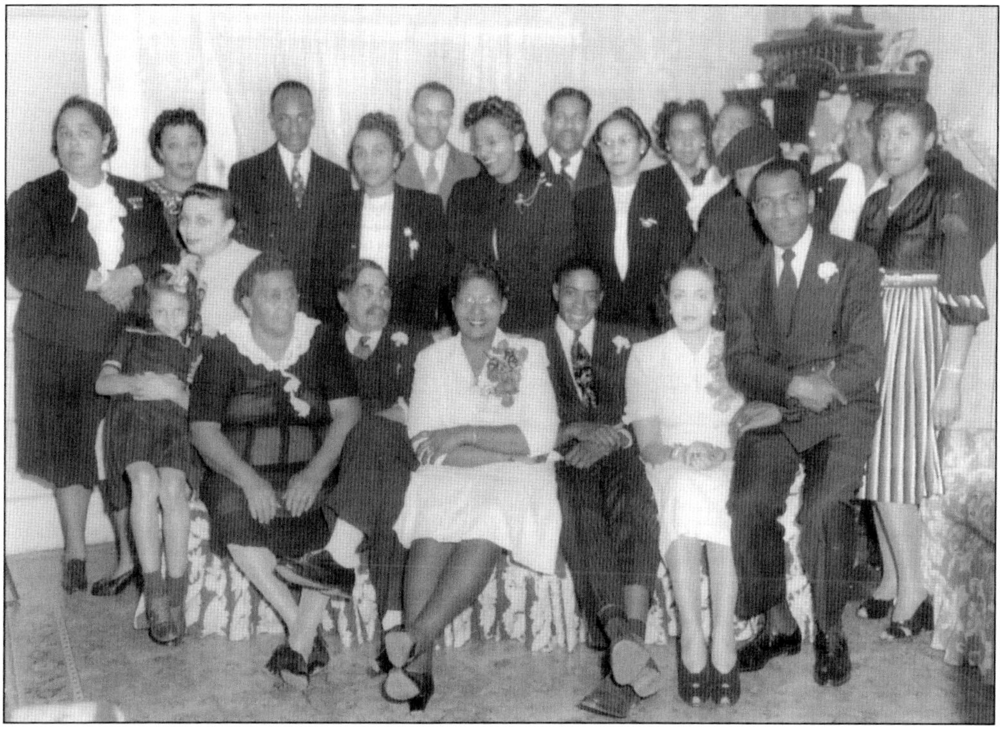

GLEANER'S CLUB. Members of the Gleaner's Club meet in one of the member's homes to discuss the next goodwill project. The members seated are, from left to right, Gladys Twyman, holding the young girl; Ida Belle; Rev. Alonzo Webb; Beatrice and Ed Chambers; Susie Curry; and Earl Dickey. Among those standing are Lula Mae Webb, Luska J. Twyman, Camilla and John Childress, Lenny Patterson, Magdalene Stockton, and Mollie Farris. (Courtesy of Alonzo Webb.)

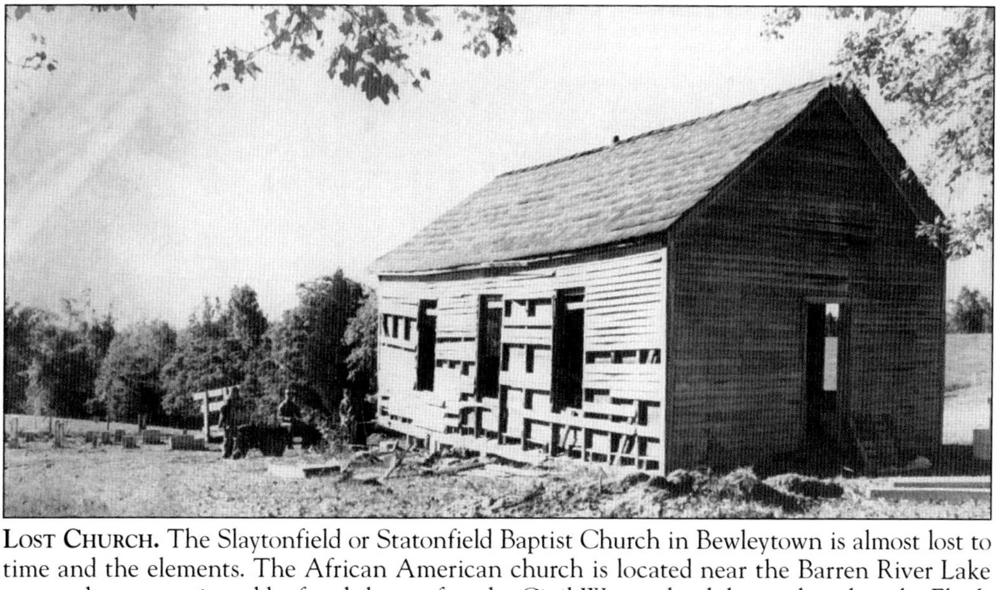

LOST CHURCH. The Slaytonfield or Statonfield Baptist Church in Bewleytown is almost lost to time and the elements. The African American church is located near the Barren River Lake area and was constituted by freed slaves after the Civil War on land donated to them by Elijah Slayton. Nearby is a cemetery where African American Civil War soldier Daniel Whitney is buried. (Courtesy of Martha Harrison.)

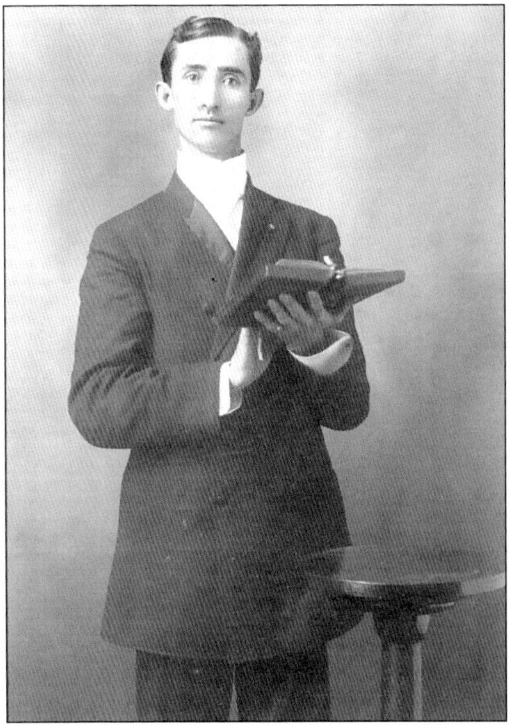

Holy Word. This unidentified young minister poses for a striking photograph, taken by Adolph Rapp. Rapp had a studio and home on the corner of Main and Race Streets in downtown Glasgow. Emigrating from Germany, Rapp started his career as a confectioner, but his intrigue with photography settled his career choice. In 1904, he represented Barren County at the World's Fair, showcasing the county in scenic pictures.

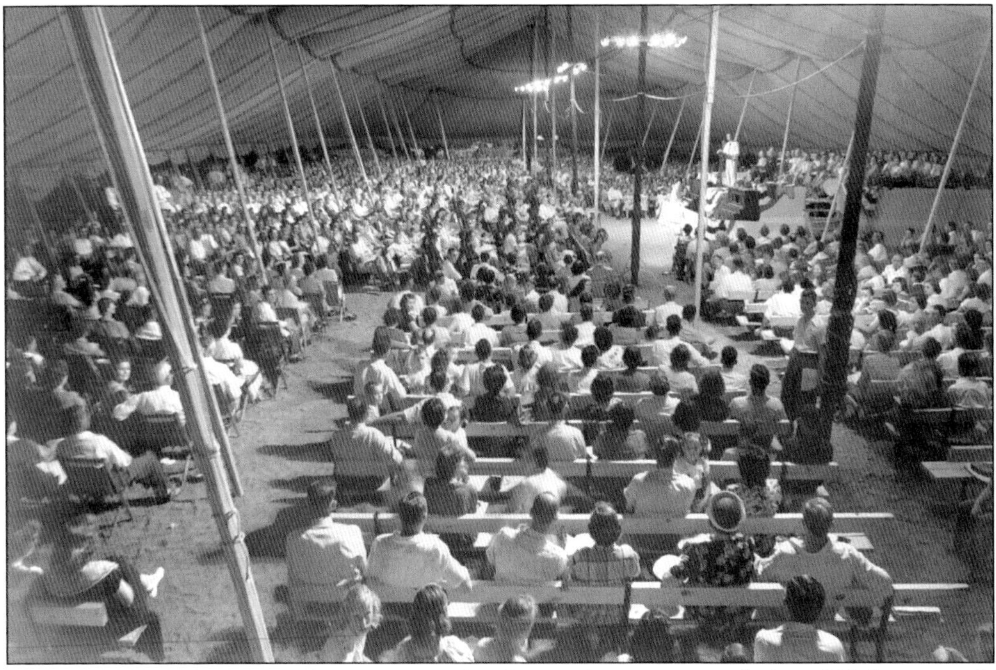

Bringing in the Sheaves. There were no churches in the county until after 1800, but an early visitor observed that the county "is celebrated for its morals, sobriety, and religion." Faith in its many forms was significant in the role and development of the county. This photograph shows efforts at ecumenism, as many churches joined in sponsoring this citywide tent revival in a show of religious unity and cooperation. (Courtesy of the Glasgow–Barren County Chamber of Commerce.)

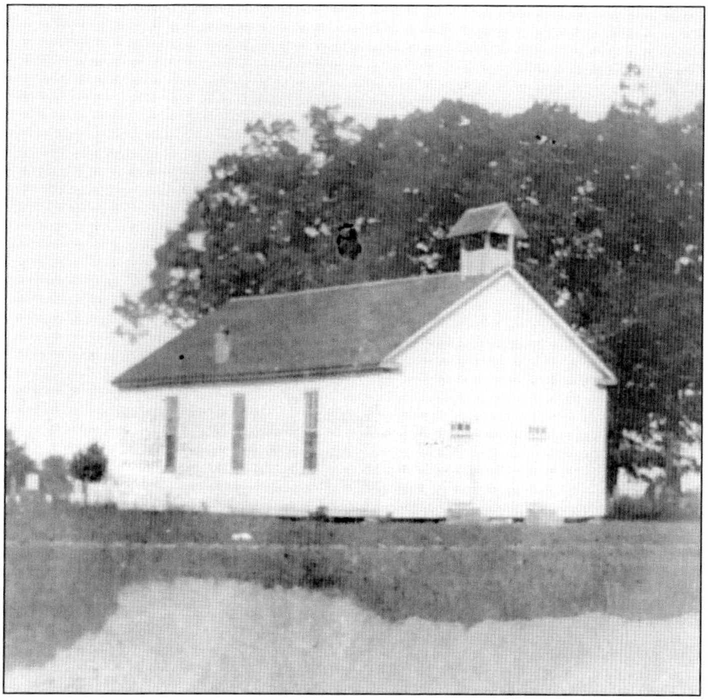

CHURCH IN THE WILDWOOD. Concord Baptist Church has a long and rich history, as do many of the churches in the county. The official constitution date is 1811, but records indicate an even earlier history date (1800) for the congregation. It is located in the southern part of Barren County, only 2 or 3 miles from the Barren River. The History of Kentucky Baptists lists John Mulkey as the church's first pastor. (Courtesy of Martha Harrison.)

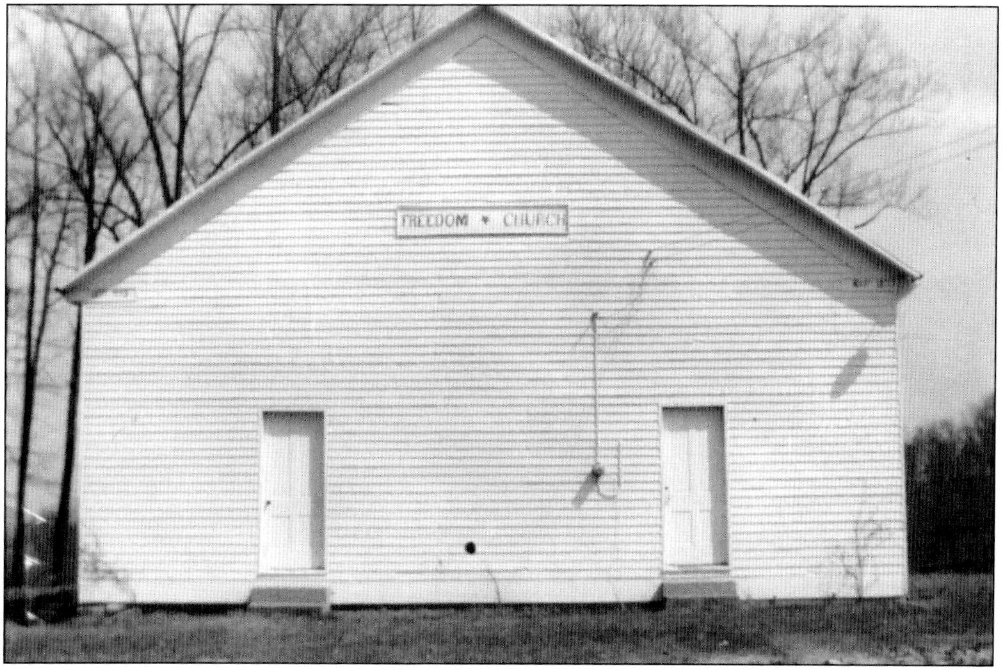

FREEDOM'S CHURCH. The little community of Freedom (originally Black Walnut) has a long and respected history, and many believe it was a stop on the Underground Railroad. So many African Americans were helped along their way to freedom that, in 1866, the community's name was officially changed. The Freedom Missionary Baptist Church was formed in 1855, and the church building shown here was completed in 1877. (Courtesy of Pastor Terrell Kingrey and members of the Freedom Church.)

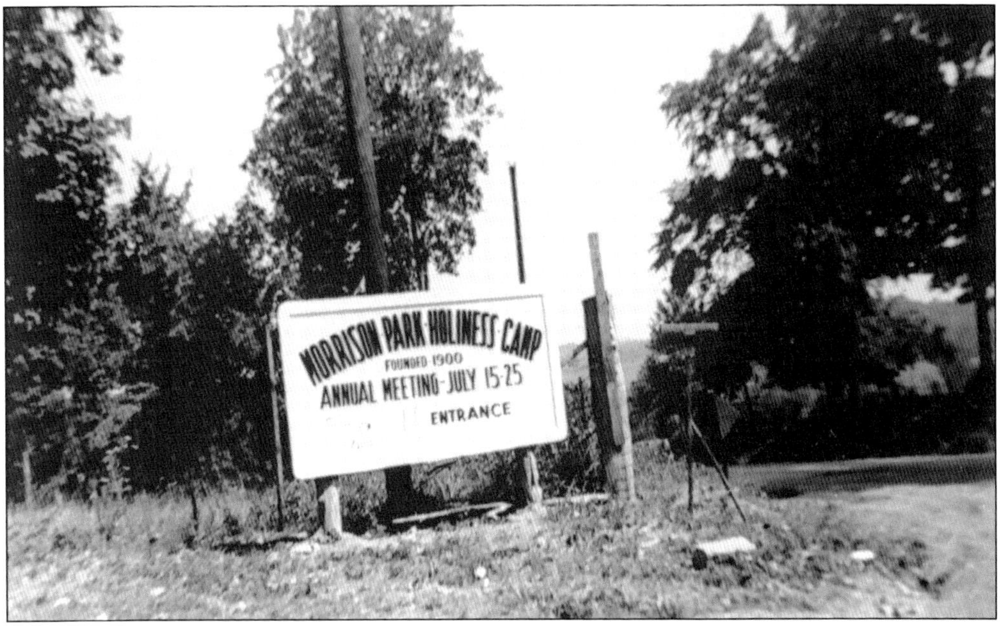

SIGN OF THE TIMES. Morrison Park Holiness Camp is located on Highway 63. Henry Clay Morrison, who grew up across the road from the land, founded it in 1900. Though he left the county in the fall of 1874, Morrison returned regularly for meetings until his death. A newspaper account from 1919 celebrates the camp and its evangelistic work, stating that "several souls were saved and good order prevailed throughout the meeting." The camp meeting site is still listed as one of the oldest sawdust camp in the United States. Meetings continued throughout the century, but the open tabernacle building shown below was destroyed by high winds in the early 1990s. The library, a small lodging cabin, and monument to Morrison are still standing. (Both, courtesy of Gary Bewley.)

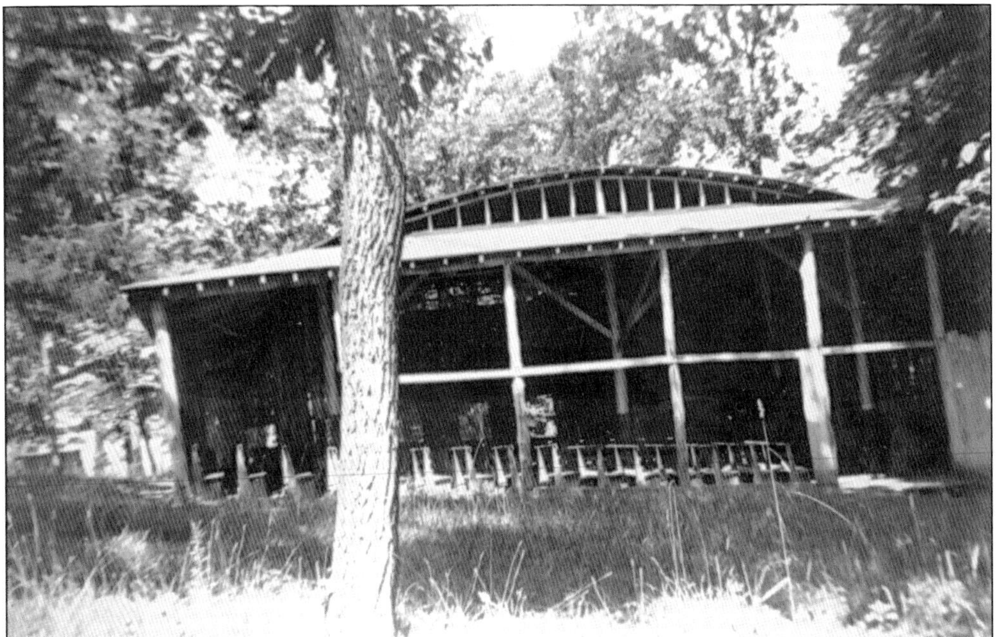

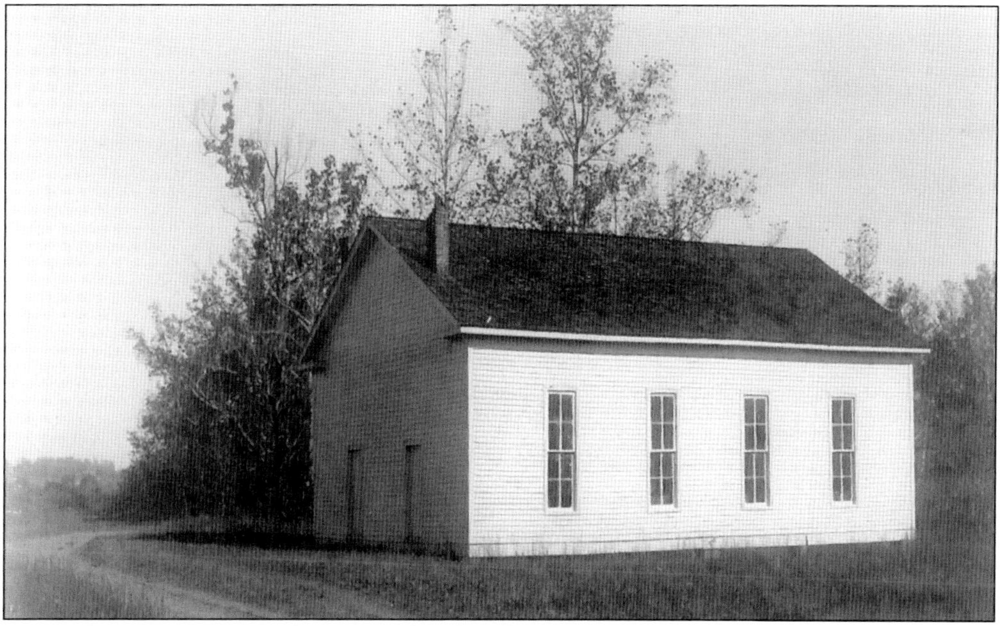

BOYDS CREEK METHODIST CHURCH. This church is one of the oldest in Barren County and is located 3 miles east of Glasgow on the Siloam Road. It was built in 1826 on land deeded by Clairy A. and Hermit Snoddy. The original building was this frame structure until 1962, when the present brick building was dedicated. There was also a Boyds Creek School on the same property until 1942. (Courtesy of Asbury Theological Seminary Archives.)

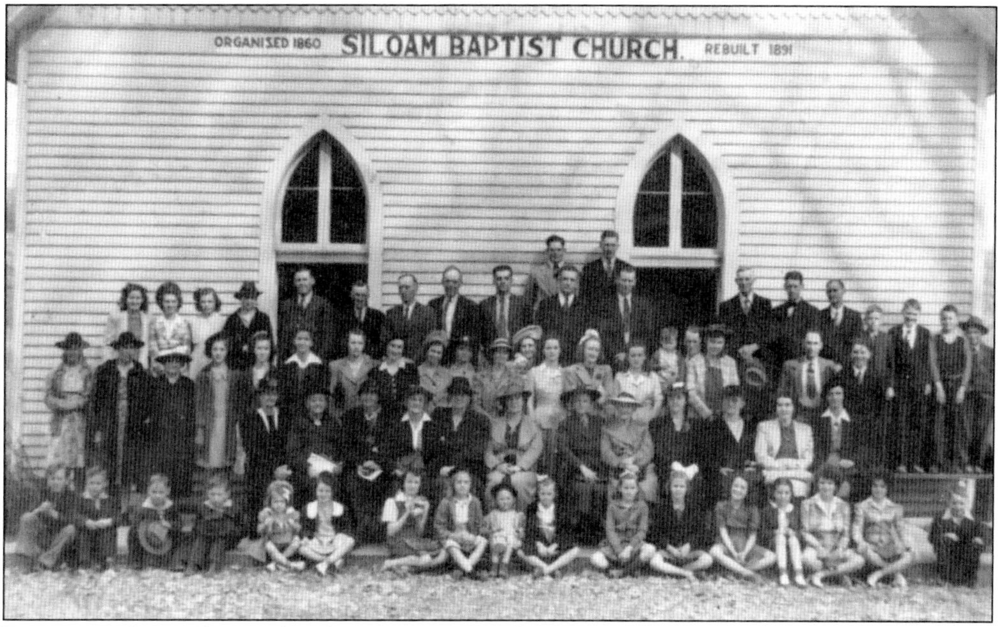

REACHING OUT. The word "Siloam" means sending, and members of Siloam Baptist Church have a long history of outreach to the community. The church's beginnings precede the Civil War, and it was originally located on Highway 90. In 1891, the church was moved to its present location on the Siloam Road. Some of the descendants of the original members are shown in this 1947 photograph.

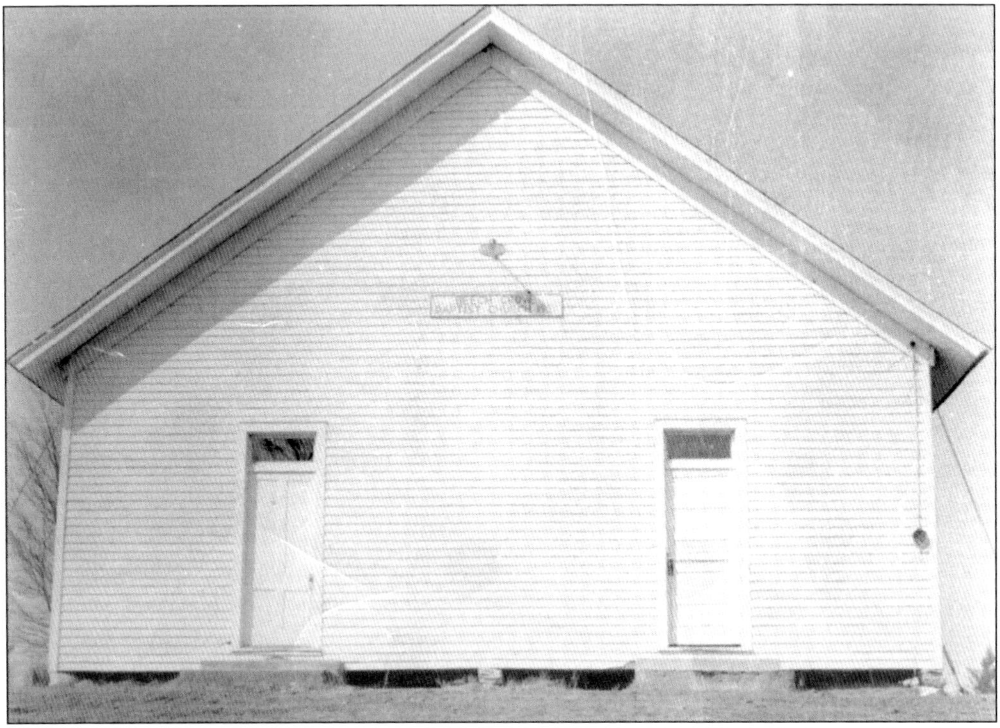

Beech Grove Church. Located on the Old Bowling Green Road, Beech Grove Church was first organized in 1892, with the church building being located about a fourth of a mile from the present site. The second building was erected in 1952 under the leadership of Pastor Raymond Kenney. Notice the condition of the church as seen in the photograph. It is being steadied and held together with cables. (Courtesy of Martha Harrison.)

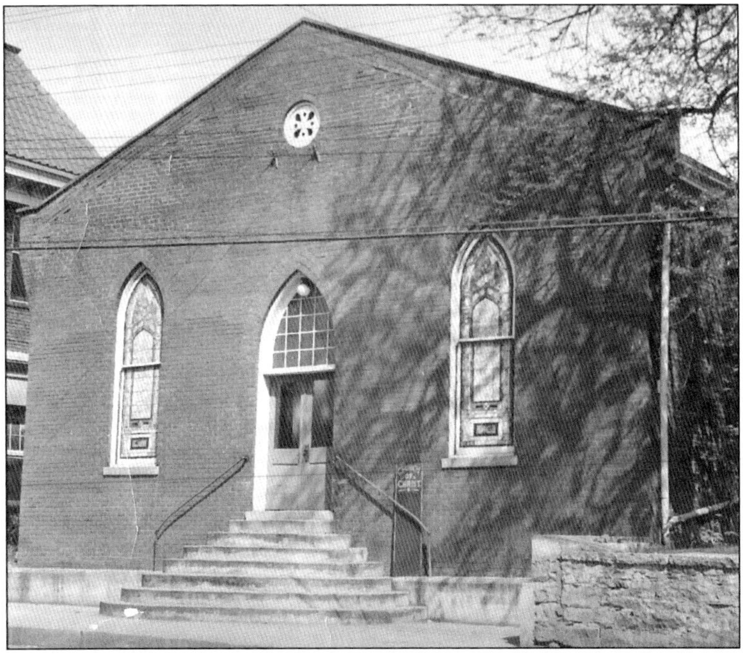

Church of Christ. It was said that a sermon by a visiting Alexander Campbell resulted in the organization of the Church of Christ, now on South Green Street. The congregation met in a member's home until a church building was completed in 1837, but it was lost to fire. This structure was erected in 1916 and was used until the present building was completed in 1948. (Courtesy of Billy Pritchard.)

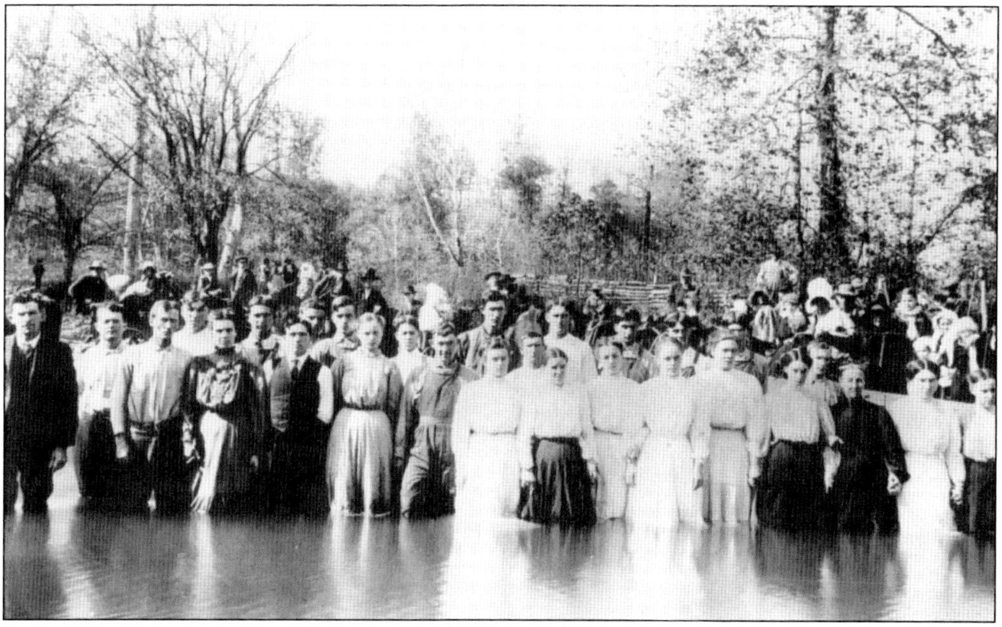

Shall We Gather at the River? Revival times at churches produced many new converts and resulted in a large number of candidates for baptism. This ceremony at Brown's Ford on the Barren River is dated October 27, 1909. Preacher L. D. Robinson had just finished a six-week revival for Pleasant Home Missionary Baptist Church when the above photograph was taken. Of particular interest is the wide range of ages represented in the group. Any available body of water could be used for the ceremony, including a farm pond, such as shown below. The Dover Baptist Church congregation and Pastor Joe Richey have gathered for the ceremony. Though this service is being held in the summer, the services were held regardless of the weather, which meant many times the ice had to be broken for wintertime baptisms. (Above, courtesy of Runell and Terry Houchen; below, courtesy of Margaret Eddings.)

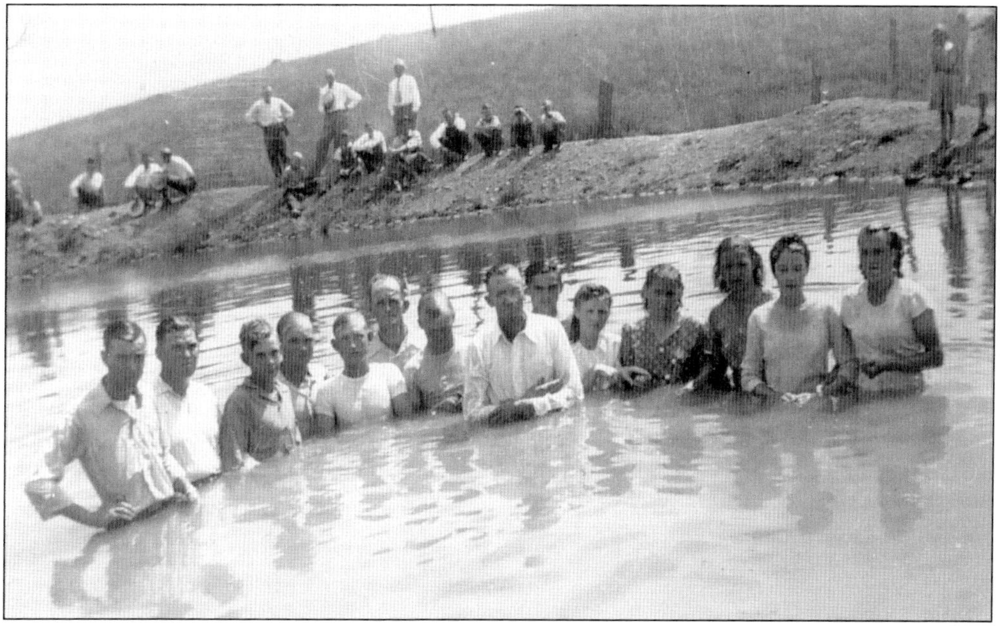

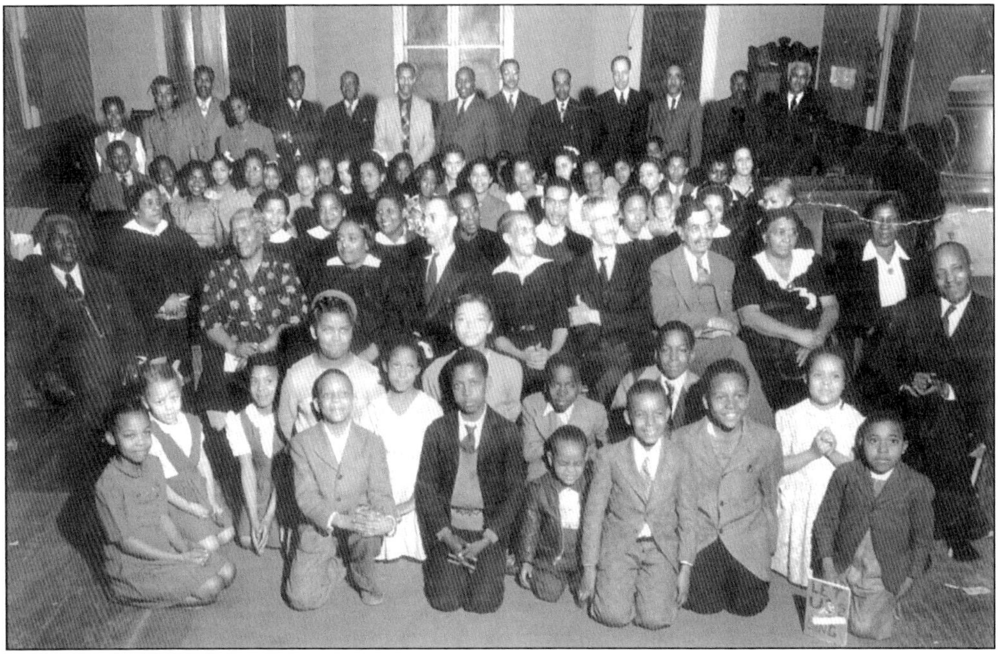

Faithful Members. Members of the First Baptist Church, which was located on Lewis Street, are shown in this photograph. This was the first African American church in Glasgow and was organized by Peter Murrell, a freed slave. The original structure seen here was destroyed by fire in 1972, but a new building was erected and dedicated in 1974. The wonderful, innocent, devout faces of the children are priceless. (Courtesy of Alonzo Webb.)

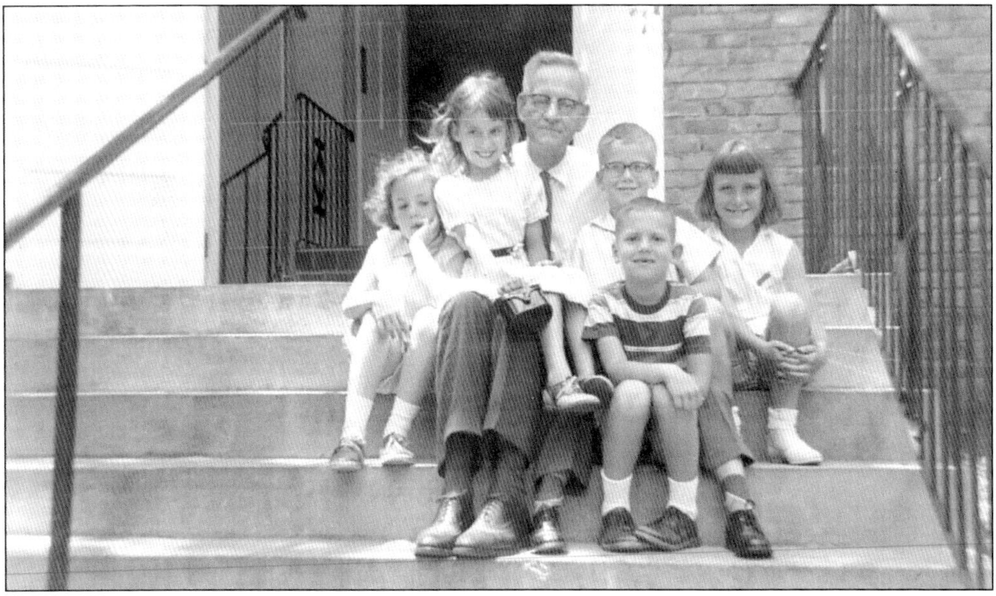

Precious Memories. Rev. W. L. Huntsman is shown with some of his youngest parishioners on the steps of Glasgow Presbyterian Church. It was the city's first church, organized in 1802. Pastor Huntsman is remembered for starting many programs to reach the children of the church and community. Pictured from left to right are Catherine Moore, Mollie Smith, Rev. William Huntsman, Donald Barrickman, Martha Carroll, and Mitch ?. (Courtesy of Perry Brantley.)

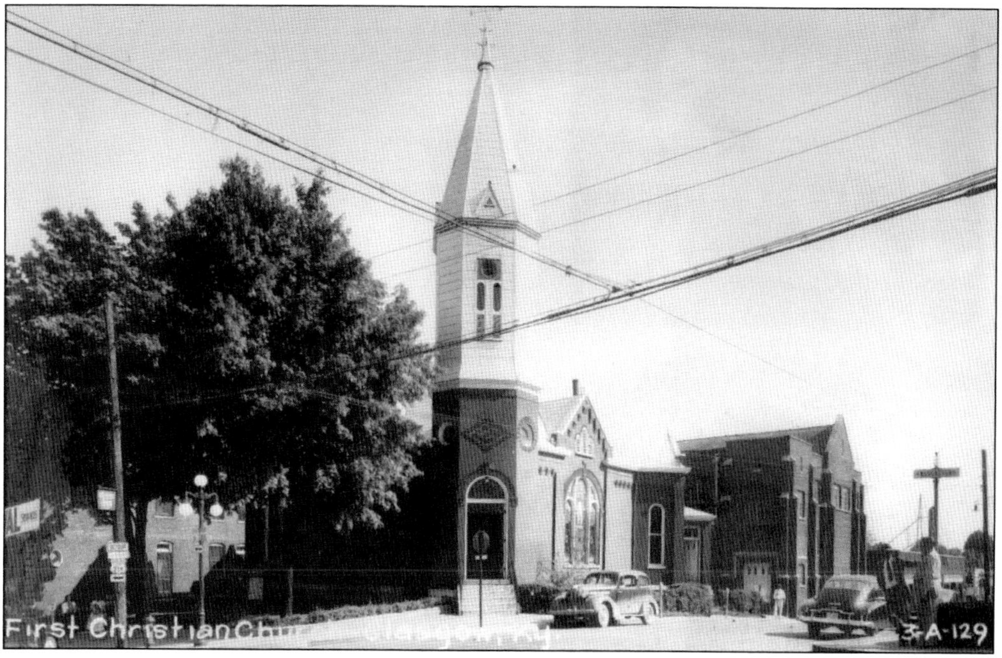

CHANGING TIMES. The First Christian Church is shown in its former location on the square. The site is now the location of Beulah Nunn Park. Nunn, the former first lady of the state, provided leadership for many historical efforts in Barren County. The park also features a marble monument to musician Billy Vaughn and a state historical marker for Luska J. Twyman. In 2009, a Glasgow–Barren County Veterans Wall of Honor was dedicated in the park.

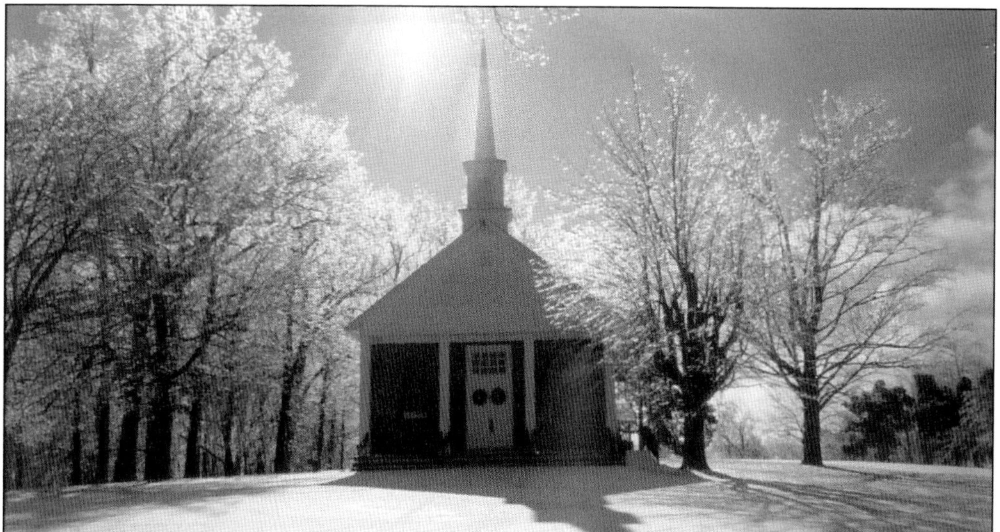

MOTHER CHURCH. Barren County's religious roots run deep as represented by Mount Tabor, the first permanent church organized in the county. The church was constituted in November 1798, and Alexander Davidson was chosen as the first pastor. Mount Tabor has also been the parent church for many other daughter churches in Barren and Warren Counties. The church was rebuilt in 1890 and was remodeled, as shown here in 1969. (Courtesy of Lanny Whitlow.)

Barren County, Kentucky

Barren County, located in the heart of south central Kentucky, was formed in 1799 and is the commonwealth's 13th largest county. Pioneers found the land without the usual, extensive wooded areas and so it looked barren to them in comparison. The area is anything but "barren," as its land and population have been productive in agriculture, commerce, education, medicine, and the military. Voted in 2007 by *Progressive Farmer* magazine as the "Best Place to Live in Rural America," the county has also produced one of the South's first African American mayors, two governors, renowned musicians, a Pulitzer Prize winner, two Congressional Medal of Honor recipients, a major television network president, and a U.S. Air Force general. Countless other citizens, equally productive, proudly call Barren County their home.

Images of America: *Barren County* includes many never before seen photographs of the area's rich historical culture, its religious and educational institutions, and ordinary family life that showcase why the county remains one of the best places to live in rural America. Nancy Richey, image librarian at Western Kentucky University's Kentucky Library and native of Barren County, uses photographs from the library, civic organizations, and private individuals to create this photographic essay showcasing the historic personality of this area.

The Images of America series celebrates the history of neighborhoods, towns, and cities across the country. Using archival photographs, each title presents the distinctive stories from the past that shape the character of the community today. Arcadia is proud to play a part in the preservation of local heritage, making history available to all.

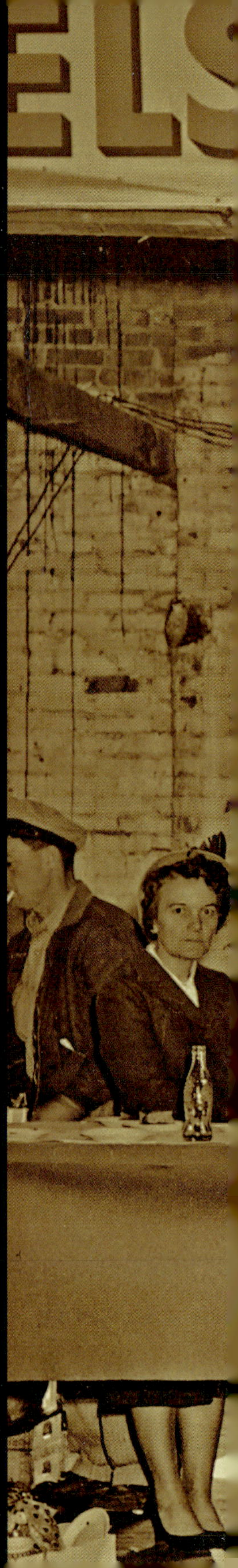

ARCADIA PUBLISHING

www.arcadiapublishing.com

MADE IN THE USA

ISBN-13 978-0-7385-8592-5 $24.99
ISBN-10 0-7385-8592-0
52499
9 780738 585925